MOTOR SKILL ACQUISITION OF THE MENTALLY HANDICAPPED:

Issues in Research and Training

ADVANCES IN PSYCHOLOGY
31

Editors

G. E. STELMACH

P. A. VROON

NORTH-HOLLAND
AMSTERDAM · NEW YORK · OXFORD · TOKYO

MOTOR SKILL ACQUISITION OF THE MENTALLY HANDICAPPED:

Issues in Research and Training

Michael G. WADE
Department of Physical Education
Southern Illinois University

1986

NORTH-HOLLAND
AMSTERDAM · NEW YORK · OXFORD · TOKYO

ISBN: 0 444 87976 5

Publishers:

ELSEVIER SCIENCE PUBLISHERS B.V.
P.O. Box 1991
1000 BZ Amsterdam
The Netherlands

Sole distributors for the U.S.A. and Canada:

ELSEVIER SCIENCE PUBLISHING COMPANY, INC.
52 Vanderbilt Avenue
New York, N.Y. 10017
U.S.A.

Library of Congress Cataloging-in-Publication Data
Motor skill acquisition of the mentally handicapped.

    (Advances in psychology ; 31)
    Papers presented at a conference held Sept. 28-29,
in Bethesda, Md., sponsored by the National Institute
of Child Health and Human Development and the National
Institute for Handicapped Research.
    Includes bibliographies and indexes.
    1. Physical education for mentally handicapped
persons--Congresses. 2. Perceptual-motor learning--
Congresses. I. Wade, Michael G. II. National
Institute of Child Health and Human Development (U.S.)
III. National Institute of Handicapped Research (U.S.)
IV. Series: Advances in psychology (Amsterdam,
Netherlands) ; 31.
GV445.M67 1986   613.7'0880826   86-4403
ISBN 0-444-87976-5

PRINTED IN THE NETHERLANDS

FOREWORD

Cognitive impairments exhibited by mentally retarded persons are frequently accompanied by a variety of motor impairments. Until recently, research in motor skills has received limited attention relative to the importance of motor skills for overall development. The past decade, however, has seen an increased research effort aimed at assisting handicapped individuals to achieve improved levels of motor skill performance.

The increased activity in motor skills research has been paralleled by growing theoretical support and consideration of the idea that perception and motor activity are intimately related. This view calls into question the separation of cognitive activity and motor activity that has characterized past research approaches. It directs research attention to determining the influences of traditional learning variables on motor performance and toward the important theoretical issues that focus on the nature of control and coordination in mentally handicapped persons.

In recognition of these developments, the National Institute of Child Health and Human Development (NICHD) jointly with the National Institute for Handicapped Research (NIHR) sponsored and convened a conference on The Development of Control, Coordination and Skill in the Mentally Handicapped, Bethesda, MD, September 28–29, 1985. This cooperative effort was made possible largely through the scientific wisdom and thoughtful concern of Dr. Douglas Fenderson, then Director of the NIHR.

Based upon the conference proceedings, this volume brings together the research and theoretical perspectives of experts in the developmental aspects of motor control, coordination, and skill in the mentally handicapped. This is accomplished within the context of cognition. The result is a unified presentation of current research and theory which should give direction and impetus to future research on motor skill development with its promise of benefits for the mentally handicapped.

Theodore D. Tjossem, Ph.D.
Chief
Mental Retardation and Developmental
Disabilities Branch
National Institute of Child Health
and Human Development

TABLE OF CONTENTS

CONTRIBUTORS

Robert ARENDT, Department of Psychology, Vanderbilt University, Nashville, TN

Susan AUFDERHEIDE, Department of Physical Education, Purdue University, Lafayette, IN

Al BAUMEISTER, Department of Psychology, George Peabody College, Vanderbilt University, Nashville, TN

Gershon BERKSON, Department of Psychology, University of Illinois-Chicago Circle, Chicago, IL

Ann BROWN, Center for the Study of Reading, University of Illinois, Champaign, IL

Joe CAMPIONE, Center for the Study of Reading, University of Illinois, Champaign, IL

Jorge DARUNDA, Department of Psychiatry and Neurology, Tulane University Medical School, New Orleans, LA

Walter DAVIS, Department of Physical Education, Kent State University, Kent, OH

Gary GALBRAITH, Neuro-Psychiatric Institute, Pacific Hospital Research Center, San Diego, CA

James HOGG, Hester-Adrian Research Center, University of Manchester, Manchester, Lancs, England

Robert HORNER, Department of Special Education, University of Oregon, Eugene, OR

Rathe KARRER, Department of Psychology, University of Illinois-Chicago Circle, Chicago, IL

Bill MACLEAN, Department of Psychology and Human Development, Vanderbilt University, Nashville, TN

Motor Skill Acquisition of the Mentally Handicapped:
Issues in Research and Training
M.G. Wade (editor)
© Elsevier Science Publishers B.V. (North-Holland), 1986

INTRODUCTION

Michael G. Wade, Ph.D.

Department of Physical Education
Southern Illinois University
Carbondale, Illinois 62901

Research on the motor behavior of persons with mental handicaps has developed only in the past twenty or so years since an early paper by Malpass (1963) in the first Handbook on Mental Deficiency. This lack of an extensive history on motor skills research of mentally handicapped individuals is due primarily to the fact that motor skills research per se has come into its own in psychology only in the past 20 or so years. While scholars have been struggling with broader theoretical issues on problems of control and coordination in human motor skills, there has been relatively little spin off in other related areas such as mental retardation. The past ten or so years has been increasing research activity among scholars concerned both with the investigation of motor skill behavior and the related motor skill deficiencies of the mentally handicapped.

The four parts of this volume capture the main elements of present research activity and have running through them a single theme; namely, the ability of persons with mental handicaps to acquire and express motor skill behavior. The first section on control and coordination, which contains chapters by Berkson, Davis, Woollacott, and MacLean and his associates, deals with the dynamics of controlling movement skill and the nature of the variables that mediate the learning of motor skills. Berkson deals with a particular problem relative to coordination and control; namely, stereotypic behaviors. Typically, these are abnormal motor behaviors, and to better understand their underlining causes, the Berkson chapter examines ways of mediating the control dynamics of such stereotypies. Davis deals with the problem that mentally handicapped individuals have in utilizing different levels of visual information as it relates to motor skill expression, in this instance, throwing. Again, the research question is the nature of the underlying processes that mediate control and coordination. Woollacott looks at a fundamental developmental motor skill, postural control. Postural control appears developmentally after the reflexive behaviors of newborns and is seen as a precursor to the normal development of voluntary motor control. Woollacott examines the control dynamics of this within children with Down's Syndrome. The fourth chapter in this section, by MacLean and his associates, examines stereotypic motor behavior and its relationship to vestibular stimulation. All of the chapters in this section deal with the amelioration of problems of control and coordination which are fundamental to the development of normal motor skill behavior.

Parts II and III examine the traditional area of research in motor behavior, that is, the speed of information processing and reaction time paradigms. The chapters in Part II by Vernon and Zelaznik deal with the cognitive aspects of response timing in motor behavior. Vernon examines

the correlates of information and intelligence and how this speed of
information relates to the ability of harness motor responses. Zelaznik
presents a closer analysis of reaction time performance, examining the
components of both response generation and movement time as two components
that contribute to the generation of rapid motor responses.

Part III focuses on the physiological, rather than the cognitive, bases of
response time in motor behavior. The Karrer and Daruna chapters together
provide data on the physiologically based deficits exhibited by persons
with mental retardation in the generation of rapid motor responses.

Part IV deals with the issue of training, perhaps one of the most popular
research areas currently under study. Training seeks to minimize the
effects on motor behavior that is manifest in mental retardation, in order
to maximize the potential of the mentally handicapped in a variety of areas
that require motor responses for appropriate behavior. Just as Parts I,
II, and III of the book lay out some of the fundamental motor skill
acquisition problems and the investigatory strategies related to those
problems, Part IV presents studies that take mentally retarded individuals
and teach those individuals to perform optimally on a variety of motor
skill behaviors necessary to lead as normal a life style as possible in the
community. Hogg and Horner confront these issues head on in their
chapters. Hogg takes a theoretical view, distinguishing between the
process and the context of paradigms that seek to train motor behaviors in
mentally handicapped individuals. The chapter by Horner is directed more
toward programmatic strategies for developing generalized motor skills with
severely handicapped learners.

Each part of the book includes a reaction paper by a well-known scientist,
each of whom has published work in the area of mental retardation. The
reaction papers place each section's contributions in perspective, provide
critical commentary, and suggest new directions for research. The chapters
taken together provide the most up-to-date research work being carried out
in the area of motor behavior in mentally handicapped individuals.
Further, it delineates the main areas of research activity; namely, control
and coordination, response timing, and training. The common theme is
obviously Motor Skill Acquisition of the Mentally Handicapped, and together
the different sections provide up-to-date knowledge of both the basic
and the applied aspects of motor skill learning as it relates to the
mentally handicapped.

Section I
Control and Coordination of Motor Skills

Motor Skill Acquisition of the Mentally Handicapped:
Issues in Research and Training
M.G. Wade (editor)
© *Elsevier Science Publishers B.V. (North-Holland), 1986*

CONTROL OF FEEDBACK FROM ABNORMAL
STEREOTYPED BEHAVIORS

Gershon Berkson and R. J. Gallagher

University of Illinois at Chicago

This paper was presented at a conference entitled, "The Development of Control, Coordination and Skill in the Mentally Handicapped", September 28-29, 1984, held at the National Institute
of Child Health and Human Development, Bethesda, Maryland. The
conference was supported by the NICHD and the National Institute
for Handicapped Research and research reported in the paper was
supported by a grant from the National Institute of Child Health
and Human Development (HD 15008). Arnold Rincover commented on
a draft of the paper. We are indebted also to the parents,
teachers, and children who participated in the research.

Although deafferentation studies have shown that movements can occur
without sensory feedback, it is clear that motor organization ordinarily
depends on the sensations associated with action. Guidance of the form of
the movement; input at the time of first development of the movement
pattern; and even schemas of how the world is organized are ways in which
sensory input associated with action manifests itself. This paper deals
with a fourth function of sensory input as a motivator. The major conclusion we wish to leave you with is that sensory input maintains certain
behaviors and that the nature of the input can be defined and adjusted to
modify behavior.

In normal children, the sensorimotor period is a time of rapid development
of cognitive and motor behaviors having to do with the child's relation
with space, time and society. Severely retarded children proceed more
slowly through this period, and some never go beyond it. Some investigators emphasize that the processes of development are fundamentally the same
in the normal and mentally retarded children. However, a truer picture
probably would be that while severely retarded children proceed more slowly
through normal stages, their behavior increasingly takes on pathological
features in addition to their delay.

One difficulty with studying development in normal children comes from the
rapid pace of their development. Even major changes in motor and cognitive
processes can occur in a matter of days or weeks so that investigators may
meet practical difficulties in carrying out analyses of the causal and
functional factors involved in the development of various behaviors in
infancy. The slower development of severely retarded children provides the
opportunity for more careful study, as long as pathology is taken into
account.

The subject of this paper is the stereotyped behaviors that appear to be an important aspect of adaptation in the sensorimotor period. These behaviors tend to be repeated frequently, and in some individuals, may involve most of their waking behavior. Normal babies may demonstrate as many as 30 different stereotyped behaviors during their first year (Thelen, 1981). Blind, autistic and severely retarded children also develop them (Berkson, 1967), and in these children they may continue beyond the sensorimotor period (Miller, 1984). Isolation-reared subhuman primates habitually engage in stereotyped behaviors (Berkson, 1967), and it is possible that cage-stereotypes of restricted animals and drug-induced stereotypes may be related (Berkson, 1983).

It is not necessary to review the literature since that has been done in a number of places recently (Berkson, 1983; LaGrow & Repp, 1984; Lewis & Baumeister, 1982; Thelen, 1981). Instead, we wish to concentrate on one concept that has guided explanations of the development and maintenance of stereotyped behaviors, that is self-stimulation. First, we will show that normal and abnormal stereotyped behaviors differ in form. We will then say that there is not much empirical support for the concept of self-stimulation but that it seems as though abnormal stereotyped behaviors are maintained by specific feedback from the behavior themselves. We will then show that self-stimulation actually involves two concepts, stimulation and control. Finally, we will show that, if one begins early enough and does a functional analysis on individuals, one can diminish pathological stereo-typed behaviors significantly and easily.

FORM OF STEREOTYPED BEHAVIORS

An assumption of many review of the literature (and of the present article) is that stereotyped behaviors of normal and abnormal children are basically the same. While there has been some questioning of this assumption, no one has actually tested it. There are several ways in which normal and abnormal stereotyped behaviors could be different. They might occur at different developmental periods. In fact, a number of people believe that abnormal stereotyped behaviors develop from the normal repetitive behaviors of infancy (Thelen, 1981). While this is probable, the necessary longi-tudinal studies to test this belief have not yet been carried out.

A second way in which the normal and abnormal behaviors might differ is that they might serve different functions. As will be shown below, func-tional analyses of stereotyped behaviors have hardly begun. At one level, their putative role as a "substrate of motor development" which accounts for the occurrence of certain stereotyped behaviors at specific transi-tional periods in motor development is countered by the observation that retarded children manifest specific stereotyped behaviors beyond a develop-mentally appropriate period. For instance, many children engage in body-rocking well past the time that they are sitting and walking efficiently.

Perhaps the simplest way of assessing whether abnormal and normal stereo-typed behaviors differ might be to look at their form. Showing that abnormal stereotyped behaviors are indeed topographically different from the normal repetitive behaviors of infancy would at least show that they are not the same in all ways and open the question of whether they are different in the ways mentioned above.

Table 1 portrays the results of a study in which Steven Schwartz analyzed

Table I

Means and Standard Deviations for Handgzing and Body Rocking
Dimensions of Retarded Children and Normal Infants

Handgazing

Dimensions	Normals (n=7)		Retarded (n=6)		Mann-Whitney U-Test	
	$\bar{x}$	SD	$\bar{x}$	SD		
Duration	3.07	1.39	11.97	11.17	3	p < .05
Extension	3.23	2.30	4.24	1.80	13	NS
Openness	1.83	0.83	1.82	0.67	21	NS
Body Position	3.00	0.00	1.89	1.06	42	p < .01
Handedness	1.70	0.59	1.36	0.63	21	NS
Handposition	1.90	1.03	2.82	0.79	10	NS
Repetition	0.00	0.00	0.76	0.59	3	p < .05

Body Rocking

Dimensions	Normals (n=7)		Retarded (n=6)		Mann-Whitney U-Test	
	$\bar{x}$	SD	$\bar{x}$	SD		
Amplitude	1.02	0.58	2.24	0.15	0	p < .01
# of Repetitions	3.40	2.17	27.69	26.66	1	p < .01
Rate	1.25	0.24	1.19	0.32	29	NS

NS = not significant

videotapes of hand-gazing and body-rocking of severely retarded and normal infants. The table shows that while aspects of the movements are similar in the two groups, they also differ significantly in other ways. This means, at the very least, that something is different about normal and abnormal stereotyped behaviors. Theories about one class of behaviors may not account completely for the other. We now need to go on and define the similarities and differences further and then find out what conditions produce the differences.

SELF-STIMULATION

The most prominent account of the maintenance of repetitive movements in infancy and abnormal stereotyped behaviors is that they are maintained by feedback from the movements, in other words, self-stimulation. Psychoanalytic theorists (Brody, 1960; Spitz & Wolf, 1949) termed these movements autoerotic reminders of characteristics of the child's parents. Piaget (1952) and Wallon (1973) saw the normal repetition of action by infants as functional in cognitive growth. The primary, and especially the secondary, circular reactions were said to produce variations of visual and proprioceptive feedback that constructed schema of the world. Finally, behaviorists (e.g., Lovaas & Newsom, 1976) speculated that sensory feedback from the stereotyped behaviors serve as reinforcers that maintained the behaviors.

All of these positions agree that feedback from the movements themselves serve as a motivator maintaining the behaviors. This contrasts with a view (e.g., Levy, 1944; Wolff, 1968; Lewis & Baumeister, 1982; Thelen, 1981) that stereotyped behaviors are intrinsically organized primitive behaviors that are maintained without important reference to the feedback they provide. It is possible, of course, that many of the stereotyped behaviors begin as early expressions of intrinsic motor development and that the feedback from them becomes important only later on. That is, the processes of initiation of these behaviors may be very different from those facilitating or maintaining them (Gottlieb, 1976).

In any case, the self-stimulation perspective suffered from three major defects until about ten years ago. The first was that the perspective tended to be post hoc and very general. Beyond the statement derived from clinical observation that the behaviors appeared self-stimulatory, there was little account of what stimulation was important and why. Second, the concept tended to be logically circular. That is, one could tell that the feedback from the behavior was maintaining stereotyped behaviors only because it seemed as if the child was interested in what he or she was receiving. Third, and perhaps most important, there was no convincing direct experimental evidence that the feedback from the movements was at all important.

Then in the 1970s, students of Ivar Lovaas reported four clinical studies (Newsom, 1974; Rincover, 1978; Rincover, Cook, Peoples & Packard, 1979; Rincover, Newsom, Lovaas & Koegel, 1977) that began to give validity to the self-stimulation concept. They showed that stereotyped behaviors could be reduced by adjusting the feedback from them. They also showed that children tended to play with toys that provide the same feedback as did their stereotyped behaviors.

SPECIFICITY OF FEEDBACK

Our studies of feedback from stereotyped behaviors have been devoted to confirming and expanding these studies and to applying what we have learned to an early intervention program for preventing the development of abnormal stereotyped behaviors.

The first issue we dealt with had to do with the specificity of the feedback. Rincover (1978) had emphasized the specificity of feedback both within and between individuals. That is, if one studies stereotyped behaviors with objects, it is possible to define a specific stimulation that the object provides, and that stimulation seems to be idiosyncratic to the individual doing the specific stereotyped behavior.

Linda Morton (1984) raised the issue of generality versus specificity in body-rocking and head-rolling. She noted that, in these behaviors, several modalities may be stimulated. Vestibular, proprioceptive, visual and even auditory feedback are all reasonable candidates for the important maintaining stimulus modalities. Stewart (1985) eliminated the auditory channel as important in maintaining body-rocking, but the other three possibilities remained. Morton reasoned that body-rocking and head-rolling might be maintained by vestibular, proprioceptive and perhaps visual feedback of different types. More important, she reasoned that if she provided head-rollers and body-rockers with linear (forward and back) and angular (rotational) stimulation, she could determine whether feedback specific to the form of the movement or more general feedback that the two types of movement shared were involved.

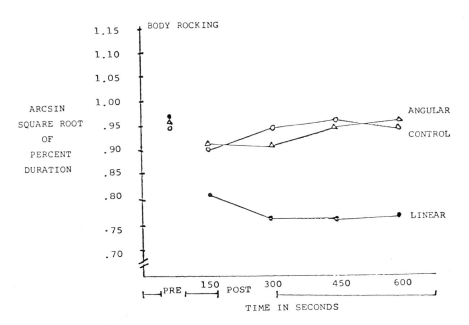

Figure 1
Body rocking before and after angular, linear and control stimulation

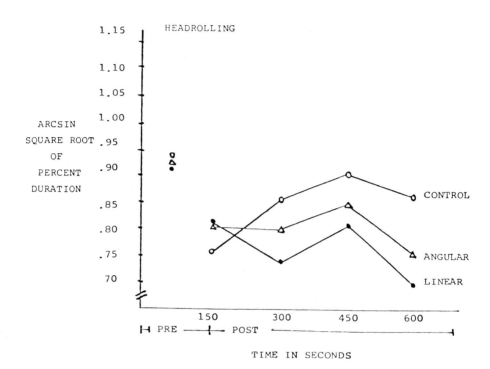

Figure 2
Head rolling before and after angular, linear and control stimulation

She presented linear and angular movement and a control condition to body-rockers and head-rollers, and she measured the amount of each stereotypy in the period preceding and following the stimulation. As can be seen from Figure 1, body-rocking was reduced only by linear treatment, a result consistent with the idea that a specific pattern of feedback is maintaining the behavior. The results with head-rollers (Figure 2) is less clear since they did not approach statistical significance.

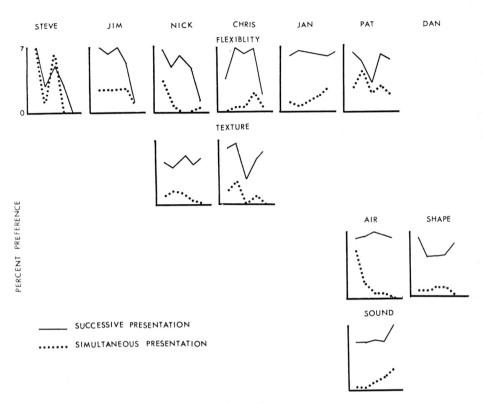

Figure 3
Preference by seven children for objects varying in flexibility, texture, air, shape or sound with two methods of presentation

Morton's results suggested that body-rocking produces a specific form of feedback which influences many subjects. Winnega and Berkson's (1984) study of feedback from object stereotypies also showed this pattern and further clarified the degree to which the effects applied to many or only particular people. She asked judges to estimate the nature of the feedback from object stereotypies (e.g., visual, texture, flexibility) and found good agreement among judges. Then she cross validated the judgments by systematically varying the characteristics of objects and measuring the child's preference for use of the object in stereotyped behavior. Figure 3 displays the graphs from this cross validation. The graphs show, first, that most children who engage in object stereotypies use flexibility as an object characteristic determining their preferences. A few children depend on other features of these objects. Thus, while assessment of individual differences is appropriate, there is also cause for making more general statements about object characteristics that maintain stereotyped behavior.

FEEDBACK AND CONTROL

The analysis of feedback from stereotyped behaviors is therefore demonstrated and can show both generality and specificity. However, the concept
of self-stimulation means more than simply providing stimulation for the
child. The child provides it to him or herself. The question is whether
stimulation and control are two separate reinforcing processes. The next
study that we report suggests that they are separate and that the effect of
these two motivators is correlated with developmental level.

Modern accounts of the child's exploration of its world emphasize that
control or mastery are intrinsically rewarding. Certain psychoanalytic
theorists also view stereotyped behavior as a way of ordering or controlling the environment (Bettelheim, 1967). Linda Buyer (Buyer, Morton,
Winnega, & Berkson, submitted) set out to ask whether controlling the
feedback from body-rocking is more or less important than the stimulation
received from it. She used a simple procedure which involved pairs of
three rocking chairs (Figure 4). One rocking chair never moved (control);
one moved only when an experimenter rocked it in the way the child would
rock the chair (passive); and one rocked normally under the child's control
(active). Buyer reasoned that if control is separate from stimulation and
is important for the child, body-rockers should prefer to sit in the active
chair.

Figure 4
The experimental situation from the point of view of the child
after he had sat in each chair experiencing each condition

We had learned from Winnega's study that n of 1 studies are necessary in
this field. So Buyer paired each condition with each other 10 times for
each child. Table 2 shows the results.

Table 2

Summary of Each Child's Preferences in Each Choice Situation
and Their Intentionality Ratings
and Vineland Adaptive Behavior Series

Child	Number of Times Active Chosen Over Passive	Number of Times Passive Chosen Over Immobile	Number of Times Active Chosen Over Immobile	Mean Rating	VABS Score
Jenny	10 ***	9 **	10 ***	3	2-11
Bryan	9 **	8 *	8 ***	3	2-3
Angela	8 *	10 ***	10 ***	2.75	2-2
Daniel	5	8 *	10	2	3-6
Kathy	7	8	7	2	1-7
Ronny	6	6	5	1.5	1-11
Michael	6	7	7	1	1-10
Scott	5	6	6	1	0-11
Lynn	5	4	7	1	1-6

*** $p < .001$ ** $p < .01$ * $p < .05$

Certain children did not prefer any chair. Others significantly preferred
the active and the passive chair over the control but did not discriminate
between the two experimental chairs. The remainder of the subjects preferred the passive rocking over the control but liked to control the
feedback most of all.

During the course of the study, it also became clear that despite the fact
that all of the children were severely or profoundly retarded, there seemed
to be definite differences in their developmental level. Therefore, we
asked judges to estimate the degree to which the subjects seemed to understand the procedure of the study, and we administered a Vineland Adaptive
Behavior Scale. The results showed quite clearly that the more mature
subjects preferred control. This means two things. First, control and
stimulation are separately reinforcing. Second, the maintaining influence
of stimulation and of control are developmentally ordered.

PREVENTION OF ABNORMAL STEREOTYPED BEHAVIORS

Summarizing to here, it is clear that abnormal stereotyped behaviors can be
distinguished from normal repetitive movements of infancy. The abnormal
behaviors, at least, are maintained separately by feedback from the movements and by control of the feedback. Analysis of the feedback is possible
and reveals that feedback patterns tend to be specific. At the same time,
some types of feedback apply to many children while some are idiosyncratic
to individual children.

G. Berkson and R.J. Gallagher

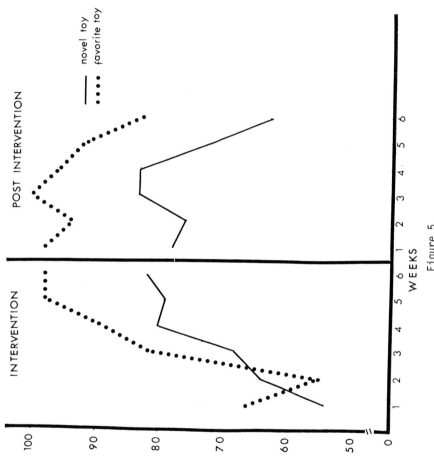

Figure 5

Object manipulation in a testing situation during and after intervention

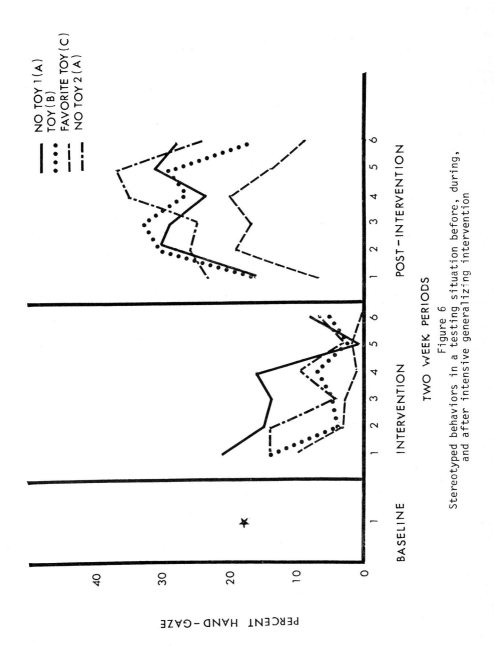

Figure 6
Stereotyped behaviors in a testing situation before, during, and after intensive generalizing intervention

In their recent review of treatment studies, LaGrow and Repp (1984) concluded that while many procedures alter the level of expression of stereotyped behaviors, there have been few demonstrations that abnormal stereotyped behaviors are eliminated from the behavior repertoire.

Since abnormal stereotyped behaviors often are inversely related to interaction with the environment (Berkson & Mason, 1964); since they can inter-
fere with learning (Koegel, Firestone, Kramine, & Dunlap, 1974); and since
they can increase with age in at least some populations (Berkson,
McQuiston, Jacobson, Eyman & Borthwick, in press), there seems to be a need
to continue to attempt to replace them with more adaptive behaviors. In
our view, doing this requires three new approaches.

The first of these approaches does not involve scientific knowledge. It is
a commitment of clinical staff to accomplish this aim. Although doing this
would seem obvious from what we have said, in fact, we have encountered
several instances during our project of clinical staff opposing a program
of therapy for abnormal stereotyped behaviors because the behaviors were
regarded as developmentally normal or at least because there seemed to be
no alternative for the child. We have even witnessed staff tell their
charges to "go rock" when the children were engaged in more normal activities. Thus, no therapy will be effective without substantial environmental
and attitudinal changes in the family or facility in which the child lives.

A second requirement for a completely successful program for eliminating
abnormal stereotypies is to begin the program early. Almost all previous
attempts to reduce stereotyped behaviors have been carried out with school-
age children or adults (LaGrow & Repp, 1984). At these ages, the behaviors
are well-established in the behavior of the person, and well-practiced
behaviors are difficult to eliminate. A reasonable approach might be to
try early intervention, probably before two years of age, as soon as the
abnormality of the behavior becomes apparent.

A third requirement of a program for preventing the development of stereotyped behaviors would be an individual assessment of the feedback they
provide. Previous studies have not been particularly sensitive to individual differences and may, as a result, have had spotty success.

We have not progressed very far to our goal of eliminating stereotyped
behavior. But we have accomplished some things. In the first place, we
have shown that the most prevalent stereotyped behaviors of severely
handicapped children in the first three years are hand-gazing, body-rocking
and sometimes head-hitting that is not self-injurious.

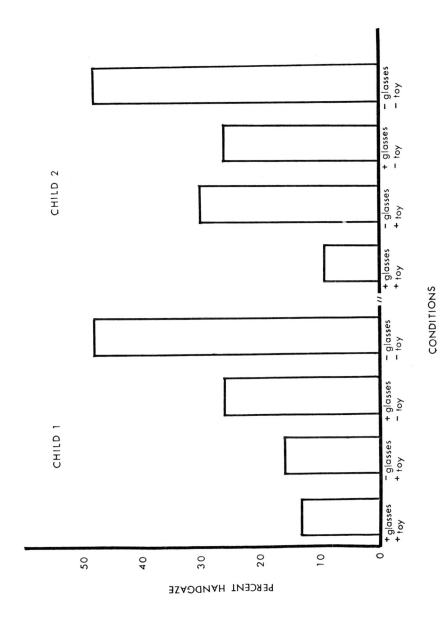

CONDITIONS

Figure 7

Handgazing by two children when toys and/or glasses were present

Second, we have shown that a massive intervention markedly reduces stereo-typed behaviors during intervention and in a testing situation. We worked with one two-year-old child who was functioning cognitively at about a two-month developmental level. He engaged in hand-gazing and head-hitting on the table in front of him. We provided him with routine caregiving and occupational and physical therapy during all of his waking hours. Figures 5 and 6 display the level of hand-gazing and object manipulation in a standard situation during which the intervention was not taking place. It is clear that undifferentiated environmental enrichment altered the child's behavior dramatically and that when treatment was withdrawn, both behaviors resumed their former level. This brief experiment showed that routine clinical procedures can be effective in reducing stereotyped behaviors, especially if carried on intensively.

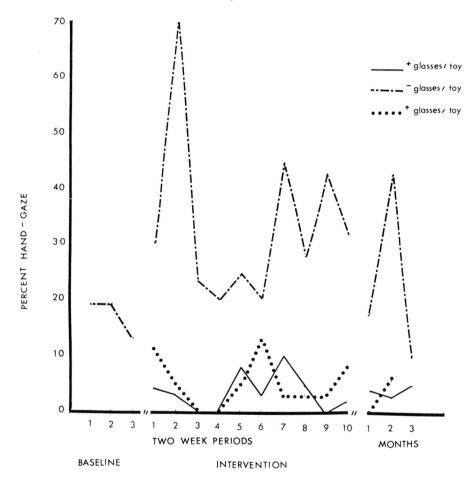

Figure 8
Handgazing with glasses on or off in the weeks after glasses
were first prescribed

However, the logic of our approach requires that a more focused treatment regime might be more effective. Reasoning that visual correction might reduce hand-gazing in visually handicapped severely retarded children, we assessed hand-gazing on two such children with glasses on and glasses off and when toys were present or absent. Figure 7 shows that both visual correction and toy presence reduced hand-gazing and that the conditions had additive effects. That is, having glasses on and toys available was maximum in reducing hand-gazing, and the reduction was dramatic. These effects, while impressive, were not necessarily permanent. To determine whether hand-gazing continued in the behavior repertoire of one of these children, we continued to observe his hand-gazing for 13 months following his first receiving glasses. Figure 8 shows that hand-gazing dwindled steadily to almost nothing as long as he was wearing his glasses. This study shows at least short-term declines in hand-gazing when glasses are prescribed in children who gaze at their hands abnormally. However, treatment must be maintained.

CONCLUSION

There are several studies that we have not met in this research. We do not know whether these studies with severely retarded children tell us anything about normal children, although we do believe that they provide indirect empirical support for the view that feedback from movements is important in maintaining normal repetitive movements of infancy.

The research also tells us little about why stereotyped behaviors of retarded children remain with them while the repetitive behaviors of normal infancy rapidly come and go. Perhaps stereotypy is a response to cognitive limitations. However, such a position awaits operational definition and empirical support.

We also have said very little about the ultimate function of self-stimulation because as we have said elsewhere (Berkson, 1983), the many theories about the "purpose" of stereotyped behaviors are as difficult to test as they are frequent and varied.

Furthermore, we have not told you whether (and if so under what conditions) abnormal stereotyped behaviors emerge from normal repetitive behaviors in humans. The alternative, of course, is that abnormal stereotyped behaviors are only coincidentally related to the normal repetitive movements of infancy. This is at least a plausible possibility since some abnormal stereotyped behaviors (e.g., head-hitting, head-rolling) are not obviously like normal repetitive behaviors. (However, see Berkson, 1968, for a relevant animal study).

Despite the fact that we have not confronted several important issues, there are some things that we have accomplished. We have shown that abnormal stereotyped behaviors can be distinguished topographically from the normal repetitive behaviors of infancy. We have also demonstrated that the feedback from stereotyped behaviors can be analyzed and that it tends to have specific form that many children use but that it also may be idiosyncratic.

Our studies revealed that self-stimulation actually involves at least two components that maintain behavior, stimulation and control, and that these two factors are developmentally ordered. The studies also show that with adequate individualized analysis, it is relatively simple to reduce stereotyped behaviors in infancy.

Finally, we have shown quite clearly that sensory feedback associated with movements can be rewarding. We hope that this study of a clinical population tells us something important about the organization and control of motor behavior.

REFERENCES

Berkson, G. (1967). Abnormal stereotyped motor acts. In J. Zubin & H. F. Hunt (Eds.), Comparative psychopathology (pp. 76-94). New York: Grune and Stratton.

Berkson, G. (1968). Development of abnormal stereotyped behaviors. Developmental Psychobiology, 1(2), 118-132.

Berkson, G. (1983). Repetitive stereotyped behaviors. American Journal of Mental Deficiency, 88(3), 239-246.

Berkson, G., & Mason, W. A. (1964). Stereotyped movements of mental defectives. IV. The effects of toys and the character of the acts. American Journal of Mental Deficiency, 68, 511-524.

Berkson, G., McQuiston, S., Jacobson, J. W., Eyman, R., & Borthwick, S. (in press). The relation between age and stereotyped behaviors. Mental Retardation.

Brody, S. (1960). Self-rocking in infancy. Journal of the American Psychoanalytic Association, 8, 464-491.

Buyer, L,, Morton, L., Winnega, M, & Berkson G. Stimulation and control as reinforcers maintaining stereotyped behaviors. Manuscript submitted for publication.

Gottlieb, G. (1976). Conceptions of prenatal development: Behavioral embryology. Psychological Review, 88(3), 215-234.

Koegel, R., Firestone, P., Kramine, K., & Dunlap, G. (1974). Increasing spontaneous play behavior by suppressing self-stimulation in autistic children. Journal of Applied Behavior Analysis, 7, 521-528.

Kravitz, H., & Boehm, J. J. (1971). Rhythmic habit patterns in infancy: Their sequence, age of onset, and frequency. Child Development, 42, 399-413.

LaGrow, S. J., & Repp, A. C. (1984). Stereotypic responding: A review of intervention research. American Journal of Mental Deficiency, 88, 595-609.

Levy, D. M. (1944). On the problem of movement restraint. American Journal of Orthopsychiatry, 14, 644-671.

Lewis, M. H., & Baumeister, A. A. (1982). Stereotyped mannerisms in mentally retarded persons: Animal models and theoretical analyses. In N. R. Ellis (Ed.), International review of research on mental retardation (Vol. II). New York: Academic Press.

Lourie, R. S. (1949). The role of rhythmic patterns in childhood. American Journal of Psychiatry, 105, 653-660.

Lovaas, O. I., & Newsom, C. D. (1976). Behavior modification with psychotic children. In H. Leitenberg (Ed.), Handbook of behavior modification and behavior therapy. Prentice-Hall.

Miller, Leon K. (1984). Stability of multiple stereotypies in handicapped children. Presented at 92nd Annual Convention of the American Psychological Association, Toronto, Ontario.

Morton, L. (1984). Effects of linear vs. angular acceleration upon stereotypic behaviors: An examination of the self-stimulation model. Unpublished master's thesis, University of Illinois at Chicago.

Newsom, C. D. (1974). The role of sensory reinforcement in self-stimulatory behavior. Unpublished doctoral dissertation, University of California at Los Angeles.

Piaget, J. (1952). The origins of intelligence in children. New York: International Universities Press.

Rincover, A. (1978). Sensory extinction: A procedure for eliminating self-stimulating behavior in developmentally disabled children. Journal of Abnormal Child Psychology, 6, 229-310.

Rincover, A., Cook, R., Peoples, A., & Packard, P. (1979). Sensory extinction and sensory reinforcement principles for programming multiple adaptive behavior change. Journal of Applied Behavior Analysis, 12, 221-233.

Rincover, A., Newsom, C. D., Lovaas, O. I., & Koegel, R. B. (1977). Some motivational properties of sensory stimulation of psychotic children. Journal of Experimental Child Psychology, 24, 312-232.

Spitz, R. A., & Wolf, K. M. (1949). Autoerotism. Psychoanalytic Study of the Child, 3, 85-120.

Stewart, J. (1985). Sound intensity and stereotypic rocking in severely profoundly retarded children: A sensory reinforcement approach. Unpublished doctoral dissertation, University of Illinois at Chicago.

Thelen, E. (1981). Rhythmical behavior in infancy: An ethological perspective. Developmental Psychology, 17, 237-257.

Winnega, M., & Berkson, G. (1984). Analyzing the stimulus properties of objects used in stereotyped behaviors. Unpublished master's thesis, University of Illinois at Chicago.

Wallon, H. (1973). The psychological development of a child. International Journal of Mental Health, 1, 29-39.

Wolff, P. H. (1968). Stereotypic behavior and development. <u>Canadian Journal of Psychology</u>, <u>9</u>, 474-484.

Motor Skill Acquisition of the Mentally Handicapped:
Issues in Research and Training
M.G. Wade (editor)
© *Elsevier Science Publishers B.V. (North-Holland), 1986*

PRECISE VISUAL INFORMATION AND THROWING ACCURACY
OF MENTALLY HANDICAPPED SUBJECTS

Walter E. Davis, Ph. D.

Kent State University

The author gratefully acknowledges the contributions of Janet
Kotyk for conducting the training sessions and Tom Edison for
assisting in the data collection. Also acknowledged are Drs.
Robert Stadulis and Stephen Langendorfer for their helpful
suggestions on an earlier version of the manuscript. Appre-
ciation is extended to the staff at Parma Developmental
Center and the Cuyahoga County Board of Mental Retardation/
Developmental Disabilities.

Support for this study was provided, in part, by grants
awarded to the author by the Office of Research and Sponsored
Programs, Kent State University and the U.S. Department of
Education, Office of Special Education, No. GOO8301260-02.

Request reprints of the author, Motor Behavior Laboratory,
Kent State University, Kent, Ohio, 44242.

INTRODUCTION

The study reported here represents an initial attempt to understand the
role of vision in controlling a complex aiming task. The importance of
vision in the control of aiming has been well known since Woodworth's
(1899) classic study. Yet, controversy still exists as to exactly how and
when vision is utilized and also as to its relative importance over other
perceptual systems in guiding movement. Research shows that vision
dominates in slowly executed aiming tasks, especially for younger perfor-
mers. However, in very rapid tasks, the importance of vision diminishes
(Posner, Nissen & Klein, 1976; Sugden, Cholewa, Cannell & Walder, 1983).
Anwar (1981) found that mentally handicapped subjects were more accurate
when both their hands and the target could be seen (visually guided) than
when only the target was visible (visually directed). However, in comparison to the non-handicapped group, they faired less well in the visually guided than in the directed situation. Anwar suggested that vision
was less useful than muscle-joint receptors in movement control for the
mentally handicapped compared to non-handicapped subjects. On the other
hand, in discrimination tasks mentally handicapped subjects have scored
relatively higher in vision/tactile system comparisons than did their
non-handicapped peers (e.g., Bilovsky & Share, 1965).

Most studies attempting to delineate the role of vision in aiming have
employed simple laboratory tasks involving only single degree of freedom

movements and/or have focused primarily on the role of feedback (e.g., Carlton, 1981; Henderson, 1977). Several researchers have recognized the need for using more natural tasks of greater complexity and for appropriately describing the concurrent visual information salient in directing the movement. This strategy is consistent with Gibson's (1966; 1979) theoretical approach to perception and action in which a functional and molar level description of the environmental information is sought. Following this approach, Lee (Lee, 1980; Lee, Lishman & Thomson, 1982) demonstrated that a "time-to-contact" variable (Schiff, 1965) is the "effective stimulus" (Gibson, 1960) in guiding such tasks as catching objects and contacting the take-off board in the long jump. Time-to-contact is specified by the optical expansion of the object as it moves toward the perceiver (as in catching) or as the perceiver moves toward it (as in long jumping).

Throwing is an aiming task similar to the tasks utilized by Lee in that it also involves a spatial target. However, an important difference is that both performer and target are relatively stationary during most throwing tasks. Thus, optical expansion of the target is not as present and the time-to-contact information is less available and presumably less relevant for movement control. Throwing is also different from most laboratory aiming tasks in which the hand (or hand-held object) lands on the target. In these tasks, vision is shown to be most effective in adjusting the movement near the end when the hand-object is in close proximity to the target (Carlton, 1979; 1981). In throwing, of course, the object is released and any final adjustment must be made when the hand-object is far from the target.

The laboratory task in Whiting and Cockerill's (1972; 1974) studies required subjects to push a small trolley up an incline a specified distance. Vision of the target was found to be important for accuracy, especially for the younger subjects. The object was thus released, as in throwing, but in a different manner and for shorter distances (100-200 cm) than generally used in overhand throwing. In both studies (Whiting & Cockerill, 1972; 1974), vision was more important when the target was at the greater distance. It would be expected, then, that visual information would be essential in the control of overhand throwing accuracy when target distance is great (over 5 m). While much research has been conducted on overhand throwing with non-handicapped subjects, few studies have considered the role of vision.

In studies by Eason and Smith (1979; 1980), the effect of color on the accuracy of throwing bean bags and darts was investigated. In the first study, they found targets with different colored concentric circles (chromatic) to be more effective than targets with white and black rings (achromatic) during a post-practice measure. However, in the second study, white targets with multi-chromatic darts produced the best accuracy. Eason and Smith (1980) suggested that the colored darts on the white background were the most distinctive and provided precise knowledge of results for subsequent performance. A difficulty with that interpretation, as they noted, is that the white target with white darts situation produced the second most accurate scores. If accuracy is best determined as the average distance from the exact center (Malina, 1963), then it would seem more intuitive to expect that information about the exact center of the target, rather than color per se, is most useful in guiding accuracy of throwing.

In a situation where throwers could see the target center prior to and during throwing a baseball but did not receive information about where their throws landed (Henderson, 1977; Malina, 1963), it was found that accuracy initially declined and then steadily improved. Malina suggested that the improvement was due to the subjects adjusting to lack of knowledge of results by utilizing target center information to guide throws. While knowledge of results is essential to improving subsequent performance, the question remains as to the importance of precise information prior to and during the throw.

The hypothesis that precise information about the center of the target is useful for guiding accuracy of the overhand throw was first tested in a preliminary study (Davis, 1984) with university students. Precise information was specified by a small red dot (5 cm in diameter) in the center of a large white target (245 cm in diameter). The dot was removed for the "no center information" condition. Two other conditions were also presented in which the dot was offset 7.5 cm in the upper left and lower right quadrants respectively. A shift in the throwing distribution corresponding to the direction of off-set was taken as further evidence the dot was being utilized.

Results indicated that subjects, particularly women, tended to be more accurate in the dot condition. Overall the difference between the dot and no dot condition was not statistically significant; however, the trend was in the direction predicted. The mean error for the condition with the dot present (precise center information) was the lowest (49.6 cm), the condition with the dot absent (no center information) was the highest at 54.6 cm and the other two conditions were in between. A significant gender by condition interaction was found. Analysis indicated that women threw with significantly greater accuracy when the dot was present. It was suggested that men were apparently able to rely on the outer dimensions of the 8 ft diameter target for center information for guiding their throws (Davis, 1984).

Further analysis of the data indicated that skill level did not effect the importance of the dot. Previous studies (e.g., Whiting & Cockerill, 1972; 1974; Sugden et al., 1983) found less skilled subjects to rely more on visual guidance in aiming. Subjects in these studies, however, were also younger. Age/experience, rather than skill alone, might have been a factor in determining the results.

From the results of the preliminary study it seemed reasonable to pursue the original question. That is, will mentally handicapped subjects, who are less experienced and less skilled than the university students, benefit from precise visual information about the target center as provided by the dot? This question was addressed in Experiment 1 of the present study, which partially replicated the method and procedures used previously (Davis, 1984). Subjects were divided into two groups, Down syndrome and non-Down syndrome on the basis of previous findings of performance differences between these groups on motor tasks (Davis, Ward & Sparrow, Note 1).

EXPERIMENT 1

METHOD

Subjects. Male and female subjects were selected from a special school
under the jurisdiction of Cuyahoga County Board of Mental Retardation/
Developmental Disabilities. The Down syndrome group consisted of nine
male and seven female subjects; eight male and ten female subjects comprised the mentally handicapped group. The mean chronological age for the
Down syndrome subjects was 14.3 years (SD = 3.0) and IQ was 39.5 (SD =
7.9). The mentally handicapped subjects' mean age and IQ measures were
15.0 years (SD = 3.3) and 45.3 (SD = 9.0) respectively. There were no
significant differences between the groups on either CA or MA. Subjects
were selected with the assistance of the adapted physical educators at the
school.

Apparatus and task. The apparatus was a large circular target 245 cm (8
ft.) in diameter and constructed from quarter-inch plywood. It was
mounted on two volleyball standards so that the center was 130 cm from the
floor. The target was painted white and covered with a plain white bed
sheet which allowed for presentation as either a blank target, i.e., no
markings to specify the exact center, or as a target with a precise center
(a small bright red dot, 20 mm in diameter, placed in the exact center).
The target was gridded in 15 cm squares drawn with a No. 3 lead pencil.
The grid was visible at close range (within 3 m) but could not be seen by
the subjects who threw from a distance of 6 m.

Subjects were given 10 warm-up throws followed by 10 experimental throws
for each of the following conditions: (1) blank target - precise center
information unavailable (NCI); (2) red dot in the exact center - precise
center information available (PCI); and (3) red dot in the center with
instructions to focus on the dot throughout the throw - precise center
information with instruction (PCWI). The first two conditions were
alternated to control for order, with the third condition always presented
last.

Subjects were instructed to: "Throw and try to hit the center of the
target." These instructions were repeated in response to any subject's
inquiry regarding the dot or the center of the target. All throws were
made overhand using tennis balls covered lightly with carbonate of mag-
nesia powder (chalk dust). When the ball struck the target, the dust left
a 5 cm impression, with a peak in the center, visible for the recorder at
close range but not visible to the subjects. After each throw the
recorder stepped in front of the target, marked the point of the throw on
a scoresheet, brushed off the dust and stepped aside for the next trial.
The scoresheet was gridded exactly as the target at a 1:15 size ratio.
Subjects could observe momentarily where their throws landed but received
no verbal feedback regarding their performance. Each subject was encouraged, prior to each block of trials, to "try and hit the center of the
target."

Design and Analysis. As in the previous study, accuracy was defined as
the distance from the center (radial error) (Malina, 1968) and measured to
the nearest 1 mm or 15 mm in real distance on the target. The mean
absolute and variable radial errors were analyzed separately using a two
(Group) by two (gender) by three (condition) ANOVA mixed design with
repeated measures on the last factor.

RESULTS AND DISCUSSION

No significant main effect or interaction was found for absolute error (Figure 1), indicating that neither group nor condition was superior for throwing accuracy. This finding suggests that precise visual information, as provided by the center dot, was not beneficial to either the Down syndrome or mentally handicapped subjects. These results contrast with the previous findings for non-handicapped subjects who did throw more accurately when the dot was present (Davis, 1984).

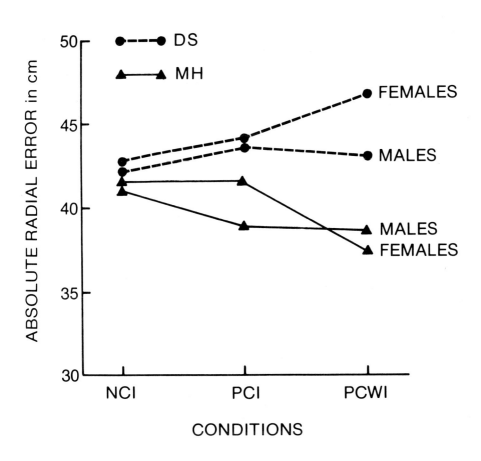

Figure 1
Group by condition effects on absolute error in throwing accuracy

It was expected that mentally handicapped subjects might be even more dependent on visual guidance than the adults in the initial study since they were younger and less experienced. Whiting and Cockerill (1974) found their youngest group (C.A. = 6-7 yrs) to perform relatively less accurately than the two older groups (C.A. = 10-11 and 19 + yrs) when vision was occluded during an aiming task. Sugden et al. (1983) found that younger subjects benefited more than older from viewing the target longer just prior to throwing underhand to a specified distance while blindfolded.

A possible reason the visual information was not effective for the mentally handicapped subjects in this study is that they simple ignored it. It is well known that mentally handicapped subjects do not necessarily spontaneously adopt effective strategies in discrimination tasks (see Zeaman & House, 1963) and recent evidence suggests this may be the case in motor tasks as well (Horgan, 1983; Reid, 1980). Using the dot might be considered a performance "strategy" and, in this instance, one that subjects did not spontaneously adopt. It is suggested here, of course, that the appropriate strategy is to focus on the dot in the center of the target. Failure to focus attention on the appropriate environmental information is a characteristic other researchers have demonstrated with mentally handicapped subjects. From the observation of the mentally handicapped subjects during the testing, it appeared that most subjects often did not focus on the target in any of the conditions. However, eye movements were not measured.

If the above interpretation is correct, one would also have to conclude that the brief "instructions" to focus on the dot throughout the throw was not effective for teaching this strategy to the subjects. Errors were not significantly reduced for either group. In fact, for the Down syndrome subjects errors were slightly, though not significantly, higher for this condition. It must be noted, however, that a similar instruction situation did not improve the throwing accuracy of the non-handicapped adults (Davis, 1984).

Figure 1 shows that mentally handicapped subjects performed slightly more accurately than the Down syndrome subjects but this difference was not statistically significant. Also, no gender differences were found in Experiment 1. Gender differences in throwing accuracy have been reported in the literature for non-handicapped throwers. Males have been shown to be more accurate than females beginning as early as pre-school (Hicks, 1930) and continuing through the elementary school years (Hoffman, Imwold & Koller, 1983; Keogh, 1965; Wilson, Silva & Williams, 1981). However, with mentally handicapped subjects, researchers (Rarick, Dobbins & Broadhead, 1976) found males to be superior to female subjects on all motor performance tasks except vertical accuracy of throwing.

Analysis of variable error produced no significant main effects; however, a significant condition by gender interaction was found, $F(2,29) = 3.8$, $p < .05$ (Figure 2).

As a complex motor task, it is not surprising to find high inter- and intra-subject variability in throwing accuracy (e.g., Dobbins & Rarick, 1977).

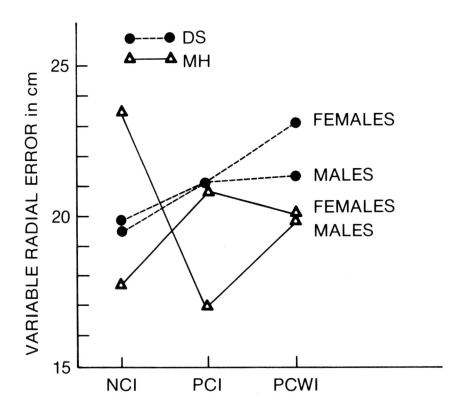

Figure 2
Group by condition effects on variable error in throwing accuracy

Since no differences between the Dot and No Dot conditions were found, the question remains as to whether precisely specifying the center information is unnecessary or whether subjects were just not using this information to improve accuracy. Experiment 2 was designed to answer this question by training subjects to focus on the dot throughout the throw. Pre- and post-tests were administered to a training group who practiced with the dot in the center and a control group who practiced the same way except the dot was absent from the target. In addition, as part of Experiment 2, subjects were tested on their understanding of "center" of the target. Prior to the throwing task, in both the pre-and post-testing situation, subjects placed a mark in the exact center of different size circles and squares cut from construction paper. The throwing task and instructions were similar to those in Experiment 1 but the subjects, conditions and procedures varied to some extent.

EXPERIMENT 2

Subjects. Forty-four subjects were selected from the same school as in
Experiment 1. Fifteen of these subjects had participated in Experiment 1.
Subjects were first pre-tested and then assigned to either a training/-
instruction group (Information) or training/control group (No Information). Groups were matched on pre-test accuracy scores. Groups were also
balanced with regard to gender, Down syndrome/non-Down syndrome (N = 7/10
& 8/11), IQ level (X = 41.1, Sd = 7.2 & X = 40.6, Sd = 6.3) and previous
participation in Experiment 1 (N = 7 & 8).

Apparatus and Task. For Experiment 2 the testing and training occurred in
a room 10 m by 8 m. A 350 cm square was marked on the blank white wall,
using a bright green border 5 cm in width, and served as the target. The
center of the target was 84 cm from the floor. All throws were made from
a distance of 6 m. All test trials were video taped using a SONY Betamax
portable videocassette recorder. A IKEGAMI color video camera (HL-79) was
positioned behind the subject such that both the subject's arm and target
were visible throughout the throw. Accuracy scores were later taken from
the video tapes. Throws that missed the target were repeated. If more
than 4 throws (33% of the trials) missed the target, data from that
subject was not used. Five subjects were eliminated from the study on
this basis.

Prior to throwing, subjects were asked to place a mark in the exact center
on circles and squares cut from construction paper. Each subject was
presented, in a random order, with 3 circles and 3 squares measuring 25
cm, 50 cm and 75 cm in diameter. Post-testing followed the same procedures. Performance was measured as radial error from the exact center of
the figure. This task was designed to determine their level of understanding of the concept of center and to determine the level of accuracy
in identifying the center on the basis of the outer dimensions alone.

Training. Both groups received an equal number of practice throws (60 per
session) given on alternate days over a two week period (six sessions each
group). All subjects practiced on the same target as used in the pre- and
post-tests. The Information group practiced with the red dot in the exact
center of the target and were given instructions to "look at the dot"
prior to and throughout the throw. The No Information group threw at the
same target without the dot and with instructions to hit the center of the
target. All training was conducted by a Graduate Research Assistant
experienced in teaching mentally handicapped students. Training and
testing sessions lasted approximately 10 minutes per subject.

Design and Data Analysis. Subjects were measured on throwing accuracy,
under two experimental conditions (with and without the dot), in a pre-and
post-training situation. As in Experiment 1, throwing accuracy was
measured as absolute and variable radial error. Accuracy scores were
taken from the video tape by the experimenter. Accuracy was measured to
the nearest 1 mm on the monitor which equaled 7 mm in real distance. Data
from the "find the center" task was analyzed using a two (group) by two
(gender) by two (time - pre and post) by two (shape - circle and square)
by three (sizes) ANOVA mixed design with repeated measures on the last
three factors.

RESULTS AND DISCUSSION

Results from the "find the center" task are first reported. There was a significant size main effect, as shown in Figure 3, $F(2,24) = 20.2$, $p <$ .01. Subjects were significantly more accurate in finding the center of the smallest figures. Accuracy was also significantly greater for 50 cm over the 75 cm figures. There were no other significant main effects and no significant interactions. This result suggests that when relying on the outer dimensions alone, the larger the target the larger the error in locating the center. From this, it would be expected that judging the center of a square target 350 cm would be relatively inaccurate.

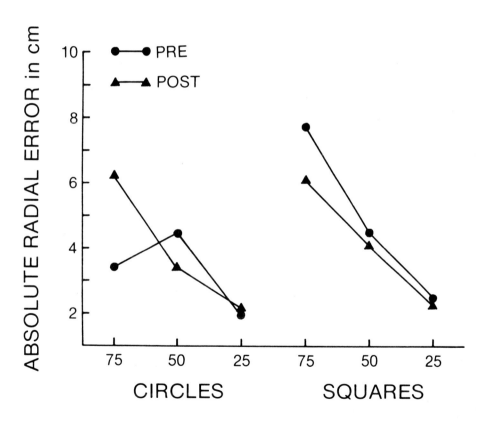

Figure 3
Size and shape differences in pre and post measures
of accuracy in finding the center

As shown in Figure 3, there was a slight but non-significant difference overall between the circle condition and square condition, the latter having a higher error score. Training in throwing at the center of a target did not improve subjects' accuracy in finding the center of the geometric shapes.

Preliminary analysis of the throwing data indicated that Down syndrome subjects were similar to the mentally handicapped subject in accuracy in each of the conditions (See Table 1) and thus, means were collapsed for subsequent analysis.

Table 1

Means and Standard Deviation of Down Syndrome
and Mentally Handicapped Subjects

			Subjects			
			DS		MH	
Group	Time	Cond	Males (N=10)	Females (N=5)	Males (N=13)	Females (N=8)
Info	Pre	Dot	63.2 (17.0)	82.5 (22.6)	77.4 (33.9)	58.8 (36.1)
		NoDot	75.9 (13.0)	78.5 (19.1)	73.0 (18.5)	62.1 (20.7)
	Post	Dot	41.2 (16.4)	37.7 (10.1)	49.0 (19.1)	36.8 (11.7)
		NoDot	52.9 (15.2)	51.4 (15.9)	66.1 (16.4)	50.6 (11.3)
NoInfo	Pre	Dot	69.3 (16.9)	56.4 (5.6)	64.3 (34.0)	62.4 (7.3)
		NoDot	78.1 (24.0)	56.1 (15.6)	77.8 (14.7)	66.5 (14.0)
	Post	Dot	66.9 (20.9)	49.7 (11.7)	50.9 (17.2)	46.9 (15.9)
		NoDot	72.7 (15.6)	68.1 (12.1)	61.4 (14.7)	55.7 (8.6)

A two (group) by two (gender) by two (condition) by two (time) ANOVA mixed design with repeated measures on the last two factors was used to determine if precise information, training and instruction decreased throwing error and throwing variability in mentally handicapped subjects. Only the data from subjects who completed the both and pre- and post-testing and all the training were used in this analysis. Results showed a significant main effect for time, $F(1,32) = 27.4$, $p < .001$ and condition, $F(1,32) = 35.4$, $p < .001$, but not for group. As shown in Figure 4, post-test scores were significantly lower than pre-test scores for both groups. In the Dot condition, error scores were significantly lower than in the No Dot condition across groups.

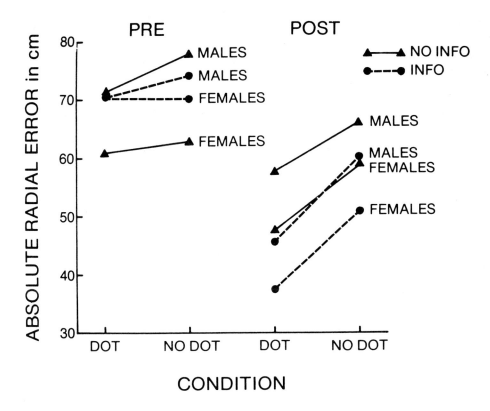

Figure 4
Gender by group by condition effects on absolute error
in throwing accuracy for pre and post measures

A time by group interaction also reached significance, $F(1.32) = 4.12$, $p <$ .05 indicating that the information group's error scores were lower in the post-test situation but not in the pre-test. There was also a significant time by condition interaction, F, $(1,32) = 8.16$, $p < .01$. Inspection of the means indicates that there was a significant condition difference during the post-test but not during the pre-test. Thus, the results of the pre-test for throwing accuracy were consistent with Experiment 1, that is, there were no differences between the Dot and No Dot conditions (Figure 4). In the post-test, throwing error was less in the Dot condition than in the No Dot condition suggesting that following practice the dot became effective in providing information to guide throwing accuracy. The three way interaction of Time by Group by Condition failed significance, $p = 1.95$. The other interactions failed to reach significance as well.

From Figure 4, it can be seen that both groups decreased throwing error from the pre- to post-testing but that the Information group decreased more. It would be expected that subjects would decrease their errors with both practice situations but that the Information group would improve more. The statistical results bore this out.

Difference scores between pre- and post-tests were calculated for the two groups and analyzed using a two (group) by two (gender) by two (condition) ANOVA mixed design with repeated measures on the last factor. These results showed a significant condition effect, $F(1.32) = 8.16$, $p < .01$ but the main effect for group just failed significance, $F(1,32) = 3.22$, $p = .08$ (Figure 5). The group by condition interaction also failed significance, $F(1,32) = 1.95$, $p = .17$.

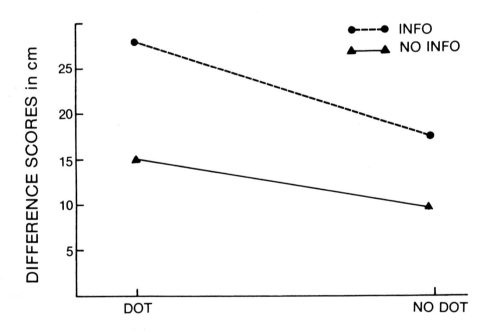

Figure 5
Group by condition effects on difference scores

In Experiment 2, as in 1, significant gender differences were not found for absolute error. However, on variable error, significance was found $F(1,32) = 6.25$, $p < .05$, with females being less variable than their male counterparts (Figure 6).

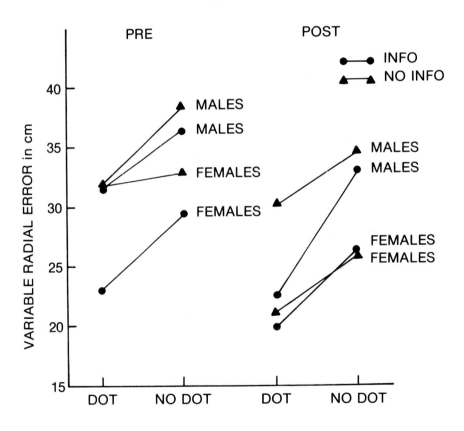

Figure 6
Gender by group by condition effects on variable error
in throwing accuracy for pre and post measures

Again, both inter- and intra-individual variability were high (See Table 2).

W.E. Davis

Table 2

Means, Standard Deviation and Difference Scores in cm

Group	Ss No.	Pre Mean	(Sd)	Post Mean	(Sd)	Difference
	1	46.4	(15.7)	32.4	(16.9)	14.0
	2	45.1	(23.6)	33.5	(16.7)	11.6
	3	75.2	(37.3)	31.2	(17.9)	44.0
	4	83.1	(44.4)	70.0	(22.4)	13.1
	5	66.2	(22.3)	39.0	(23.0)	27.2
	6	93.1	(55.9)	38.5	(19.7)	54.6
	7	92.1	(46.6)	61.4	(25.4)	30.7
Info	8	130.8	(26.6)	81.3	(46.8)	49.5
	9	42.5	(20.7)	43.4	(23.1)	- 0.9
	10	51.3	(26.5)	28.6	(14.3)	22.7
	11	54.6	(27.9)	40.6	(23.2)	14.0
	12	77.6	(30.9)	48.9	(24.8)	28.7
	13	107.1	(39.5)	29.2	(15.1)	77.9
	14	62.8	(19.7)	35.0	(12.8)	27.8
	15	54.7	(16.0)	46.4	(31.9)	8.3
	16	24.9	(12.8)	23.7	(13.8)	1.2
	17	96.7	(20.5)	40.3	(20.7)	56.4
	Totals	70.7	(27.4)	41.4	(21)	29.4
	18	58.1	(36.0)	60.6	(42.3)	- 2.5
	19	65.8	(27.5)	60.6	(30.7)	5.2
	20	58.5	(24.6)	56.9	(40.9)	1.6
	21	65.4	(40.9)	52.4	(32.8)	13.0
	22	98.9	(48.7)	103.7	(36.4)	- 4.8
	23	74.7	(40.7)	48.7	(23.0)	26.0
	24	87.3	(29.8)	34.4	(20.7)	52.9
NoInfo	25	64.5	(26.4)	74.0	(42.0)	- 9.5
	26	68.5	(36.9)	51.8	(21.7)	16.7
	27	109.5	(25.9)	35.5	(27.2)	74.0
	28	34.9	(10.5)	37.5	(13.3)	- 2.6
	29	68.7	(26.8)	74.3	(31.5)	- 5.6
	30	67.0	(34.9)	68.4	(28.0)	- 1.4
	31	60.3	(44.6)	58.0	(27.4)	2.3
	32	52.5	(23.1)	41.4	(14.7)	11.1
	33	51.2	(30.1)	28.3	(9.8)	22.9
	34	66.0	(27.4)	37.1	(16.5)	28.9
	35	68.9	(45.9)	56.6	(22.6)	12.3
	36	58.8	(16.0)	44.1	(29.2)	14.7
	Totals	66.0	(31.7)	52.6	(25.8)	13.3

Dot Condition

Table 2--Continued

		No Dot Condition				
Group	Ss No.	Pre Mean	(Sd)	Post Mean	(Sd)	Difference
Infor	1	72.0	(41.2)	41.9	(25.9)	30.1
	2	62.8	(32.3)	45.0	(22.4)	17.8
	3	67.6	(27.9)	43.4	(35.7)	24.2
	4	95.6	(53.8)	78.2	(65.7)	17.4
	5	81.7	(36.3)	56.2	(32.9)	25.5
	6	91.4	(30.1)	53.2	(29.7)	38.2
	7	72.9	(34.0)	85.2	(39.2)	-12.3
	8	97.6	(45.7)	85.0	(25.4)	12.6
	9	54.9	(42.6)	60.4	(26.9)	- 5.5
	10	52.4	(23.6)	45.6	(23.0)	6.8
	11	68.9	(35.0)	67.2	(36.8)	1.7
	12	87.9	(32.6)	68.5	(28.6)	19.4
	13	91.0	(40.7)	37.1	(28.1)	53.9
	14	56.5	(22.9)	48.5	(21.9)	8.0
	15	67.7	(29.5)	63.4	(30.0)	4.3
	16	39.1	(14.6)	41.8	(18.9)	- 2.7
	17	79.4	(35.8)	46.7	(30.4)	32.7
	Totals	72.3	(33.)	55.5	(29.7)	16.8
NoInfo	18	49.9	(24.1)	60.0	(23.5)	-10.1
	19	92.2	(55.2)	64.2	(35.0)	28.0
	20	71.7	(44.3)	68.1	(29.5)	3.6
	21	65.3	(29.0)	70.2	(42.4)	- 4.9
	22	111.2	(57.0)	99.8	(40.4)	11.4
	23	80.6	(31.1)	66.7	(32.2)	13.9
	24	93.1	(44.1)	49.8	(32.5)	43.3
	25	71.9	(26.4)	91.0	(49.9)	-19.1
	26	76.7	(51.6)	54.4	(28.4)	22.3
	27	90.2	(43.7)	59.4	(33.5)	30.8
	28	48.8	(16.2)	47.3	(29.8)	1.5
	29	83.2	(38.9)	61.3	(39.0)	21.9
	30	68.2	(44.1)	63.4	(48.0)	4.8
	31	62.5	(27.1)	76.7	(43.2)	-14.2
	32	49.6	(27.7)	59.5	(13.6)	- 9.9
	33	52.0	(25.9)	58.0	(9.6)	- 6.0
	34	82.9	(40.5)	41.9	(15.8)	41.0
	35	76.8	(34.0)	61.7	(33.5)	15.1
	36	52.5	(31.1)	53.5	(18.0)	- 1.0
	Totals	70.7	(35.7)	62.6	(30.3)	8.1

Perhaps more important to this study was the finding of a significant time, $F(1,32) = 12.5$, $p < .01$, and a significant condition effect, $F(1,32) = 19.9$, $p < .001$, indicating that subjects were not only more accurate but also less variable with the dot present. A Group main effect and Group interactions all failed significance suggesting that both groups benefited from practice and from the presence of the dot in reducing variable error. No other interactions were significant.

In summarizing the findings of Experiment 2, results indicate that both groups improved following practice, as would be expected. This was the case for both absolute and variable radial error. Both groups improved most under the Dot condition, with the Information group demonstrating an even greater improvement than the No Information group. The fact that the dot significantly effected the accuracy scores for both groups during the post-test may indicate that all subjects became more conscious of the dot. It was reported by the Graduate Assistant who conducted the training sessions that subjects expressed an awareness of the dot and no dot training situations.

GENERAL DISCUSSION

The results of this study support the hypothesis that precise visual information will increase throwing accuracy for mentally handicapped subjects. These findings are consistent with previous research, with both handicapped and non-handicapped populations, demonstrating the effectiveness of vision in controlling movement during aiming tasks. In this case, the task involved with multi-degrees of freedom. The overhand throwing task may also be considered a ballistic movement. Recent evidence shows that even in rapid goal-directed movements, visual information is important in modifying the movement (Gielen, van den Heuvel & van de Gon, 1984). Gielen and colleagues found that muscle activation patterns of rapid tracking movements are modified during the movement.

It is not clear from the present study whether the visual information provided by the center dot allowed subjects to modify the movement during the throw or was used as a reference in providing outcome information (knowledge of results) for guiding subsequent throws. Subjects were able to observe, at least momentarily, where their throws landed and the dot could have served as a reference in providing more precise outcome information. Henderson (1977) found that such knowledge of outcome was important in improving accuracy in a dart throwing task. Subjects, in her study, who did not receive knowledge of outcome (i.e., could not see where the darts landed) but could see the location of the target prior to and during the throw also reduced their throwing errors, however, not to the same extent as subjects with both target and outcome information. In considering the combined results of these studies, it is likely that subjects utilized both means of controlling throwing movements.

The present study demonstrated that while precise visual information can be effective for reducing errors it is not automatic with mentally handicapped persons. Subjects required training before they effectively utilized the visual information. The findings here support previous research (Horgan, 1983; Reid, 1980) showing that mentally handicapped subjects do not always spontaneously adopt an effective strategy during motor tasks.

Anwar (1981) suggested that mentally handicapped subjects may be relatively more accurate in target localization using haptic information rather than visual information as compared to non-handicapped subjects. However, it may also be the case that the handicapped subjects would have benefited from the visual information to the same extent as the non-handicapped subjects had they been provided instructions. The results from the present study suggests that these differences in performance may be reduced with training.

REFERENCES

Anwar, F. (1981). Visual-motor localizations in normal and subnormal development. British Journal of Psychology, 72, 43-57.

Bilovsky, D., & Share, J. (1965). The ITPA and Down's syndrome: An exploratory study. American Journal of Mental Deficiency, 70, 78-82.

Carlton, L. G. (1979). Control processes in the production of discrete aiming responses. Journal of Motor Behavior, 5, 115-124.

Carlton, L. G. (1981). Processing visual feedback information for movement control. Journal of Experimental Psychology: Human Perception and Performance, 7, 1019-1030.

Davis, W. E. (1984). Precise visual information and throwing accuracy in adults. Perceptual and Motor Skills, 59, 759-768.

Dobbins, D. A., & Rarick, G. L. (1977). The performance of intellectually normal and educable mentally retarded boys on tests of throwing accuracy. Journal of Motor Behavior, 9, 23-28.

Eason, B. L., & Smith T. L. (1979). Effects of chromatic targets on a throwing task for subjects referred for learning disability. Perceptual & Motor Skills, 48, 229-230.

Eason, B. L., & Smith, T. L. (1980). Effects of multichromatic and achromatic target and darts on throwing. Perceptual & Motor Skills, 51, 519-522.

Gibson, J. J. (1960). The concept of the stimulus in psychology. American Psychologist, 15, 694-703.

Gibson, J. J. (1966). The senses considered as perceptual systems. Boston: Houghton-Mifflin.

Gibson, J. J. (1979). An ecological approach to visual perception. Boston: Houghton-Mifflin.

Gielen, C. C. A. M., van den Heuvel, P. J., & Denier van der Gon, J. J. (1984). Modification of muscle activation patterns during fast goal-oriented arm movements. Journal of Motor Behavior, 16, 2-19.

Henderson, S. E. (1977). Role of feedback in the development and maintenance of a complex skill. Journal of Experimental Psychology: Human Perception and Performance, 3, 224-233.

Hicks, J. A. (1930). The acquisition of motor skill in young children. Child Development, 1, 90-105.

Hoffman, S. J., Imwold, C. H., & Koller, J. A. (1983). Accuracy and prediction in throwing: A taxonomic analysis of children's performance. Research Quarterly for Exercise & Sport, 54, 33-40.

Horgan, J. S. (1983). Mnemonic strategy instruction in coding, processing and recall of movement related cues by the mentally retarded. Perceptual and Motor Skills, 57, 547-557.

Keogh, J. F. (1965). Motor performance of elementary school children. Los Angeles: University of California, Department of Physical Education.

Lee, D. N. (1980). Visuo-motor coordination in space-time. In G. E. Stelmach & J. Requin (Eds.), Tutorials in motor behavior (pp. 281-295). Amsterdam, Holland: North-Holland.

Lee, D. N., Lishman, J. R., & Thomson, J. A. (1982). Regulation of gait in long jumping. Journal of Experimental Psychology, 8, 448-459.

Malina, R. M. (1963). Performance changes in a speed-accuracy task as a function of practice under different conditions of information feedback. Unpublished doctoral dissertation, University of Wisconsin.

Malina, R. M. (1968). Reliability of different methods of scoring throwing accuracy. Research Quarterly, 39, 149-160.

Posner, M. I., Nissen, M. J., & Klein, R. M. (1976). Visual dominance: An information processing account of its origins and significance. Psychological Review, 83, 157-171.

Rarick, G. L., Dobbins, D. A., & Broadhead, G. D. (1976). The motor domain and its correlated in educationally handicapped children. Englewood Cliffs, NJ: Prentice-Hall.

Reid, G. (1980). The effects of memory strategy instruction in the short-term motor memory of the mentally retarded. Journal of Motor Behavior, 12, 221-227.

Schiff, W. (1965). The perception of impending collision. Psychological Monographs, 79, (Whole No. 604), 1-26.

Sugden, D. A., Cholewa, J. P., Cannell, A. J., & Walder, P. J. (1983). Development of use of vision between 8 and 16 yrs. of age on performance of slow continuous and fast discrete motor tasks. Perceptual and Motor Skills, 57, 1263-1269.

Whiting, H. T. A., & Cockerill, Z. M. (1972). The development of a simple ballistic skill with and without visual control. Journal of Motor Behavior, 4, 155-162.

Whiting, H. T. A., & Cockerill, I. M. (1974). Eyes on hand--eyes on target? Journal of Motor Behavior, 6, 27-32.

Wilson, J. G., Silva, P. A., & Williams, S. M. (1981). An assessment of motor ability in seven year olds. Journal of Human Movement Studies, 7, 221-231.

Woodworth, R. S. (1899). The accuracy of voluntary movement. Psychological Monographs, 3(2), (Whole No. 13), 1-113.

Zeaman, D., & House, B. J. (1963). The role of attention in retardate discrimination learning. In N. R. Ellis (Ed.), Handbook of mental deficiency. New York: McGraw-Hill.

Motor Skill Acquisition of the Mentally Handicapped:
Issues in Research and Training
M.G. Wade (editor)
Elsevier Science Publishers B.V. (North-Holland), 1986

THE DEVELOPMENT OF THE POSTURAL AND VOLUNTARY MOTOR CONTROL SYSTEMS
IN DOWN'S SYNDROME CHILDREN

Marjorie H. Woollacott, Ph.D.[1] and Anne Shumway-Cook, R.P.T., Ph.D.[2]

[1]Institute of Neuroscience and
College of Human Development and Performance
University of Oregon
Eugene, OR 97403

[2]Department of Physical Medicine and Rehabilitation
Good Samaritan Hospital and Medical Center
1015 NW 22nd Avenue
Portland, OR 97210

INTRODUCTION

When motor development of the Down's syndrome child is compared to that of
the normal child, a consistent delay is observed in the acquisition of
both postural and voluntary components of motor control (Cowie, 1970;
Frith & Frith, 1974; Knight et al., 1978). Molnar (1978) studied motor
control in a population of mentally retarded children and found both a
delay in emergence of postural adjustments and increased variability in
age of onset of postural adjustments. In tests of gross motor skills,
Down's syndrome children perform consistently below their normal peers,
with their worst performance in the area of static and dynamic balance
(Cratty, 1969; Rarick & McQuillan, 1977).

Neuromuscular abnormalities in Down's syndrome children which have been
observed to be coincident with developmental delays include: generalized
muscular hypotonus, hyperextensibility of joints, decreased deep tendon
reflexes, increased persistence of primitive reflexes, delay in the
emergence of higher level balance and equilibrium reactions and slowed
reaction times during voluntary movement (Benda, 1960; Brinkworth, 1975;
Carr, 1970; Cowie, 1970; Davis & Kelso, 1982; Donoghue et al., 1970;
Penrose & Smith, 1966; Share et al., 1964).

It has been hypothesized that the transition from primitive spinally
controlled muscle response patterns to more integrated and coordinated
movement patterns is delayed and/or absent in Down's syndrome children due
to poor myelination of the descending cerebral and brainstem neurons and a
reduction in the number of neurons in the higher nervous centers leading
to a paucity of higher center control over lower more primitive centers
(Cowie, 1970; Molnar, 1978).

Examples of neuropathology associated with Down's syndrome include: 1)
reduction in the number of neurons of cerebellum and brainstem as indicated by a 40% decrease in brain weight of cerebellum and brainstem
compared to normals; 2) decreased size of cerebral hemispheres, especially
frontal lobes; 3) fewer and smaller convolutions of the brain, suggesting
neurological immaturity (Benda, 1960; Crome & Stern, 1972; Loesch-
Madzeuska, 1968; Penrose & Smith, 1966); 4) structural abnormalities in

the dendritic spines of pyramidal neurons in the motor cortex (Marin-Padilla, 1976); 5) lack of myelinization of nerve fibers in the precentral, frontal lobe area, and cerebellum (Benda, 1960); 6) connective tissue abnormalities which contribute to joint laxity and hyper-extensibility (Smith & Berg, 1976; Zellweger & Simpson, 1977), and have been hypothesized to contribute to decreased deep tendon reflexes (Harris, 1981).

A number of research projects involving early therapeutic intervention with Down's syndrome children have been conducted based on behavioral observations of developmental delay. Bricker and Bricker (1971), Dmetriv (1973), Decoriat et al. (1967), Hanson (1978), and Harris (1981) have facilitated normal mental and motor development through a variety of stimulation techniques with mixed results. While these and other studies accurately describe the behavioral deficits and delays in Down's syndrome children, few studies have explored the specific motor control deficits which could underlie postural instability and subsequent developmental delay in motor coordination. Many researchers attribute deficits in motor skills to underlying hypotonia; however, recent work by Davis and Kelso (1982) casts doubt on this hypothesis. They tested the ability of 7 Down's syndrome subjects and 6 normal subjects to set and/or voluntarily modulate muscle stiffness, and found the two groups comparable. While the Down's syndrome subjects did show altered movement parameters such as increased movement time and oscillation about the final end position, Davis and Kelso concluded that underlying muscle response organization is normal. It is possible that ability to voluntarily control muscle stiffness may not be indicative of the degree of stiffness in a task utilizing non-voluntary or automatic postural responses.

The above studies seem to be consistent in describing the behavioral deficits associated with Down's syndrome, including developmental delays and balance problems, but do not provide evidence to help unravel the underlying problems in the organization of sensory and motor systems.

However, recent research by Butterworth and Cicchetti (1978) has begun to examine these questions, looking at the ability of Down's syndrome children to solve problems of intersensory conflict in balance control. They used balance conditions involving both sitting and standing and studied a population of normal and Down's syndrome children with experience in standing ranging from 1 to 20 months. (Mean age range was 29 to 42 months.) Using an experimental approach in which they moved the visual surround of the child without moving the base of support, they showed that Down's syndrome children were more influenced by incongruent visual and proprioceptive-vestibular input than normal children as evidenced by increased sway and numbers of falls. This tendency to differentially respond to inappropriate visual cues decreased with age and experience in standing. In the seated posture the youngest population of Down's syndrome children performed better than normals during the sensory conflict task. However, over time the Down's syndrome children did not improve significantly as did their normal peers. These findings led Butterworth to conclude that "magnitude of response to discrepant visual information is a function of the particular posture. Down's infants do not differ from normals in their ability to perceive optic flow patterns, but they do differ in the way they make use of the information depending on whether they are sitting or standing" (Butterworth, 1982, p. 62).

In order to better understand research on functional balance problems in children with Down's syndrome, a brief review of the neural basis of normal posture control will be presented.

NORMAL POSTURE CONTROL AND ITS DEVELOPMENT

The development and maintenance of stability is critical to the acquisition of complex motor skills and requires the maturation of two potentially separate, though interactive, processes within the postural control system: (1) those responsible for coordinating muscles and joints into appropriately organized response patterns, and (2) those responsible for ensuring that responses remain consistently context dependent. This involves organizing, integrating, and acting upon redundant visual, vestibular and support surface-somatosensory inputs providing orientational information to the postural control system.

Previous research with normal adults, using a moveable platform to experimentally test balance, has shown that the central nervous system coordinates muscles responding to loss of balance through stereotypically organized sway synergies which minimizes body sway and maintain the center of mass within the base of support (Nashner, 1976; 1977). These sway synergies consist of multiple muscles constrained to act together as a functional unit with fixed temporal and special parameters.

In addition to sway synergies, postural stability depends upon the organization and integration of orientation inputs from visual, vestibular and somatosensory systems. Previous work on sensory integration and balance control in normal adults suggests that the controlling sensory inputs to the postural control system are context specific. In a well practiced position, when the support surface is stable, mechanical somatosensory inputs provide the primary though not the sole input to balance. Vision plays a more important role in novel situations, or in situations where support surface inputs are minimally helpful (as on a compliant surface) (Lee & Lishman, 1975). Vestibular inputs serve a reference function and are critical in resolving conflict between somatosensory and visual inputs (Nashner et al., 1982).

Research on the development of posture control in normal children has demonstrated that directionally specific response synergies are present in children as early as 15 months. However, variability in timing and amplitude relationships between proximal and distal muscles suggests that structural organization of the synergies is not yet fully developed until about seven years of age (Shumway-Cook & Woollacott, 1983; in press; Forssberg & Nashner, 1982). Transition from immature to mature postural synergies does not occur in a linear fashion but rather has stage-like properties, with variability in synergic responses greatest in children aged four to six. In addition, with development there appears to be a shift in the controlling inputs to posture from visual dependencies to a more adult-like dependence on a combination of support-surface somatosensory and visual inputs at about four to six years of age. Neural processes which are responsible for resolving multi-modal sensory conflict are not fully developed before the age of seven. Hence, it has been suggested that the age of four to six represents a transition period in the development of posture control. It is hypothesized that this is a time when the nervous system uses visual-vestibular postural inputs to

fine tune ankle and foot proprioception and concomitant synergic responses
leading to the emergence of mature postural control by the age of seven to
ten years.

The present study tested the hypotheses that deficits in static and
dynamic balance skills found in Down's syndrome children are in part the
result of abnormalities within the automatic postural control system.
Specifically, experiments were designed to: 1) quantify deficiencies in
the long latency automatic postural response system; and 2) determine if
deficiencies exist in the sensory integration mechanisms underlying the
organization of orientation information from somatosensory, visual and
vestibular systems.

METHODS

SUBJECTS

A total of 17 children, ages 15 months to six years were tested (eleven
normal children and six children with Down's syndrome). Parameters for
selection of the children with Down's syndrome included: Presence of
trisomy-21 or mosaic Down's syndrome, normal vision and hearing, absence
of congenital heart defects, no history of seizures, absence of current
medications, and independence in stance and/or ambulation. The purpose,
procedures, risks and benefits of the study were explained to parents, and
informed consent given.

Normal and Down's syndrome children were divided into two groups: 1) a
group of older children aged four to six, who were given all experimental
tests and evaluation procedures. This group contained four Down's syndrome and six normal children; 2) a group of younger children, ages 15-31
months, consisting of two Down's syndrome children and five normal
children who were evaluated on only the simpler experimental procedures.

INITIAL CLINICAL EVALUATIONS

Following selection, but prior to experimental sessions, each child with
Down's syndrome in the older group was independently clinically assessed
by two pediatric therapists experienced in evaluating and treating
children with developmental disabilities. The tests of developmental and
motor control which were used were the Bayley Scales of Infant Development
and the Brigance Diagnostic Inventory of Early Development (birth to seven
years) (Bayley, 1969).

The Down's syndrome children were found to be functioning 18 to 24 months
behind their age level with significant performance decrements in both
static and dynamic balance tests. All children were judged moderately
hypotonic by clinical assessment based on test of resistance to passive
stretch, joint extensibility, muscle consistency and anti-gravity postur-
ing.

Table 1 presents a summary of the clinical evaluation results. When data
were normalized for variability in chronological age, all four children
performed at the same overall developmental level, demonstrating a surprising homogeneity of behavioral performance across these children.

Table 1

Clinical Evaluation Summary

Down's Syndrome Subjects	Chrono- logical Age	Developmental Age		Balance Tests		Muscle Tonus*	Fine Muscle
		Brigance	Bayley	Static	Dynamic		
1. Mosaic Downs	5.5	2.11	3.6	3	3.6	2	4
2. Trisomy 21	3.5	2.0	2.3	2	1.5	2	3.6
3. Trisomy 21	5.3	3.0	3.6	3.0	3.0	1	2.5
4. Trisomy 21	5.8	3.4	2.5	2	1.6	2	2

*Muscle Tonus Scale

  1 2 3 4 5

hypotonus normal hypertonus

APPARATUS

A hydraulically controlled platform capable of both horizontal (anterior-posterior) and rotational (about an axis colinear with the ankle joint) movements was used to elicit postural responses. The platform consisted of a base plate (50 cm x 52 cm) suspended at the four corners on strain gauge sensors. The strain gauge sensors measured total load ($\pm$ 0.005 kg/meter linearity $\pm$ 5%) and torque (the difference between the forces detected by the anterior and posterior strain gauges). Anterior or posterior platform displacements were $\frac{1}{2}$ sine waves, 2 cm in amplitude with a duration of 250 msec. Rotational displacements which caused ankle dorsiflexion or plantarflexion were also $\frac{1}{2}$ sine waves of 6 degrees amplitude and 250 msec duration. The measurement of anterior-posterior sway was made through the use of a rod attached to the subject's hips with a velcro strap and connected to the base of the platform via a potentiometer.

For experiments analyzing postural and voluntary interactions, a handle was placed vertically in front of the child at waist height, and via a metal tube, attached to the floor in front of the base plate; the child was asked to push or pull on the handle in response to a light signal while standing on the platform.

Surface electromyograms (EMG's) were used to measure the responses of the gastrocnemius (G), tibialis anterior (T), hamstrings (H), and quadriceps

(Q) muscles during all postural perturbations. Each raw EMG signal was processed by full-wave rectification and filtering (0-40 Hz) to obtain an envelope of activity whose level was related to the amplitude of muscle contraction.

High speed (100 frames per second) film analysis was completed using a camera placed seven meters from the primary sagittal plane of action with the optical axis set at a height to maximize the subject within its field of view. Cinematographic data were smoothed using a cubic spline smoothing process and digitized using every fifth frame. Biomechanical analysis included quantification of joint angles at hip, knee and ankle during initial stance and subsequent sway. Sway motion was separated into two components: 1) platform induced motion, and 2) compensatory motion, and was represented graphically, utilizing stick figures constructed from digitized data points.

PROCEDURES

Each child was tested at least three separate 45-minute sessions, conducted during different weeks to assure replicability of observations over time. The first two sessions were used for evaluation of postural responses to platform translations and rotations. Ten anterior and 10 posterior horizontal platform translations were sequenced randomly during the session. In addition, ankle dorsiflexing perturbations were given in a linear sequence of five trials each, in order to study the adaptation mechanisms of each child.

The final session was used to examine postural responses under varying sensory conditions, and used only the children above three years of age since younger children would not tolerate the unstable support surface and eye closure without crying. Table 2 summarizes the different configurations of sensory inputs utilized and whether each condition represented a multi-modal sensory conflict or non-conflict condition.

Children were asked to stand for five seconds under four different sensory conditions (see Table 2). These included: 1) normal stable platform surface with eyes open ($S_N V_N$); 2) normal platform surface, eyes closed ($S_N V_C$), a situation representing loss of redundancy among sensory inputs but not inter-sensory conflict; 3) platform surface servoed, vision normal ($S_S V_N$), a condition in which the platform was rotated in direct proportion to AP sway motion as measured by the potentiometer. This procedure minimized orientational input from ankle and feet by maintaining a fixed 90 degree ankle joint angle despite body sway; as a result support surface inputs were perceptually correct but incongruent with orientationally correct vision and vestibular inputs, resulting in an intersensory conflict situation. In the final condition ($S_S V_C$) children were asked to balance with their eyes closed, platform surface servoed. This provided orientationally incorrect somatosensory inputs in conjunction with an absence of visual inputs leaving only orientationally correct vestibular inputs to mediate balance and thus represents both a measure of vestibular input efficacy and a multi-model sensory conflict.

Table 2

Sensory Conditions

Condition	Configuration of Sensory Inputs to Posture	Conflict
$S_N V_N$	Congruent Support Surface-Somatosensory, Vision and Vestibular	No Conflict
$S_N V_C$	Congruent Somatosensory and Vestibular, No Vision	No Conflict
$S_S V_N$	Congruent Vision and Vestibular, Incongruent Somatosensory	Conflict
$S_S V_C$	Vestibular Input, Incongruent Somatosensory, No Vision	Conflict
Rotational Perturbations	Congruent Vision and Vestibular; Incongruent Somatosensory	Conflict

DATA ANALYSIS

Muscular responses to platform tests were analyzed using rectified and filtered electromyograms (EMG's). EMG onset latency was determined by visual inspection while EMG amplitude was calculated by numerically integrating the first 76 msec of the EMG response, providing a relative measure of muscle contractile activity. Pearson product moment correlation was used to express the stability of the amplitude relationship between distal and proximal muscles.

Body sway measures were used to determine a "Stability Index" which reflected children's stability in response to postural perturbations. Potentiometer data were numerically integrated and scaled to the theoretical limits of sway of each child. Theoretical limits of sway were determined by first measuring the height of each child and calculating center of mass. Foot measurement from heel to ball of foot was taken to determine total base of support. Theoretical limits for forward and backward sway were calculated separately since the larger base-of-support (3/5 of total) in the forward direction produces greater stability in that direction. Angle of sway was calculated using an arc tangent function relating height of center of mass to base of support. In addition to integrated sway data, maximum excursion of sway during a trial was recorded. Increasing scores on the Stability Index indicate decreasing stability, with 100 representing loss of balance.

Due to the small sample size and the lack of homogeneity of variance, the Mann Whitney U Test was used on all tests of statistical significance.

All normal adult data used for comparison of response latencies and amplitudes were taken from a previous study in the laboratory (Woollacott et al., 1982).

RESULTS

POSTURAL CONTROL - MOTOR COORDINATION

Monosynaptic Stretch Reflex. Normal standing adults compensate for externally induced body sway through the activation of automatic postural responses with latencies on the order of 100 msec. These longer latency postural responses have been shown to be more effective than monosynaptic stretch reflexes in returning the center of mass to within the base of support (Nashner, 1976; 1977). Previous studies have shown that in normal adults the excitability level of the myotatic (monosynaptic) reflex is considerably reduced in the upright standing posture (Gurfinkel et al., 1971).

In this study normal children, ages four to six years, showed incomplete suppression of the monosynaptic stretch reflex in response to dorsiflexing rotational perturbations in 40% of the trials. Down's syndrome children tested also showed incomplete inhibition of the stretch reflex during stance. Two of the four older Down's syndrome children evidenced myotatic responses in 40% of the trials (two showed no myotatic response).

Postural Sway Synergies. In response to platform translations, children with Down's syndrome produced postural response synergies which, in the majority of cases, were appropriately directionally specific, though more variable than the postural synergies of adults. There were no significant differences between normal and Down's syndrome children of ages four to six in the preferential selection of response patterns; however, both groups showed greater variability of response patterns than did adults or a population of normal children ages 15-31 months. Figure 1 displays EMG activity from four lower extremity muscles in a normal child and a child with Down's syndrome in response to a platform perturbation producing forward sway. The platform moves back, causing the subject to sway forward, with a resultant primary response in gastrocnemius and hamstrings and a secondary response in the antagonist muscles tibialis anterior and quadriceps. Gross sequencing of muscles in response to platform movement was comparable in both normal and Down's syndrome children, though patterns of muscular activation over sequential trials were more variable than normal adult synergies. However, when compared to normal children, children with Down's syndrome showed subtle differences in timing and force relationships between synergic muscles.

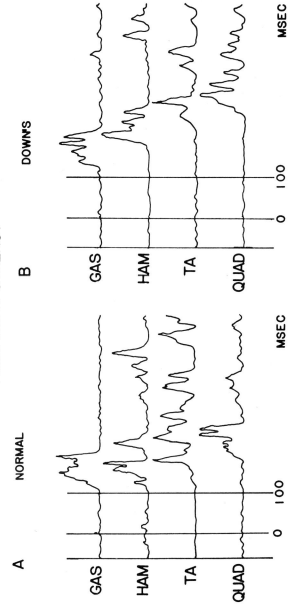

Figure 1

EMG activity in response to a plus (forward) sway translation,
showing the similarity in muscle sequencing
between Down's syndrome and normal children

Distal-Proximal Muscle Temporal Delay. In normal adults the response to
platform translation usually begins in distal muscles at the perceived
base of support, and progresses to proximal muscles with a 10 to 25 msec
delay (Woollacott et al., 1982). Both Down's syndrome and normal children
displayed an increased temporal delay in the recruitment of proximal
muscles. Figure 2 shows the temporal delay between distal and proximal
muscles in adults, normal children and children with Down's syndrome in
response to a forward sway (Gastrocnemius-hamstrings) and backward sway
(tibialis anterior-quadriceps) perturbation. Zero msec represents time of
onset for distal muscles. In adults, proximal muscles were activated
10-25 msec later. In normal children proximal muscle delays of 36 ± 18
msec in forward sway and 58 ± 16 msec in backward sway were common.
Children with Down's syndrome showed a delay of 57 ± 13 and 36 ± 17 msec
for forward and backward sway respectively. Children's delays were
significantly slower in comparison to adult data (p < .01) but not with
respect to one another.

TEMPORAL DELAY
DISTAL-PROXIMAL MUSCLES

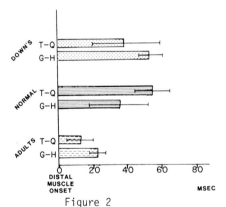

Figure 2
Comparison of temporal delay between distal and proximal muscles
in normal and Down's syndrome children. Delays in both groups are
significant when compared to adults, but not with respect to one another.

Distal-Proximal Muscle Amplitude Correlations. Synergic muscles in adults
are tightly coupled and despite trial to trial amplitude variations,
contract in fixed proportion to one another (Woollacott et al., 1982).
Significantly lower (p < .001) inter-muscle amplitude correlations were
found for both forward and backward sway synergies for normal children
compared to adults and for children with Down's syndrome compared to
normal children. Figure 3 presents the correlation data for gastrocnemius
and hamstrings muscles in response to plus sway perturbations from six
adults, six normal children and four older children with Down's syndrome.
Note that correlations were high (r̄ = .85) for adults indicating a tight
synergic coupling between gastrocnemius and hamstrings muscles over all
trials. Normal children demonstrated a smaller correlation (r̄ = .45) and
Down's syndrome children showed the least correlation (r̄ - .22). This
suggests that unlike adults, automatic postural response synergies in
children ages four to six were not as clearly established, and this was
especially true of Down's syndrome children.

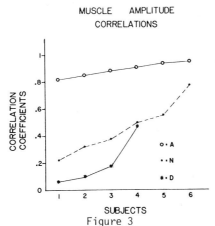

Figure 3

Digital-proximal muscle amplitude correlations for adults, normal and Down's syndrome children. Correlations are high ($\bar{r}$ = .85) for adults, smaller for normal children ($\bar{r}$ - .45) and least for Down's syndrome children ($\bar{r}$ = .22) suggesting synergic coupling between proximal and distal muscles is not well established in Down's syndrome children.

Onset Latencies. The onset latencies of postural muscle responses of Down's syndrome children were significantly slower (p < .001) than normal children in response to externally produced perturbations to balance. Normal children were slightly slower than adults (112 ± 12 msec as compared to 100 ± 4 msec), while Down's syndrome were considerably slower (136 ± 32 in forward sway and 162 ± 40 in backward sway). Figure 4 displays the average distal muscle onset latency for all three populations to both forward and backward sway perturbations. Delayed activation of postural patterns in Down's syndrome children could not be attributed to decreased motor neuron excitability as analysis of EMG records showed monosynaptic stretch reflex responses at normal latencies, and low level tonic background activity in many trials indicative of supra-threshold motor neuron excitability.

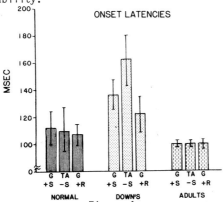

Figure 4

Distal muscle onset latency in response to forward (+S), backward (-S) sway and toes up rotation (+R). Down's syndrome children are significantly slower (p < .001) than normal children or adults in responding to externally induced body sway.

Motor Coordination - Newly Walking Down's Syndrome Children. Figure 5
compares postural responses to three forward sway translations in the two
youngest Down's syndrome children, a 15 month old, and a 22 month old
normal child. Two Down's syndrome children, age 22 months, were exposed
to platform tests. One had been walking independently for one week, the
other for one month. In the child with Down's syndrome who had been
walking one week, postural responses to platform induced sway were poorly
organized. No response was found in four of the eight trials (falls
resulted), while in the remaining trials the response was limited to
activation of the distal muscle of the appropriate synergy.

Latencies were also quite slow (gastrocnemius = 160 msec; tibialis
anterior = 190 msec). The 22 month old child with Down's syndrome who had
been talking one month showed by comparison better organized responses.
Distal muscle activation of the appropriate synergy was consistently
present at latencies between 140 and 160 msec. Proximal muscle coupling
was still poor but was present on occasion. Latency and amplitude variability of the proximal muscle was great.

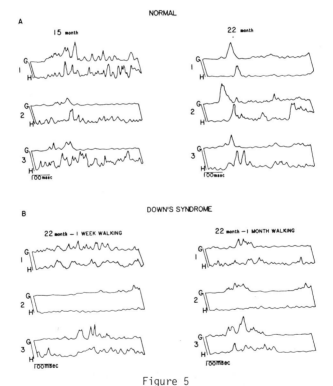

Figure 5
Postural response patterns to three forward sway translations in newly walking Down's syndrome children and young normal children. Response patterns in
young Down's syndrome children are limited to activation of directionally
appropriate distal muscle. Lack of good synergic organization in this age
may represent an ontogenetic difference in postural control between Down's
syndrome and normal children.

Biomechanical Correlates of EMG Activity. Joint angle-segment motion.
Analysis of angular position at hip, knee and ankle indicated that no
significant change occurred in initial body stance position over sequential trials. This rules out change in initial position as an explanation
for EMG pattern variability in the four to six year old normal child, and
in the child with Down's syndrome.

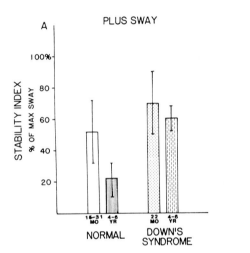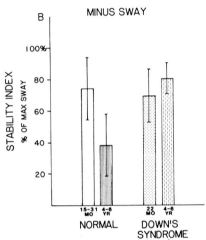

Figure 6
Comparison of body sway in response to platform translation in normal
and Down's syndrome children. Down's syndrome children (ages four to
six) swayed significantly more than did normal children and more often
reached their limits of stability in response to platform induced sway.

BIOMECHANICS OF TRANSIENT SWAY

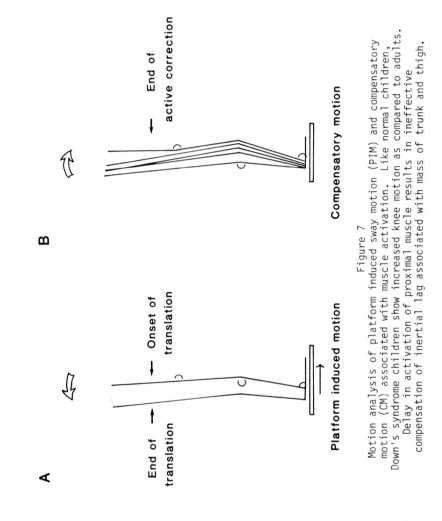

Figure 7

Motion analysis of platform induced sway motion (PIM) and compensatory motion (CM) associated with muscle activation. Like normal children, Down's syndrome children show increased knee motion as compared to adults. Delay in activation of proximal muscle results in ineffective compensation of inertial lag associated with mass of trunk and thigh.

Figure 6 is a graphic representation constructed from digitized data points which presents body motion associated with platform induced backward sway and compensatory muscular action.

Biomechanical analysis of joint angle changes associated with platform induced body motion indicated that both groups of children, like adults, sway initially like inverted pendulums, with motion principally about the ankle joints (6A) (Horak & Nashner, 1983). However, in most adults compensation for body sway involves movement primarily at the ankle joint as torque exerted by ankle musculature propels the center of mass back to a point of stability and synergistic action by proximal thigh and trunk muscles minimizes antiphase motion at the hips resulting in little movement at knee (Shumway-Cook & Woollacott, in press). This is not the case in normal and Down's syndrome children aged 4-6 who show considerable differential motion at knee and hip. Figure 6B displays body motion associated with compensatory muscle action in response to backward sway and illustrates increased movement of body segments with concomitant flexion at knee and hips. Motion analysis combined with EMG data suggests that differential motion at the hip and knee was the mechanical consequence of diminished temporal coupling between proximal and distal muscle synergists. Activation of proximal muscles was not sufficiently rapid to minimize inertial lag associated with the mass of the thigh and trunk.

Body Sway. Figure 7 compares average sway to a forward and backward postural perturbation across age groups of normal children and children with Down's syndrome.

In response to both forward and backward platform translations normal children ages 15 to 31 months swayed on the average closer to their limits of stability and more often reached their maximum point of stability during a trial than did normal children ages four to six years (p < .01). This is consistent with developmental literature indicating that stability normally increases as a function of age. Down's syndrome children ages four to six swayed on the average closer to their limits of sway than did normal children ages four to six (p < .01) and, in addition, more often reached their limits of stability in response to platform induced sway.

POSTURAL CONTROL - SENSORY INTEGRATION

Platform rotations, like translations, result in ankle rotation and stretch to ankle muscles, but without the concomitant shift in the center of mass and resultant body sway. As a result, while somatosensory inputs from lower extremities associated with translation are congruent with visual and vestibular inputs in signalling body sway, somatosensory inputs secondary to rotation are in conflict with vision and vestibular inputs, which do not signal sway. Previous research has shown that, in normal adults and children above the age of seven, somatosensory inputs without concomitant visual/vestibular inputs are sufficient to produce a synergic response. However, this response, in the absence of actual body sway, is destabilizing and, in the normal adult and child above seven, attenuates within three to five trials.

Consistent with normal children ages four to six, all of the children with Down's syndrome ages four to six showed postural response patterns to rotational perturbations, indicating that somatosensory inputs in isolation were sufficient to bring automatic postural responses to threshold. However, unlike their normal counterparts, none of the children with Down's syndrome showed adaptive attenuation of postural responses to rotational perturbations within 15 trials. In addition, three of the four children lost balance during the first three rotational trials, none of the normal children lost balance. The two youngest children with Down's syndrome (20 months), similar to normal children under the age of three, did not show long latency postural responses, and in addition, lost balance in response to all rotational trials (Shumway-Cook & Woollacott, in press). Figure 8 presents examples of adaptive attenuation of inappropriate rotational responses in the normal adult and child, and lack of adaptation in the child with Down's syndrome.

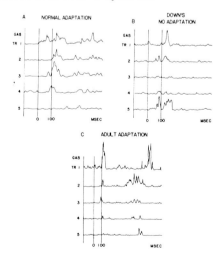

Figure 8
Comparison of adaptive attenuation of inappropriate rotational responses in adults, normal and Down's syndrome children. Normal children exhibit appropriate adaptation within 10 to 15 trials while Down's syndrome children did not.

<u>Inter-sensory Conflict and Sway</u>. Both normal and Down's syndrome children (ages four to six years) were asked to stand quietly for five seconds during four different conditions: surface and visual inputs normal ($S_N V_N$); surface input normal, eyes closed ($S_N V_C$); surface inputs uncorrelated with body sway (due to servoed platform) vision normal ($S_S V_N$); and surface servoed, eyes closed ($S_S V_C$). Results presented in Figure 9 represent change in stability across the four sensory conditions in both normal children and children with Down's syndrome.

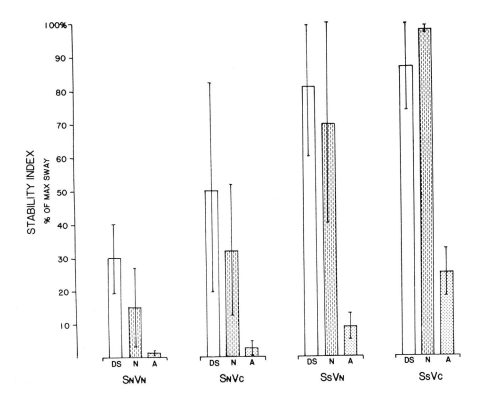

Figure 9

Stability Index for continuous stance trials under altered sensory conditions in normal, Down's syndrome children and adults. Down's syndrome children exhibited diminished stability under all conditions when compared to adults and normal children. Greatest number of falls were in situations presenting inter-sensory conflict ($S_S V_N$ and $S_S V_C$) suggesting processes responsible for resolution of inter-sensory conflict are not yet developed in the four to six year old Down's syndrome child.

Under the first condition where all three inputs to the postural control system were present ($S_N V_N$), children with Down's syndrome were signifi-cantly (p .05) more unstable than normal children or adults, although they were still well within their limits of stability. When redundancy of inputs was reduced by removing visual inputs through eye closure ($S_N V_C$), both normal and Down's syndrome children showed diminished stability although again they were well within their limits.

When the support surface was rotated in direct proportion to anterior-posterior sway resulting in fixed angle joint angle and somatosensory inputs which were incongruent with visual and vestibular inputs ($S_C V_N$), two of the four children with Down's syndrome fell, while one of the five normal children fell. When visual inputs were removed leaving only vestibular inputs and orientationally incorrect somatosensory inputs to mediate balance reactions, three of the four Down's syndrome children fell. Four of the five normal children fell under the same condition. This suggests that conditions presenting the greatest threat to stability in both normal and Down's syndrome children under six are those with incongruent inputs representing multi-modal sensory conflict.

POSTURAL-VOLUNTARY INTERACTION

Experiments designed to look at the relationship between voluntary move-ments and posture control required the children to push or pull on a non-compliant handle in response to a visual light signal (see Figure 9).

Previous researchers (Paltsev, 1967; Cordo et al., 1980) using similar paradigms have shown that in normal adults voluntary effort is always preceded by activity in postural muscles so as to minimize instability associated with voluntary movement. This anticipatory postural activity is consistent with a feedforward control mechanism between the voluntary and postural systems since initiation of postural activity is not depen-dent upon feedback from the voluntary activity as would be true in a compensatory-feedback system.

Four normal adults were tested with the apparatus and all showed direc-tionally specific activity in distal leg muscles preceding activity in the upper extremity prime mover.

In four of five normal children, previously tested (Shumway-Cook & Woollacott, in press), upper extremity voluntary responses were always preceded by postural responses in the lower extremities. In all cases, the postural responses were specific to the direction of arm movement rather than consisting of a general increase in activity in both lower extremity muscles. The fifth child showed preparatory activity in 80% of her trials.

The four oldest Down's syndrome children were tested using the handle apparatus. One of the children was unable to understand the instructions sufficiently to perform the task; the remaining three were able to perform a pull in response to the visual cue combined with an auditory cue. The Down's syndrome children showed adequate anticipatory postural activity prior to voluntary movement in less than 50% of the trials as compared to 100% in the four normal children, and, in addition, were considerably slower in making their voluntary movement. In those cases where postural activity preceded voluntary activity, it was specific to the arm movement required rather than consisting of a general coactivation of lower extremity muscles. Figure 10 compares one push and one pull trial from a Down's syndrome child and a normal child. In the normal child, activity in lower extremity muscles (gastrocnemius for pull; tibialis for push) which preceded upper extremity muscle activation is consistent with an anticipatory <u>feedforward</u> control process. Postural activity in the Down's syndrome child <u>follows</u> upper extremity voluntary effort in a compensatory or feedback manner.

Figure 10
Handle apparatus used to test the interaction between the voluntary and the postural control systems.

DISCUSSION

Clinical evaluation of the four older children with Down's syndrome indicated they were functioning 18 to 24 months behind age level with significant performance decrements in both static and dynamic balance tests. This is consistent with existing literature documenting delays in the longitudinal development of Down's syndrome children. All four children with Down's syndrome were determined to be moderately hypotonic, also consistent with existing literature. Presence of short latency myotatic reflexes in response to platform rotations at latencies comparable to normal children is not consistent with clinical findings of <u>hypoactive</u> deep tendon reflexes and reduced motoneuron pool excitability. Rather these data support Davis and Kelso in suggesting that children with Down's syndrome show muscle stiffness and motoneuron pool excitability comparable to that of normal children (Davis & Kelso, 1982). Presence of short latency myotatic reflexes (normally suppressed in the standing adult) lends only weak support to the hypothesis that children with Down's syndrome show decreased higher center modulation of more primitive patterns controlled at lower centers as normal children of the same age also show incomplete suppression of short latency myotatic responses (Cowie, 1970; Molnar, 1978).

POSTURAL RESPONSE SYNERGIES

Down's syndrome children, ages four to six, produced directionally specific though highly variable synergic responses to induced postural sway. Analysis of the structural organization of postural responses in children with Down's syndrome showed significantly poorer amplitude correlation and more variable temporal relationship between proximal and distal muscles. This suggests that postural synergies responding to externally induced sway are poorly formed in comparison to normal children of the same chronological age. In addition, postural synergy onset latencies were significantly slower in Down's syndrome children. As stated previously, delayed activation of postural patterns in Down's syndrome children could not be attributed to reduced segmental motoneuron excitability in light of (1) normal myotatic latencies, and (2) presence of low level tonic background activity in many trials indicative of supra-threshold motoneuron excitability.

The presence of myotatic reflexes at normal latencies in conjunction with significant delays in long latency postural responses presents an interesting paradox. It suggests that currently held views in rehabilitation literature which attributes the developmental delays and balance problems found in Down's syndrome children to decreased segmental motoneuron pool excitability and pathology of the stretch reflex mechanism leading to hypotonia should be questioned. Instead these data suggest support for Burke who critically questions the validity of traditional views on the role of the muscle spindle in disorders of muscle tonus (Burke, 1983).

In children with Down's syndrome, deficiencies in structural organization of postural responses in combination with slowed onset of response resulted functionally in significantly increased body sway and, in some instances, loss of balance in response to external disturbance to stability.

POSTURAL RESPONSES IN NEWLY WALKING DOWN'S SYNDROME CHILDREN

There was considerable difference in the organization of postural patterns in very young children with Down's syndrome as compared to very young normal children. Unlike normal children under three years who showed reasonably consistent though unmodulated sway synergies in response to platform translations, the two 22 month old Down's syndrome children showed very inconsistent and poorly organized sway responses, which were also quite slow. This difference in postural response organization between young normal and Down's syndrome children is particularly surprising when one examines the ontogenesis of postural control in normal children. Here the normal child under three years appears to have more consistently organized and less variable postural responses than does the four to six year old. However, the young child's inability to appropriately modulate postural responses can result in instability due to overcompensation and subsequent oscillation (Forssberg & Nashner, 1982).

Thus, the finding that postural synergies in the young 22 month old Down's syndrome child were more poorly organized than the four to six year old Down's syndrome child may represent a difference in the ontogenetic development of postural control between Down's syndrome and normal children. Possibly equilibrium problems found in Down's syndrome children are

not just the result of delayed, albeit normal, development -- but in fact
represent a difference in the evolution and development of postural
control. More research on the development of posture control in children
under three years is needed to confirm this.

SENSORY INTEGRATION

Results from experiments which tested balance under altered sensory
conditions demonstrated that Down's syndrome children, ages four to six
years, had difficulty maintaining balance with loss of redundant sensory
inputs, and that situations presenting the greatest threat to stability
were those with incongruent inputs representing multi-modal sensory
conflict. This, in conjunction with the results from rotational perturbation trials, suggests that the organizational processes underlying
adaptation and resolution of sensory conflict may be less developed in the
four to six year old Down's syndrome child than in the normal child.
These data are consistent with previous work on stance balance control in
patients with cerebellar pathology (Nashner & Grimm, 1977; Nashner et al.,
1983).

POSTURAL-VOLUNTARY INTERACTION

Several studies on postural-voluntary interaction have demonstrated the
role of lower extremity postural activity preceding upper extremity
voluntary activity preceding upper extremity voluntary activity in providing a stable base for movement. The Down's syndrome children (four to
six years) able to perform the task demonstrated anticipatory postural
activity in only 50% of their trials as compared with 100% in four normal
children previously tested. In the remaining 50% of the trials activity
in postural muscles followed upper extremity motion.

This suggests that Down's syndrome children were more consistently relying
upon a feedback strategy for controlling interaction between posture and
voluntary systems rather than a feedforward control process more commonly
used in normal children and adults.

THERAPEUTIC IMPLICATIONS

This research suggests that therapeutic remediation of balance problems in
Down's syndrome children should focus on two primary areas: 1) improving
motor coordination by assisting children in developing and refining
postural synergies; this requires improving th spatio-temporal coupling
between multiple muscle groups which act together; 2) improving the
organizational processes responsible for integrating and acting upon
redundant and conflicting sensory inputs. Specifically, Down's syndrome
children need to develop strategies for dealing with loss of redundancy of
sensory inputs as well as strategies for the resolution of multi-modal
sensory conflict.

It should be emphasized that in the normal child neither process -- the
formation of postural synergies of the integration of sensory inputs -- is
a voluntary or conscious process. This is an important understanding when
considering therapeutic intervention. The maintenance of stability

requires the execution of fast (automatic) postural responses with onset latencies below those of voluntary reaction time responses. It is unlikely that techniques which rely upon voluntary or consciously acquired balance responses will ensure stability unless the learned response becomes automated -- that is, not requiring conscious processing. The same may be said for strategies for adapting to multi-modal sensory conflict.

Paillard (1966) differentiates between innate and learned synergies of action and suggests that the functional usefulness of new synergies will depend on 1) the degree to which existing but inappropriate synergies can be fractionated, and 2) the ability to automate the new synergies. When considering the remediation of balance deficits in Down's syndrome children one is not dealing with existing but inappropriate synergies which must be broken down prior to building new synergies. Rather the problem appears to be in decreasing the onset latency and improving the structural organization of existing postural responses.

One current approach to habilitating the Down's syndrome child is the Neurodevelopmental Therapy Approach (NDT). The NDT approach focuses on normalization of hypotonia and subsequent facilitation of equilibrium reactions through specific handling and movement of the child (Harris, 1980). Our research suggests that segmental motoneuron pool excitability and concomitant hypotonia may not be the controlling factor in slowed or delayed postural responses. This may explain why pharmacological approaches which improve muscle tonus in Down's syndrome children nonetheless show little functional gains in the acquisition of developmental skills (Bazelon et al., 1967).

Previous research on adult postural responses suggests that onset latencies are variable depending on context. This suggests that the delayed onset latencies in Down's syndrome children should be responsive to change. Woollacott et al. (1980) have shown that the combination of providing prior information about direction of sway and repetition of trials was successful in decreasing latencies of postural responses in normal adults. These experiments leave unanswered the question of long term retention of change and transfer to new situations. While practice alone may improve response latencies, it is not known whether practice alone would improve the structural organization of response synergies. There are a number of current therapeutic techniques which purport to influence and improve the coordination of muscles acting together including Proprioceptive Neuromuscular Facilitation (Knott & Voss, 1968), Functional Electrical Stimulation (Teng et al., 1976), Sensory Feedback Technique (Brudny, 1976). Only further research can determine the efficacy of these techniques in improving the structural integrity of postural responses.

There has been considerable research in the area of adaptation or compensation to sensory distortion. Lackner (1981) suggests that sensory adaptation can occur only if the necessity for performance correction is recognized at some level of representation. However, Kravitz and Wallack (1966) suggests that adaptation is not dependent upon conscious awareness of discordance among sensory channels.

Research on sensory adaptation has led to the emergence of several concepts with potential impact on improving the integration of multi-sensory input in the child with Down's syndrome. Held and Hein (1963) looked at sensory adaptation and movement in kittens. Their work suggests that active sensori-motor experience may be a necessary prerequisite to sensory adaptation. This concept is further supported by Lacour and Xerri (1979) who examined vestibular compensation in primates. They demonstrated that sensori-motor restrictions during early recovery severely hampered the compensatory process and suggest that the multi-sensory substitution process requires that the subject engage in sensori-motor activity.

Work by Graybill and Wood (1969) on adaptation to vestibular stimuli in humans demonstrated that incremental exposure to sensory discordance can facilitate adaptation and long term retention of adaptation. However, Graybill and Wood note that adaptation was situation specific and did not transfer to new environs.

These studies would suggest some approaches to facilitating the process of adaptation to sensory conflict in Down's syndrome children. Actively engaging the child in gradually increasingly complex environments which progress from loss of redundancy of sensory inputs to conflicting sensory inputs may have a positive impact on the organizational processes underlying sensory integration and result in a functional improvement in balance. Further research is needed to test this and other techniques.

The major contribution of this study has been to provide insight into specific deficits of postural control in Down's syndrome children. The ability to quantify deficits should improve our ability to develop and test the efficacy of therapeutic techniques designed to improve postural control in the Down's syndrome child.

REFERENCES

Bayley, N. (1969). Bayley Scales of infant development. New York: Psychological Corp.

Bazelon, M., Paine, R., Cowie, V., Hunt, P., Houck, J., & Mahanand, D. (1967). Reversal of hypotonia in infants with Down's syndrome by administration of 5-hydroxytryptophan. The Lance, 1130-1133.

Benda, C. E. (1960). Mongolism: A comprehensive review. Archives of Pediatrics, 391-407.

Bricker, W., & Bricker, D. (1971). Toddler research and intervention project. Paper from Institution of Mental Retardation, George Peabody College.

Brinkworth, R. (1975). The unfinished child: Early treatment and training for the infant with Down's syndrome. Royal Society Health Journal, 95(2), 73-78.

Brudny, J. (1976). EMG feedback therapy: Review of treatment of 114 patients. Archives of Physical Medicine Rehabilitation, 57, 55-61.

Burke, D. (1983). Critical examination of the case for or against fusimotor involvement in disorders of muscle tone. In J. Desmedt (Ed.), Motor control mechanisms in health and disease.

Butterworth, G. (1982). The origins of auditory-visual perception and visual proprioception in human development. In R. Wark & H. Pick (Eds.), Intersensory perception and sensory integration, New York: Plenum Press.

Butterworth, G. E., & Cicchetti, D. (1978). Visual calibration of posture in normal and motor retarded Down's syndrome infants. Perception, 7, 513-525.

Carr, J. (1970). Mental & motor development in young mongol children. Journal of Mental Deficiency Research, 14, 205-220.

Cordo, P. J., & Nashner, L. M. (1982). Properties of postural adjustments associated with rapid arm movements. Journal of Neurophysiology, 47, 287-302.

Cowie, V. (1970). A study in the early development of mongols. London: Pergamon Press.

Cratty, B. J. (1969). Motor education and the education or retardates. Philadelphia: Lea & Feiger.

Crome, L., & Stern, J. (1972). Pathology of mental retardation (2nd Ed.). Edinburgh: Churchill Livingstone.

Davis, W., & Kelso, J. A. S. (1982). Analysis of "invariant characteristics" in the motor control of Down's syndrome and normal subjects. Journal of Motor Behavior, 14(3), 194-212.

DeCoriat, L., Theslenco, L., & Waksman, J. (1967). The effects of psychomotor stimulation in the IQ of young children with Trisomy-21. In B. W. Richards (Ed.), Proceedings of the first congress of the international assoc. for scientific study of mental deficiency. Surrey, England: Michael Jackson.

Dmetriv, V. (1973). Early education for the child with Down's syndrome. Paper presented at Region I AAMD, Portland, Oregon.

Donoghue, E. C., Kirman, B. H., Bullmore, G. H., Laban, D., & Abbas, K. (1970). Some factors affecting age of walking in a mentally retarded population. Developmental Medicine and Child Neurology, 12, 781-792.

Forssberg, H., & Nashner, L. (1982). Ontogenetic development of postural control in man: Adaptation to altered support and visual conditions during stance. Journal of Neuroscience, 2(5), 545-552.

Frith, V., & Frith, C. D. (1974). Specific motor disabilities in Down's syndrome. Journal of Child Psychology and Psychiatry, 15, 293-301.

Graybill, & Wood. (1969). Rapid vestibular adaptation in a rotating environment by means of controlled head movements. Aerospace Medicine, 40, 638-643.

Gurkinkel, V. S., Kots, Y. M., Paltsev, Y. I., & Feldman, A. G. (1971). The compensation of respiratory disturbances of the erect posture of man as an example of the organization of interarticular interaction. In I. Gelfand, V. S. Gurkinkel, S. Fomin, & Tsetlin (Eds.), Models of the structural-functional organization of certain biological systems. Cambridge: MIT Press.

Hanson, M. J. (1978). A longitudinal, descriptive study of the behaviors of Down's syndrome infants in an early intervention program. Unpublished doctoral dissertation.

Harris, S. (1981). Effects of N.D.T. on improving motor performance in Down's syndrome infants. Unpublished doctoral dissertation.

Held, R., & Hein, A. (1963). Movement produced stimulation in the development of visually guided behavior. Journal of Comparative and Physiological Psychology, 56, 872-876.

Horak, F. B., & Nashner, L. M. (1983). Two distinct strategies for stance posture control: Adaptation to altered support surface configurations. Neuroscience Abstracts, 9, 65.

Knott, M., & Voss, D. (1968). Proprioceptive neuromuscular facilitation. New York: Harper & Row.

Knight, R. M., Atkinson, B. R., & Hyman, J. A. (1978). Tactual discrimination and motor skills in mongoloid and non-mongoloid retarded and normal children. American Journal of Mental Deficiency, 83, 213-222.

Kravitz, T., & Wallack, H. (1966). Adaptation to displaced vision contingent upon vibrating stimulation. Psychonomic Science, 6, 465-466.

Lackner, J. (1981). Some aspects of sensory-motor control and adaption in man. In R. D. Wark & H. L. Pick (Eds.), Inter-sensory perception and sensory integration. New York: Plenum Press.

Lacour, M., & Xerri, C. (1979). Compensation of postural reactions to fall in the vest. neurectomyal monkey. Role of remaining lab afference. Experimental Brain Research, 37, 563-580.

Lee, D. N. & Lishman, J. R. (1975). Visual proprioceptive control of stance. Journal of Human Movement Studies, 1, 87-95.

Lee, W. A. (1980). Anticipatory control of postural and task muscles during rapid arm flexion. Journal of Motor Behavior, 72(3), 185-196.

Loesch-Madzeuska, D. (1968). Some aspects of neurology of Down's syndrome. Journal of Mental Deficiency Research, 12, 237-246.

Marin-Padilla, M. (1976). Pyramidal cell abnormalities in the motor cortex of a child with Down's syndrome. A Golgi study. Journal of Comparative Neurology, 63-81.

Molnar, G. E. (1978). Analysis of motor disorder in retarded infants and young children. American Journal of Mental Deficiency, 83, 213-222.

Nashner, L. M. (1976). Adapting reflexes controlling the human posture. Experimental Brain Research, 26, 59-72.

Nashner, L. M. (1977). Fixed patterns of rapid postural responses among leg muscles during stance. Experimental Brain Research, 30, 13-24.

Nashner, L. M., Black, F. O., & Wall, C. (1982). Adaptation to altered support and visual conditions during stance: Patients with vestibular deficits. Journal of Neuroscience, 2, 536-544.

Nashner, L. M., & Grimm, R. J. (1977). Analysis of multi-loop dyscontrols in standing cerebellar patients. Progress in Clinical Neurophysiology, 4, 300-319.

Nashner, L. M., Shumway-Cook, A., & Marin, O. (1983). Experimental Brain Research, 49, 393-409.

Paillard, J. (1966). The patterning of skilled movements. In Handbook of physiology (Vol. 3). Baltimore: Williams & Wilkens.

Paltsev, Y. (1967). Interaction of the tendon reflex arc in the lower limbs in man as a reflexion of locomotor synergism. Biophysics, 12, 1045-1059.

Penrose, L. S., & Smith, G. F. (1966). Down's anomaly. Boston: Little Brown & Co.

Rarick, G. H., & McQuillan, J. P. (1977). The factor structure of motor abilities of TMR children: Implications for curriculum development. Final report for Dept. HEW and BEH.

Share, J., Kock, R., & Webb, S. (1964). The longitudinal development of infants and young children with Down's syndrome. American Journal of Mental Deficiency Research, 68d, 658-692.

Shumway-Cook, A., & Woollacott, M. H. (in press). The growth of stability: Postural control from a developmental perspective. Journal of Motor Behavior.

Smith, G. F., & Berg, J. M. (1976). Down's anomaly. Edinburgh: Churchill Livingstone.

Teng, E. L., McNeal, D. R., Kralj, A., & Waters, R. L. (1976). Electrical stimulation and feedback training: Effects on the voluntary control of paretic muscles. Archives of Physical Medicine and Rehabilitation, 57, 228-232.

Woollacott, M., Marin, O., & Nashner, L. (1980). Modifiability of human long latency (90-100 ms) muscle responses to postural perturbation by expectancy. Neuroscience Abstracts, 6, 463.

Woollacott, M. H., Shumway-Cook, A., & Nashner, L. M. (1982). Postural reflexes and aging. In Mortimer, Pirozzolo, & Maletta, The aging motor system. New York: Prager Publishers.

Zellweger, H., & Simpson, J. (1937). <u>Chromosomes of man</u>. London: Heinemann.

Motor Skill Acquisition of the Mentally Handicapped:
Issues in Research and Training
M.G. Wade (editor)
© *Elsevier Science Publishers B.V. (North-Holland), 1986*

EARLY MOTOR DEVELOPMENT AND STEREOTYPED BEHAVIOR:
THE EFFECTS OF SEMI-CIRCULAR CANAL STIMULATION

William E. MacLean, Jr., Robert E. Arendt, and Alfred A. Baumeister

George Peabody College of
Vanderbilt University

This paper was presented at a conference entitled, "The Development of Control, Coordination and Skill in the Mentally Handicapped", September 28-29, 1984, held at the National Institute of
Child Health and Human Development, Bethesda, Maryland. The
conference was supported by the NICHD and the National Institute
for Handicapped Research. Work on this paper was supported by
NICHD grants (HD17650 and HD07226).

The authors wish to thank Ellen Perrin and Daniel Ashmead for
their insightful comments on previous drafts of this manuscript.
We also wish to acknowledge the contribution of Penny Brooks,
David Weatherford, Linda Ashford, Richard A. Laine, David N.
Ellis, Holly N. Galbreath, Leslie F. Halpern, Jon T. Tapp, and
Grant A. Youngquist in the collection of the data reported in
this manuscript.

It has been frequently observed that early motor development of mentally
retarded children is delayed in comparison with their chronological age
peers (Bruininks, 1974; Cratty, 1970; Donoghue, Kirman, Bullmore, Laban, &
Abbas, 1970; Howe, 1959; Molnar, 1974, 1978; VonWendt, Makinen, &
Rantakallio, 1984). While such a delay can be explained fairly readily in
cases of clear neuromuscular dysfunction, such as cerebral palsy, there is
a high incidence of delay among children of other etiological groups.

Table 1 contains data combined from a study of 53 mentally retarded
children conducted by Molnar (1974) and a normative sample reported by
Knoblock, Stevens, and Malone (1980). The retarded children, ages 10 to
23 months, exhibited delayed motor development without evidence of neuromuscular disability. These children were followed for up to 3 years and
the chronological age at which they attained the various motor milestones
was recorded. Clearly the retarded children lagged behind their normally
developing peers. There have been at least two attempts to explain the
etiology of this delay. One proposes that the delay is a manifestation of
minimal brain damage to the brainstem, basal ganglia, mid-brain, and
cerebellum (Donoghue et al., 1970) and the other hypothesizes a functional
maturational lag (Molnar, 1974). While there is some support for the
minimal brain damage hypothesis given the likelihood that many mentally
retarded children have experienced some degree of central nervous system
insult (Baumeister & MacLean, 1979), the functional maturational lag
hypothesis appears to be a more parsimonious explanation of the delays.
This conclusion follows from Molnar's observation that the majority of

W.E. MacLean, Jr. et al.

Table 1

Attainment of Motor Milestones[a]

Motor Milestone	Retarded Children[b]	Normal[c]
Rolling over	12	4
Sitting	16	8
Crawling	21	9
Standing	25	10
Walking	37	15

[a]Mean ages in months

[b]From Molnar's (1974) study of 53 nonphysically handicapped retarded children

[c]From Knobloch, Stevens, & Malone (1980)

these children do eventually achieve the major motor milestones character-istic of the first few years of life. However, Molnar (1974) is silent as to the nature of the difficulty that produces the observed lag.

While considerable emphasis has been placed upon the remediation of the cognitive deficits characteristic of mentally retarded children, relative-ly little attention has been directed toward intervening upon their delayed motor development. Our view, however, is that early intervention directed at motor development might have implications for other aspects of development. This hypothesis follows from the observation that motor activity does seem to influence cognitive development. For example, Wachs and Gruen (1982) concluded from their comprehensive review of the early experience literature that the amount floor freedom given to children by their parents is positively related to intellectual development. Similar-ly, parental encouragement of exploration is directly related to cognitive development. In both of these examples, a prerequisite skill for explora-tion would be a normal degree of motoric development. We further argue that this relationship extends beyond the fact that measurement of early cognitive development typically is wholly dependent on measurement of motor performance.

There exists in the contemporary literature strong theoretical differences over the nature and extent of the relationship between motoric ability and cognitive development. The Piagetian position, as interpreted by develop-mental psychologists in the United States, fixes sensory-motor inter-actions with real objects in the environment as the foundations of cogni-tion (Flavell, 1963). Objects must be acted upon in order to be known

(Piaget, 1970). Early cognition, therefore, consists of operative schemes for doing rather than schemes for perceiving. The implication is that the more frequent and the more varied motor behaviors an infant can perform, the more knowledge the infant possesses and the faster the infant will develop new knowledge.

A contrasting model for later infant development, espoused by Zelazo (1983), is that advances in motor behaviors are the results of preceding cognitive development. He provides support for the possibility that changes in motor development, specifically walking, may be dictated by the development of the infant's cognitive capacity to generate ideas or access memory. He further suggests that not only may cognitive changes influence motor development but that cognitive and motor development may be two separate processes that proceed asynchronously.

Another theory of cognitive development that is even further removed from the Piagetian model on the role motor development plays is that of Gibson (1966, 1979). The major premise of this position is that perception rather than motor activity is the primary means of cognitive development. Information is available directly from an object amodally without the necessity of action. Perception of that information is cognition. Experience, including increasingly complex motor interactions, serves to attune the perceptual systems to increasingly finer aspects of a stimulus that differentiate it from other stimuli.

Given the nature of the relationships between motor development and cognitive development advocated by various people it appears that the only conclusion that can be drawn is that there is no clear answer. Kopp's (1975) remark that this state of affairs exists because there are little data is about as true today as it was a decade ago. All of the theories postulate some role for motor activity in cognitive development. What has yet to be investigated is the strength of this relationship and which of the components may be antecedent in the developmental process. Here, we shall first discuss developmental issues of motor behavior and then present the case that the motor development of preambulatory developmentally delayed children may be enhanced through the systematic introduction of rotational vestibular stimulation.

THEORIES OF MOTOR CONTROL

Early motor development is characterized by the sequential attainment of motor milestones such as rolling over from prone to supine, independent sitting, and walking alone. Traditionally, the debate about motor theory has focused on the central versus peripheral models of motor control (Kelso & Stelmach, 1976). The central control position proposes that movement is produced by a command originating from the higher centers of the central nervous system and errors are detected when sensory feedback is compared to an internal referent. This feedback, or closed-loop system, is contrasted with a feed forward, or open-loop system, in which feedback from the movement is unnecessary for motor control. According to the latter model, the higher centers of the central nervous system preplan the movement and they do not need further information to complete the action.

A contemporary theory of motor control, called the process or dynamic

approach (Kelso, 1982), is an attempt to resolve the inadequacies of a
strict feed-back or feed-forward model by a comprehensive model or motor
control. Briefly, this basic information-processing model seeks to
address two fundamental problems in motor control: (a) How can the
nervous system regulate all the independent units in order to produce a
certain motor sequence?, and (b) Because a fixed relationship cannot be
assumed between muscle states and movements, how does the motor system
account for context-conditioned variability?

In order to answer the first question, the model builds upon the "degrees-
of-freedom" construct formulated by Bernstein (1967) to explain motor
control. From this perspective motor control is viewed as a problem in
the regulation of the degrees-of-freedom inherent in the skeletomuscular
system (Turvey, Fitch, & Tuller, 1982). In this model the degrees of
freedom are regulated by the synthesis of the individual variables of the
system, i.e., the muscles and the joints, into larger functional groups
(Turvey, 1977). Individual parts of the body need not, therefore, be
controlled by a one-to-one correspondence with higher-order motor control
units because they are constrained to act as a unit by their links with
the other elements.

In answering the question of how the motor system accounts for context-
conditioned variability, the timing aspect of movements has become a key
issue. Kugler, Kelso, and Turvey (1982), and Thelen (1985) have noted the
necessity to determine whether there exists any component of movement
that, in the presence of variable contexts, give the movement its fundamental form. Only after a way is found to demonstrate that certain motor
acts are part of the same topology will it be useful to consider how the
infant is able to develop control over the various parameters influencing
the movement in response to environmental demands. Thelen (1985) presents
evidence that one good candidate for...

> the solution to this problem is that the timing relationship
> among muscles remains constant, whereas speed or force is
> subject to metrical change. Thus, our ability to distinguish
> one class of actions as distinctive may be the result of this
> relatively invariant timing among its components, which
> preserves the character of the movement as a reach or a kick,
> for example, within the range of speeds or forces of the
> movement's performance (p. 3).

It follows, then, that proper sequencing or timing of the motor unit
activity becomes an essential feature of motor development, particularly
in gross motor activities that involve a cyclic pattern. The early
stereotyped movements of infants are a primary example of such rhythmical
activities.

A further implication of the theoretical variability between muscle
excitation and the actual movement outcome is the essential contribution
of the physical properties of the system. Berstein (1967) has described
three major sources of context-conditioned variability: anatomical
factors, mechanical laws of motion, and physiology. From a developmental
perspective, Thelen (1984, 1985) extends this emphasis on biomechanical
properties to include another source of variability -- maturation. She
has argued how anatomical features, such as the body's center of gravity,
that change as children grow can account for changes in motor behavior,

such as walking. She suggests that developmental psychology has unnecessarily limited itself to the study of neural development and has overlooked biomechanical determinants. We agree that such factors can contribute to variability in motor behavior and that such issues warrant further research. It is our opinion, however, that the dynamic state or structure of the nervous system is especially important to any study of intervention methods purporting to improve motor abilities in children who are commonly suspected of having neurological deficits. We shall attempt to demonstrate that physiological integrity, maturation of reflex behavior, and rhythmical motor activity are crucial elements of any comprehensive theory of early motor development.

PROCESSES OF EARLY MOTOR DEVELOPMENT

PHYSIOLOGICAL INTEGRITY

Motor activity is generally regarded as an index of the integrity of the central nervous system. Indeed, the assessment of motor activity is a major component of standard neurological examinations. The interdependence between the nervous system and motor activity is perhaps most apparent in cases where the operating efficiency of the central nervous system has been compromised by a lesion in the motor cortex, basal ganglia, or the cerebellum. For example, damage to the motor cortex or to the pyramidal tract usually leads to spasticity that makes voluntary movement extremely difficult. From another perspective motor development can be viewed as an index of central nervous system maturation.

In a comprehensive review of perinatal brain development, Parmelee and Sigman (1983) assert that neural functioning at any point in development is dependent upon several factors. These include:

(a) Number and location of neurons in the brain.
(b) Maturity of structure and metabolism of these neurons.
(c) Their ability to generate action potentials spontaneously or when stimulated.
(d) Number of connections between axons and dendrites.
(e) Development of synapses.
(f) Neurochemical transmitters.
(g) Organization of the total network for sensory reception, information processing, and action response. (Parmelee & Sigman, 1983, p. 103).

In the case of the developmentally delayed youngster, some of these factors have been shown to differ qualitatively and quantitatively from nondelayed children. For example, deficits in number, length, and spatial arrangement of dendrites and synapses have been reported among cases of severe mental retardation (Huttenlocher, 1975; Purpura, 1974). While it remains to be determined whether the extent of neuronal interconnectivity is directly related to neuronal operating efficiency, it is known that interconnectivity does increase with maturation (Purpura, 1975). With regard to neurotransmitters, there is good evidence for significant biochemical disruption of the balance between GABA, dopamine, seratonin and acetylcholine in the brains of Lesch-Nyhan patients (Lloyd, Hornykiewicz, Davidson, Shannak, Farley, Goldstein, Shibuya, Kelley, & Fox, 1981). This disruption is believed to be responsible for the

movement disorders, including self-injurious behavior, associated with
this disorder (Baumeister, Frye, & Schroeder in press). Finally, in cases
where morphological observations of the brain result from genetic influences, infections, intoxications, or the like, it is highly probable that
there is a reduction in the number of available neurons and concomitant
losses in operating efficiency. People with Down's syndrome are known to
have CNS irregularities that are fairly homogeneous within the group
(Scola, 1982). Of particular interest in this discussion is the under-
development of the brainstem and cerebellum relative to total brain weight
described by Crome, Cowie, and Slater (1966). The relative under-
development of the brainstem and cerebellum could account for several
specific deficits, such as muscular hypotonia, poor coordination of
voluntary movements, and immature righting and equilibrium reactions
(Donoghue et al., 1970; Eastham & Jancar, 1968) that combine to delay
motor development.

REFLEXIVE MATURATION

At birth, infant behavior is largely reflexive in nature. Within the
first year after birth substantial changes occur as the infant's motor
behavior becomes less reflexive and less symmetrical. A critical factor
in achieving motor milestones such as locomotion is the maturation of
reflexive behavior. This maturation is characterized by the decline of
the earliest reflexes and the appearance of postural adjustment reactions.

The earliest reflexes include the Moro, tonic labyrinthine in supine and
prone, asymmetrical tonic neck, symmetrical tonic neck, positive support,
segmental rolling both head on body and body on body, and galant. These
reflexes have a relatively brief role in motor development as the persistence of these early reflexes beyond the first six months of life is
suggestive of significant neurological disturbance such as cerebral palsy
(Capute, Palmer, Shapiro, Wachtel, Ross, & Accardo, 1984).

For a time, it was generally thought that these "primitive" reflexes
disappeared as motor development and CNS maturation ensued. In some
cases, such as the asymmetric tonic neck and tonic labyrinthine (supine),
there is a fairly predictable curvilinear function where the reflexes
increase in prevalence up to three months of age and then decrease over
the next several months (Capute et al., 1984). It was frequently reported
that they were replaced by voluntary programmed actions. Chief among the
proponents of this view was McGraw (1943), who wrote extensively about the
role of the cortex in inhibiting the function of the subcortical nuclei.
In contrast, Zelazo (1976), among others, proposed that these reflexes do
not disappear but become incorporated into a hierarchy of controlled
behavior.

Although the primitive reflexes are a universal characteristic of early
motor development, their role in the developmental process is not well
understood. Fiorentino (1981) has observed that newborn infants are
largely flexor dominant and that primitive reflexes serve to equalize
flexor/extensor movement patterns. Primitive reflexes appear to serve a
similar function with regard to the symmetrical motor behavior of
newborns. For example, Fiorentino (1981) maintains that the asymmetric
tonic neck reflex (ATNR) serves to disrupt symmetrical flexion and
extension patterns of movement. In short, the child experiences that

he/she use each side of the body independently. Fiorentino argues that this reflex is "fundamental in the development of visually directed reaching and eye-hand coordination" (p. 79). While Fiorentino's conclusions do suggest specific functions for the primitive reflexes, her observations are nonetheless speculative. It may not be possible to say with any certainty how primitive reflexes influence motor development although there is a concomitancy between the two phenomena that is suggestive of a relationship.

Postural adjustment reactions, categorized as equilibrium, protection, and righting, are reflexive responses that typically begin to appear within the first year of life. The development of these reactions is described as a continuous process (Capute et al., 1984) and has a clear relationship to motor development (Molnar, 1978). The significance of postural adjustment reflexive patterns for early motor development arises directly from the observation that motor milestones follow closely the emergence of specific postural adjustment reactions (Molnar, 1974).

RHYTHMICAL MOTOR ACTIVITY

An additional aspect of early motor development is the rhythmical motor activity characteristic of the first two years of life. These motor actions include sucking, body rocking, head rolling, head banging, and complex hand movements. These behaviors are highly repetitive, rhythmical motor activities that have a very characteristic temporal and topographic invariance (Berkson & Gallagher, this volume; Kravitz & Boehm, 1971; Lourie, 1949; Thelen, 1981; Wolff, 1967). Early on, authors interpreted repetitive behaviors as manifestations of a deficient psychological or emotional development process. Examples of such hypothetical explanations include ego development (Lourie, 1949), attempts to form a bond with an absent or ambivalent mother (Brody, 1960; Spitz & Wolf, 1949), or an attempt to recreate the prenatal environment (Kris, 1954). Other investigators postulated a tension or anxiety reduction model (Kubie, 1941; Lourie, 1949; de Lissovoy, 1962). As it became evident that such behavior was frequently observed in normally developing infants, stereotyped mannerisms increasingly appeared in theories of typical human development (Kravitz, Rosenthal, Teplitz, Murphy, & Lesser, 1960; Sallustro & Atwell, 1978). Piaget (1952) used examples of stereotyped motor activity when he referred to secondary circular reactions as the basis for the development of higher-order cognitive structures. Several authors (Gesell, 1939; Lourie, 1949; Wolff, 1967) incorporated rhythmic motor patterns of children into a theoretical sequence of motor development. Despite the abundance of speculation as to the origin and function of stereotypy, there was however, little systematic study of the developmental course of infant rhythmical behavior until Thelen published her findings on rhythmical stereotypies in normal human infants (Thelen, 1979; 1980; 1981).

Thelen proposed two ways in which the rhythmical motor acts operate to enhance motor development. First, Thelen (1981) has stated that infant rhythmical stereotypies are likely to be one source of a timing mechanism in gross motor behavior. This point was discussed earlier in regard to context-conditioned variability. Second, she contends that intrinsic rhythmical motor patterns specify spatial and temporal patterns. In so doing, they are essential for movement coordination and postural stability, and as such, are "called forth" by the infant to serve those adaptive functions before full voluntary control develops. She suggested, for example, that the non-reflexive, spontaneous stereotypic leg kicking of infants reflects an endogenous motor program that specifies the spatial and temporal pattern of the leg movement.

Thelen followed a group of 20 normally developing infants from the age of 1 month to 1 year. Approaching rhythmical stereotypies from an ethological perspective, she assembled a taxonomy using naturalistic observation. The infants engaged in a great deal of stereotypy, both in terms of variety and quantity. She listed and described 47 distinct movements. When the stereotypies were subsequently grouped by body part and posture, a number of developmental profiles emerged. For example, stereotyped movements involving the legs gradually increased in frequency to a peak between 14 and 32 weeks; whereas those involving the hands increased sharply at 24 weeks and then declined through week 52. Moreover, Thelen (1979) observed a significant correlation between the mean age of stereotypy onset for each infant and that infant's average Bayley Motor Scale score. These findings led Thelen to conclude that rhythmical motor acts peak in frequency at transition points of motor growth. Thus, stereotyped movements may represent transitional behavior, a bridge from one point in development to the next.

STEREOTYPY AND EARLY MOTOR DEVELOPMENT

While the previous discussion supports the repetitive aspect and the temporal and topographic invariance of infant rhythmical behavior, the assumption that the behavior is abnormal must be questioned given its close association with early motor development. Thelen's perspective places stereotyped behavior in an intrinsic role for normal motor development. Such a view stands in stark contrast to the typical perspective that stereotyped behavior is largely irrelevant and without adaptive significance.

It should be pointed out, however, that the rhythmical stereotypies exhibited by preambulatory infants may be fundamentally different from the stereotyped behavior characteristic of severely mentally retarded children and adults (Berkson, 1983). Berkson and Gallagher (Chapter this volume) make the case that the stereotyped behaviors exhibited by the two groups of children are topographically different and, therefore, it is possible that they may also differ in function. We are impressed with the possibility that abnormal stereotyped behaviors may develop from the stereotyped motor behavior of preambulatory children. In the case of the developmentally delayed child, the repetitious patterns probably occur over a longer period of time and may become highly practiced behaviors. There is, of course, the possibility that, by virtue of their longer duration among developmentally delayed children, the behaviors could come under operant control or take on the function of maintaining an optimal level of arousal (Berkson, 1967; 1983).

An additional possibility is that some rhythmical motor stereotypies provide vestibular stimulation and that the stimulation enhances motor development. There is some support for this hypothesis. Sallustro and Atwell (1978) found that normally developing babies who exhibited body rocking and head banging attained several motor milestones somewhat earlier than babies who did not regularly engage in this behavior. They reasoned that body rocking and head banging might have produced vestibular stimulation that, in turn, enhanced the motor development of their subjects.

Another line of evidence also suggests a relationship between vestibular stimulation and stereotyped movements. Mason and Berkson (1975) demonstrated that the development of abnormal stereotyped body rocking by isolation-reared rhesus monkeys could be prevented by providing proprioceptive-kinesthetic stimulation in the form of a mechanically driven, mobile, artificial mother. Mason and Berkson suggested that frequent application of noncontingent maternal stimulation over a long period of time might serve to suppress stereotyped movements, particularly body rocking, among human infants with developmental delays. It is also possible that the mobile mother provided vestibular stimulation and that the movement experience served to enhance motor development, thus preventing the emergence of pathological stereotypies. There is some additional support for this view. Thelen (1980), in a stepwise regression analysis of her observational data, discovered that the amount of stereotypy exhibited in the biweekly observations were inversely related to the amount of vestibular stimulation included rocking, jiggling, bouncing, and carrying the infant.

VESTIBULAR STIMULATION

PHYSIOLOGY

The term "vestibular stimulation" has been used in a variety of contexts to describe a broad range of sensory experiences. The common factor across these experiences was stimulation of the vestibular apparatus, depicted in Figure 1. Therefore, as a preliminary step the basic physiological operation of the vestibular system will be reviewed. The following description is adapted from previous accounts (Kandel & Schwartz, 1981; Parker, 1980).

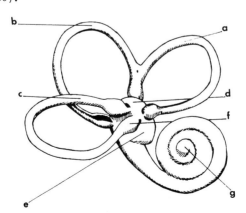

Figure 1
Artist's sketch of vestibular apparatus depicting principal components.
Semicircular canals: superior(a), posterior(b), horizontal(c).
Otilith organs: utricle(d), saccule(e). Ampulla(f). Cochlea(g).

The vestibular receptors are located within the inner ear's membranous labyrinth. This area is a series of sacs and tubes filled with a viscous fluid called endolymph. There are two types of receptors behind each ear: the otolith organs and the semicircular canals. The otolith organs are composed of the saccule and the utricle. They combine to detect linear acceleration, that is, changes in the velocity of the head traveling in a straight line. The otolith organs also detect the action of gravity, specifying head position under static conditions. Gravity is detected by hair cells aligned vertically and horizontally within the otolith organs.

The other vestibular receptor organs are the three semicircular canals. These canals lie in orthogonal planes. They respond to the angular acceleration that results from rotational motion of the head. That is, they do not respond to rotation at a constant angular velocity, but rather to increases or decreases in angular velocity. In each canal, all of the hair cells are oriented in a single direction. Angular movement in the plane of the canal causes a movement of the hair cells. Nerve impulses from these peripheral receptors are relayed by the two vestibular ganglion portions of the eighth cranial nerve to the four vestibular nuclei in the brain stem and to certain regions of the cerebellum. The four different subdivisions of the vestibular nuclear complex are in turn connected in a complex manner with the motor nuclei of the extraocular muscles, with the spinal cord, and with the cerebellum. Each of these four distinct nuclei, named the superior, lateral (Deiter's), medial (triangular), and inferior (descending), has a distinctive cellular structure and set of neural connections.

RESEARCH ISSUES

There are several methodological aspects of research on the vestibular system that should also be considered. First, it is a practical impossibility to manipulate experimentally the force of gravity. That is, gravity cannot be turned off and on with a switch like a light or a sound. As a result, the portion of the vestibular apparatus that detects static position is constantly being stimulated. Rotational stimulation is most frequently manipulated in studies involving stimulation of an intact vestibular system. This particular form of stimulation can, of course, be varied along with dimensions of speed, direction and duration. How this particular form of vestibular stimulation is related to that produced by more ecologically valid means, such as rocking in a rocking chair or by bouncing a baby, has yet to be determined. Probably for the sake of brevity, most authors, including us, have referred to head rotation as vestibular stimulation. The more accurate description would, however, improve clarity and eliminate the error of reasoning from a specific to a more general case.

Second, the vestibular system is tightly coupled with other sensory systems and rarely is its operation consciously experienced as a discrete "vestibular" event. While human subjects generally are able to report their perceptions of visual, auditory, or tactile stimuli along a variety of scales, vestibular stimulation produces more subjective, less specifiable data.

A related difficulty is the limited availability of vestibular function measures. The most common measure in intervention studies is post-rotary

nystagmus. Characteristics of the nystagmus response include the duration, amplitude, and speed (Tibbling, 1969). In most instances direct
observation of the eye yields a reasonable estimate of the vestibular
response magnitude. However, more precise measures can be derived through
electronystagmographic techniques. The caveat is that while observation
of postrotary nystagmus provides data on the functioning on the vestibular
end organ and the integrity of the vestibular-ocular reflex, this measure
does not assess the functioning of the vestibular system beyond the
vestibular nuclei.

The final issue has to do with external validity. That is, the vast
majority of studies of vestibular stimulation have employed subjects with
normal neurological functioning in abnormal situations. While studies
conducted in an abnormal situation may reveal how the normal vestibular
apparatus functions, these findings may not generalize to abnormal
vestibular functioning in a normal environment. This, of course, is an
empirical question that has yet to be addressed in research with developmentally disabled people.

VESTIBULAR STIMULATION AS AN INTERVENTION

It is well known that vestibular stimulation of normal infants has a
soothing effect. In this regard, rocking appears to be more effective
than other forms of stimulation (Korner & Thoman, 1972). The causal
factors relating vestibular stimulation to soothing remain obscure;
however, Korner (1979) points out that "vestibular-proprioceptive stimulation may be ontogenetically one of the most adequate and relevant forms of
stimulation at the pre- and full-term infants' level of neurophysiological
development" (p. 103). In addition, infants receiving vestibular stimulation exhibit more mature performance on measures of visual tracking
behavior (Gregg, Haffner, & Korner, 1976), motor development (e.g., Burns,
Deddish, Burns, & Hatcher, 1983; Neal, 1968), state organization (Burns,
et al., 1983; Korner, Schneider, & Forrest, 1983; Rosenfeld, 1980;
Solkoff, Yaffe, Weintraub, & Blase, 1969), and auditory responsiveness
(Korner et al., 1983; Neal, 1968). Additionally, it has been reported
that vestibular stimulation reduces apnea in premature infants (Korner,
1979). Given the clear effect of vestibular stimulation on infant
development, we should like to focus more closely on the studies
concerning vestibular stimulation and motor development.

MOTOR DEVELOPMENT

Premature Infants. The first systematic study of the effects of vestibular stimulation on early motor development was reported by Neal (1968).
The rationale for her investigation was that the fetus in utero receives
vestibular stimulation through movements of the mother, stimulation to
which premature infants perhaps have less exposure. If this is the case
and if vestibular stimulation is important for motor development then
treatment with vestibular stimulation should enhance the development of
the premature infant. Neal's regimen consisted of rocking the infant in a
hammock-like device for three 30-minute periods during each day, beginning
on the fifth day after birth until the 36th week of life, i.e., gesta-
tional age plus chronological age. Sixty-two premature infants were
divided between control and treatment groups and tested on a number of

measures at the 36th week. Neal found 30% higher scores in motor development, 10% higher scores in auditory functioning, and 47% higher scores in visual functioning among the children receiving the treatment beyond those evidenced by the control infants. The treated babies also gained an average of 65 grams more weight after 50 days and experienced no late edema, a symptom observed among seven of her control subjects.

Similar results have been reported by Burns et al., (1983). In that study, premature infants were given 4-weeks of continuous waterbed oscillation and maternal heart beat sounds while in the nursery incubator. When assessed at discharge by an examiner who was unaware of group assignment, the 11 randomly assigned treatment infants exhibited 23% higher scores on state and motor clusters, derived from the Brazelton Neonatal Behavior Assessment Scale, over the scores of the 11 control group infants.

Normally Developing Infants. Clark, Kreutzberg, and Chee (1977) conducted a study in which highly specific and quantifiable rotational semicircular canal stimulation was provided to 26 preambulatory normally developing infants. These children were randomly assigned to a treatment group or one of two control groups. The treatment group received 16 sessions of semicircular canal stimulation over a 4-week period. Significant increases were apparent in the motor and reflex scale scores of the treatment group relative to the two control groups. The children in the control conditions demonstrated a 3.8% improvement on the reflex test and a 6.7% improvement on the motor test over the 4-week period. The children who received the vestibular stimulation regimen demonstrated a 12.2% improvement on the reflex scale and a 27.4% improvement on the motor scale over a comparable 4-week period. While the actual motor gains were not presented in the results, it was reported in the original dissertation (Kreutzberg, 1976) that the control groups had caught up to the treatment group by the end of a 6-week follow-up period.

Children with Cerebral Palsy. There have been two studies of the effects of rotational vestibular stimulation upon the motor functioning of children with cerebral palsy. Despite fairly comparable treatment regimens, very different findings were obtained in the two studies Chee, Kreutzberg, and Clark (1978), using the same procedures and measures as Clark et al. (1977), found that children who received semicircular canal stimulation evidenced significant increases in both motor skills and reflexive maturation as compared with two control groups (handled and non-handled). Among the treatment subjects, greatest improvement was evident in the prone, supine, sitting, and creeping motor abilities. In addition, the labyrinthine righting reflexes and equilibrium reactions of the head, neck, and trunk, were benefitted the most.

Sellick and Over (1980) conducted an investigation involving cerebral palsy children that followed closely the procedures outlined by Clark et al. (1977). However, there was no significant difference in motor development, as assessed with the Bayley Scales of Infant Development, between the treatment and control children. Although Sellick and Over found it difficult to establish the basis for their failure to replicate the findings of Chee et al. (1978), the two investigations differed on several important dimensions. First, the possibility existed that the participants in each of the investigations represented different populations. The diversity of disabilities represented in the population of children with cerebral palsy is well known (Scherzer & Tscharnuter, 1982). Chee et al. listed three diagnostic categories represented in their treatment group whereas Sellick and Over listed six. Seven of the children in the Chee et al. study were described as hypertonic quadriplegia whereas Sellick and Over listed no such classification among their treatment group. The latter also included at least two blind children.

Secondly, the differences in the dependent variables used in the two investigations were highly salient and probably of considerable importance. Sellick and Over (1980) used the Bayley Scales and divided the items into subscales designed to measure different aspects of motor functioning. Chee et al. (1978), used the preambulatory motor scale constructed by Clark, Chee, Kantner, and Kreutzberg (1980). It could be that the differences in outcome may be a function of the sensitivity of the motor measure in detecting small changes in motor performance and reflex profile. The preambulatory motor measure is simply a more finely grained measure than the Bayley Motor Scale. On the other hand, the psychometric properties of the Bayley have been well established while the characteristics of the Clark scale are not well known. Taken together, the results of Sellick and Over (1980) and Chee et al. (1978) raise questions as to the efficacy of vestibular stimulation as a treatment to facilitate motor development in children with cerebral palsy. The rotation regimen may be effective in enhancing the motor development of preambulatory children of some diagnostic subcategories and not of others.

Children With Other Developmental Delays. In another investigation, children with Down's syndrome treated with rotational vestibular stimulation. Kantner, Clark, Allen, and Chase (1976), examined three normal infants between 6 and 9 months of age and four Down's syndrome children between 6 and 24 months of age. Owing to the small number of participants, subject attrition, the absence of long-term follow-up data, and the anexdotal nature of the parent's reports, the investigation must be considered descriptive and its contributions mainly procedural. However, there was some indication from this investigation that the results achieved with normally developing preambulatory children could also be achieved with Down's syndrome children.

In our own laboratory, we have recently completed two investigations of the effects of vestibular stimulation on early motor development. In our first study, we examined the effects of a vestibular stimulation regimen on the stereotypic behavior and reflex and motor development of four developmentally delayed children (MacLean & Baumeister, 1982). The study included two children with Down's syndrome, aged 17 and 30 months with developmental levels of 8 and 15 months, respectively. Other genetic and congenital disorders were displayed by the other two children who were 42 and 34 months of age. Their developmental levels were 3 and 5 months, respectively. All of the children exhibited excessive stereotypic responding including rocking, hand movements, head rolling, and leg kicking. The motor and reflex tests, identical to those used by Clark and his associates, were administered the week prior to treatment, after 1 week of treatment, after 2 weeks of treatment, and at a 4-week follow-up. Observational data on the stereotypic behavior were collected the week prior to treatment, 1 week subsequent to treatment, after 2 weeks of treatment, and at a 1-week follow-up period 1 month after the conclusion of treatment.

The regimen of vestibular stimulation was similar to that used by Clark
and his associates. The one notable difference concerns the way in which
the vestibular stimulation was administered. In the studies by Clark an
adult held the baby in his lap while another experimenter rotated the
chair. Our apparatus, on the other hand, was designed to accommodate the
baby in different body positions in an adapted car seat without an adult
having to hold the baby. Our procedure appears to have at least three
advantages: (a) it reduces the possibility of a possible experimental
confounding in that the child does not also receive handling from the
experimenter and the associated social contact, (b) it avoids the discom-
fort generally experienced by most adults who do not tolerate the vestibular stimulation well, and (c) permits better quantitative control of the
stimulation.

Three of the four children improved substantially in motor skills following 1 week of treatment. The amount of improvement increased after
completion of 2 weeks of treatment and was maintained at the 4-week
follow-up. The improvement was evident in head righting and equilibrium
skills. In addition to change in control abilities, some subjects
achieved major developmental milestones during the course of the intervention. One subject was able to sit independently for long periods of time
and to move his limbs while sitting. Another subject was able to achieve
a standing position by pulling up, to cruise along furniture, and to
ambulate with minimal support.

It should be emphasized that these children had demonstrated a very slow
rate of spontaneous motor development prior to the study. In an effort to
show that the observed increases in motor development were produced by the
vestibular stimulation and were not a function of maturation alone, the
motor scale results were rescored using the Griffiths scale (1976) and
were compared to scores from a Griffiths scale that had been administered
at least 2 months prior to the baseline assessment. For each child, the
previous value was within one item of the baseline value. The consistency
of the scores over this rather long time period (2 to 4 months) indicated
a slow rate of development that can be contrasted with the sudden
increases in motor performance observed after the relatively brief period
of semicircular canal stimulation (2 weeks).

Three of the children exhibited similar gains in reflex functioning. One
Down's syndrome child was already sufficient mature in his reflex behavior
at the beginning of treatment of obtain the maximum possible score on the
Clark et al. (1980) reflex measure. The stereotypic behavior of the
severely delayed children showed no systematic change, although the body
rocking of the Down's syndrome children decreased. The two severely
delayed children received an additional 2-week treatment period after the
4-week follow-up. The child who previously showed no gain motorically
improved 36% from the second pretest to the second posttest assessment.
The second child showed an 11% increase in motor functioning during the
second treatment.

We concluded that rotational vestibular stimulation had a lasting effect
upon the motor and reflex abilities of preambulatory developmentally
delayed children. The design of the study included follow-up posttests
that indicated the relative maturation of the children over time, a
feature not included in Kanter et al. (1976) investigation. One of the
profoundly involved children developed the ability to sit independently,

Table 2

Subject Descriptions for Study II

Subject	Age[a]	Diagnostic Information
1	10	Down's syndrome
2	16	Rare 5th chromosome defect
3	22	Cornelia deLange
4	15	Unknown etiology - apnea, seizures, herpes zoster
5	14	Microcephaly - unknown etiology
6	12	Down's syndrome
7	19	Premature - otherwise normally developing
8	19	Cerebral palsy - 14 weeks premature

[a] In months.

having been in prone and supine positions for the three years of his life. Such a substantial gain indicated the potential of vestibular stimulation for enhancing the development of multihandicapped children, a potential that is relatively unassessed experimentally.

Our second study included eight children, ranging in age from 9 to 32 months. This group exhibited a wide variety of disabilities including Down's syndrome, Carnelia deLange syndrome, microcophaly, and cerebral palsy. One subject was a child who had been born prematurely and exhibited some slight developmental delays. The subjects are described further in Table 2. Measures included the Peabody Developmental Motor Scales (Folio & Fewell, 1983) and the Bayley Mental Scale (Bayley, 1969). The Peabody Motor Scales were used in this particular study because the scales are purported to measure both fine and gross motor skills. On the basis of previous work, it appeared that fine motor skills might also be affected by semicircular canal stimulation. Each baby was assessed four times: (a) 1-month prior to the stimulation, (b) immediately before the stimulation, (c) immediately after the stimulation, and (d) 1-month after the stimulation. Through this schedule of testing we hoped to be able to separate vestibular stimulation effects from maturation with each baby serving as her/his own control. The treatment regimen was identical to that used in our earlier study (MacLean & Baumeister, 1982).

Our primary interest in this study was to elucidate further the effects of quantifiable semicircular canal stimulation upon the motor development of handicapped children. Figure 2 contains the gross motor data from the Peabody Development Motor Scales. It is apparent from these data that modest gains in gross motor skills were present for four of the children and that the gains evident following the 2-week period of semicircular canal stimulation exceeded the children's rate of growth over the month previous to stimulation. Such gains were not evident among the remainder of the children, that is, there was no regression discontinuity evident in their time series. Fine motor skill data for the subjects were not indicative of treatment effects as most subject's scores over the stimulation period were consistent with their prestimulation rate of growth. With the exception of Subject 4, the Bayley Mental Scale data did not suggest a stimulation effect as the change from pretest to posttest for the remainder of the subjects was negligible. Subject 4 exhibited a relatively large gain on the Mental Scale, from raw scores of 7 and 6 prior to stimulation to a score of 14 following the 2 weeks of stimulation. These gains were not accompanied by increases in either fine or gross motor skills for Subject 4. Anecdotal reports from the parents suggested that they observed some positive changes in alertness and motor coordination.

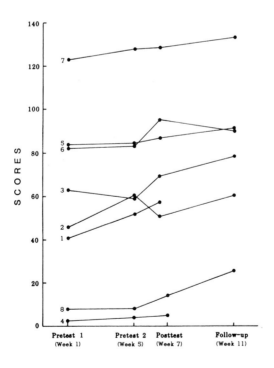

Figure 2
Peabody Developmental Motor Scale raw scores (Gross Motor)
for eight developmentally delayed children.

The results of our second study were not as conclusive as our first investigation. The stimulation procedures were identical but the subjects were more variable in terms of diagnoses, chronological ages, and developmental level. The stimulation was associated with atypical gains in gross motor development for the Down's syndrome subjects, a child with Cornelia deLange syndrome, and a child with cerebral palsy who had been born 14 weeks prematurely, and a child with cerebral palsy who had been born 14 weeks prematurely. The rates of development for the remainder of the subjects were approximately continuous throughout the study period. One possible conclusion could be that the stimulation is less effective for some children, e.g., those whose CNS is fairly well integrated (Subject 7) of those who may have considerable brain injury (Subjects 2, 4, 5). Alternatively, the findings may have been affected by our selection of outcome measures. That is, the Peabody Developmental Motor Scales may not be sufficiently sensitive to detect changes in motor functioning of all preambulatory children resulting from semicircular canal stimulation. The same point has been raised concerning the Bayley Motor Scale employed by Sellick and Over (1980) in a study of children with cerebral palsy. There is, of course, the possibility that the treatment period was too brief for some of the children. The period of time might lead to measurable gains on the Peabody or Bayley that exceed those present in control groups.

Our present research also focuses on the extent to which specific quantifiable rotational vestibular stimulation accounts for positive changes in the motor and reflex development of preambulatory infants. This study differs from our previous work in that it is a longitudinal project involving a large number of children. Three groups of 20 babies each will eventually participate in the study. The groups are composed of normally developing infants, infants with Down's syndrome, and infants with atypical motor development (such as cerebral palsy). We are employing a cross-over longitudinal design in an effort to determine the extent to which the stimulation affects motor development relative to maturation. The study requires approximately 36 weeks for each participant. There is a cross-over at approximately the 18th week where subjects change from the experimental condition to the control condition or vice versa. Half of the babies in each diagnostic group are randomly assigned to initial treatment or control conditions. The cross-over design has the advantage of doubling the number of subjects exposed to the stimulation regimen. Additionally, it resolves the ethical issues of withholding potentially beneficial treatment from the control group.

The treatment consists of rotating the infant for ten 1-minute periods in a darkened room in three different orientations according to the regimen reported by Clark et al. (1977). Each orientation places a different portion of the semicircular canals in the horizontal plane. Sessions are conducted 10 times over an approximately 2-week long period, on three different occasions during the experimental portion of the study. The control condition consists of the same procedure except that the infant is rotated at a speed reported to be below an infant's threshold for the detection of movement in a darkened room. Outcome measures are taken before and after each of the three 2-week experimental and control conditions.

One of the primary outcome measures is the Bayley Scales of Infant Development (Bayley, 1969), including the Mental Scale, the Motor Scale, and the Infant Behavior Record. Because of some discrepancies in previous studies, the reflex and motor scales developmented by Kreutzberg and his associates at Ohio State University (Kreutzberg, 1976; Clark, et al., 1980) are also administered by a certified physical therapist. Additionally, we are attempting to determine whether the treatment has an effect on physiological indices, particularly post-rotary nystagmus, heart rate, heart rate variability, respiration, and muscle tone. Further, we plan to describe in detail the developmental course of stereotyped behavior in these and the normally developing infants. To do this, we are conducting biweekly in-home behavioral observations using a scoring system modeled after Thelen's (1980) work. All motor and reflex assessments, Bayley assessments, and stereotypy observations are conducted by assistants who are blind to the child's experimental status. Finally, the infants' caregivers are required to keep an ongoing behavioral log in the home. They are instructed to record on a form provided any changes in a variety of behaviors, such as the infants' interest in their environment, feeding and sleeping patterns, general mood, or adaptive skills. Four children have recently completed the 36-week long protocol. Their data are summarized in the following section.

The subjects included three children with Down's syndrome (A, B, & C) and one child with an undetermined chromosomal disorder and severe motor delay (D). Table 3 contains demographic data collected at the beginning of the study. All of the children were white females from largely middle class homes. Each was attending the Kennedy Center Experimental School for early intervention services throughout the duration of the study.

Table 3

Demographic Data for Subjects in Longitudinal Study

Subject	Relevant Diagnosis	CA^c	Bayley MDI	PDI
A^b	Down's syndrome & prematurity	5	90^d	75^d
B^a	Down's syndrome	21	50	50
C^a	Down's syndrome	11	52	50
D^a	Undetermined chromosomal disorder	38	50	50

[a]Experimental condition first.

[b]Control condition first.

[c]In months.

[d]Corrected for prematurity.

With the exception of MacLean and Baumeister (1982), all previous investigations reported data following a single period of semicircular canal
stimulation. In that study, we provided two successive 2-week periods of
stimulation to our most severely mentally retarded subjects. In one case,
the second 2-week period resulted in sustained measurable gains while the
first period did not. The second subject exhibited additional gains
during the second phase. Our present study provides an opportunity to
analyze data from three separate stimulation periods and a comparable
control period.

In our initial analyses, it was apparent that the three Down's syndrome
subjects evidenced greater motor development during the experimental
period as contrasted with their rate of development during the control
period. The overall gains for each subject are presented in Table 4. It
was apparent that the younger, less delayed subjects evidenced the
greatest overall gains. The reflex scale data were less impressive. The
data for the remaining subject indicate that the semicircular canal
stimulation had almost no measurable effect upon her motor or reflex
development.

Table 4

Gain Scores for Motor and Reflex Scales

Subject		Motor Scale	Reflex Scale			Motor Scale	Reflex Scale
	Control Phase				Experimental Phase		
A	5 months	+12	+16		5 months	+22	+11
	Experimental Phase				Control Phase		
B	5 months	+7	+12		6 months	+3	+4
C	5 months	+29	+6[a]		5 months	+22	0[a]
D	5½ months	+8	0		6½ months	+16	+2[a]

(Crossover)

Note: The months refer to length of phase.

[a]Subject at ceiling of assessment scale.

While our analyses of the present data are at a preliminary stage, it does
appear that gains derived from semicircular canal stimulation exceed the
typical rate of maturation for the Down's syndrome subjects. In each
case, vestibular stimulation appeared to enhance their development.
Further analyses of these data are planned. For the purposes of this
chapter, this preliminary analysis provides additional support for the
relationship between vestibular stimulation and motor development.

MECHANISM OF ACTION

Despite the abundance of intervention reports demonstrating the effectiveness of semicircular canal stimulation in enhancing the motor development
of preambulatory children, relatively little is known regarding the
mechanisms involved. One attempt to address this deficiency is reported
by Holmes, Nagy Reich and Pasternak (1984). They provided an interesting
synthesis of the various early intervention reports for premature infants
(See Figure 3). They proposed that the supplemental stimulation,
including vestibular stimulation, could produce effects along two possible
pathways. First, it could be that the supplemental stimulation has a
direct effect upon the central nervous system by strengthening neural
pathways. They cited the work of Rosenzweig and others (Levine, 1960;
Rosenzweig, Bennett, & Diamond, 1972) on environmental complexity and
brain development of rats in support of their hypothesis. Briefly,
environmental enrichment has been associated with physiological changes
such as greater weight and thickness of the cerebral cortex, increased
number of glial cells, larger brain cell bodies and nuclei, and increased
metabolic activity (Rosenzweig et al., 1972). Levine (1960) reported that
rats provided with extra stimulation exhibited physiological and
behavioral effects. Similarly, Kreutzberg (1976) argued that semicircular
canal stimulation enhances the maturation of synaptic connectivity within
the inhibitory centers of the cerebellum. The difficulty with these
explanations is that there is no direct evidence that semicircular stimulation produces quantitative or qualitative changes in brain structure.
Carefully controlled animal studies would be helpful in understanding this
process.

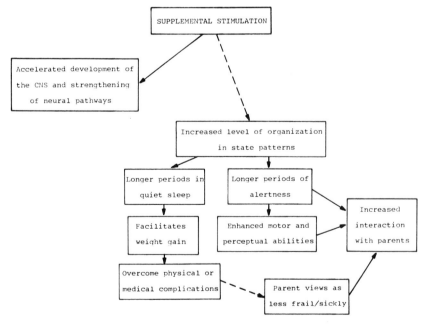

Figure 3
Model based on Holmes et al. (1984).

Holmes et al. (1984) also proposed an indirect path where immediate changes in state organization lead to enhanced physical status and greater responsivity issue is especially important for preterm infants in that there are several studies that document interactional differences between parent-fullterm and parent-preterm dyads (Beckwith & Cohn, 1980; Brown & Bakeman, 1980; Divitto & Goldberg, 1979; Field, 1977a, 1977b, 1979; Goldberg, 1978; Klaus, Kennell, Plumb, & Zuehlke, 1970; Leifer, Leiderman, Barnett, & Williams, 1972). It has been reported that a major factor contributing to these differences is that preterm infants are far less alert and responsive to social stimulation than fullterm infants (Beckwith & Cohn, 1980; Brown & Bakeman, 1980; Divitto & Goldberg, 1979; Field, 1977a, 1977b, 1979). Holmes et al. (1984) suggested that the readiness of the infant to interact more fully following intervention would contribute greatly to their interactions with parents. There is some additional support for this view. It has been shown that a responsive, well-organized infant is more rewarding to his/her parent (Sameroff, 1978) and probably is more able to respond to the environment (Korner et al., 1983). Lipsitt (1979) proposed that increased responsivity of the infant triggers more frequent and complex behavior on the part of the parent that in turn leads to more sophisticated interactions. This increase in quality and quantity of interaction might, in turn, potentiate the effects of supplemental nursery stimulation.

CONCLUSION

In summary, we have reviewed the role of primitive reflexes, postural adjustment reactions, and stereotyped behavior in early motor development. We have also presented data that suggest rotational vestibular stimulation may serve to enhance the motor development of preambulatory children. There are several implications of these data that warrant further research. First, if the motor development of retarded children can be facilitated by an intervention there may be positive effects upon their development in other skill areas. Second, early intervention of this sort may have implications for the development of so-called pathological stereotypies. That is, if rhythmical behaviors of infancy carry over and become the stereotyped behaviors exhibited by older mentally retarded persons, then a more normal motor development course could decrease the likelihood that these children would later manifest stereotyped behavior.

In general, measures of motor functioning and reflexes have shown that the rotational vestibular stimulation produces changes beyond those to be expected simply as a function of maturation. Anecdotal information obtained from parents and other caregivers also suggests that the participants were, as a whole, more attentive, less restless, and better coordinated. In considering the available data, it appears that while the effects of rotational vestibular stimulation are fairly modest in terms of magnitude among normal babies these effects could have a profound influence upon the development of developmentally disabled children.

REFERENCES

Baumeister, A. A., Frye, G. D., & Schroeder, S. (in press). Neuro-
    chemical correlates of self-injurious behavior. In J. A. Mulick & B.
    L. Mallory (Eds.), Transitions in mental retardation: Advocacy,
    technology, and science. New York: Ablex.

Baumeister, A. A., & MacLean, W. E., Jr. (1979). Brain damage and mental
    retardation. In N. R. Ellis (Ed.), Handbook of mental deficiency,
    psychological theory and research (2nd Ed., pp. 197-230). Hillsdale,
    NJ: Erlbaum.

Bayley, N. (1969). Bayley scales of infant development: Birth to two
    years. New York: Psychological Corp.

Beckwith, L., & Cohn, S. E. (1980). Interactions of preterm infants with
    their caregivers and test performance at age 2. In T. M. Fields, S.
    Goldberg, D. Stern, & M. Sostek (Eds.), High-risk infants and
    children. Adult and peer interactions (pp. 155-178). New York:
    Academic Press.

Berkson, G. (1967). Abnormal stereotyped motor acts. In J. Zubin & H.
    F. Hunt (Eds.), Comparative psychopathology - Animal and human (pp.
    76-94). New York: Grune & Stratton.

Berkson, G. (1983). Repetitive stereotyped behaviors. American Journal
    of Mental Deficiency, 88, 239-246.

Berkson, G., & Gallagher, R. P. (in press). Control of feedback from
    abnormal stereotyped behaviors.

Bernstein, N. (1967). The coordination and regulation of movement.
    London: Pergamon Press.

Brody, S. (1960). Self-rocking in infancy. Journal of the American
    Psychoanalytic Association, 8, 464-491.

Brown, J. V., & Bakeman, R. (1980). Relationships of human mothers with
    their infants during the first year of life: Effects of prematurity.
    In R. W. Bell & W. P. Smotherman (Eds.), Maternal influence and early
    behavior (pp. 353-373). New York: Spectrum.

Bruininks, R. H. (1974). Physical and motor development of retarded
    persons. In N. R. Ellis (Ed.), International review of research in
    mental retardation (Vol. 7, pp. 209-261). New York: Academic Press.

Burns, K. A., Deddish, R. B., Burns, W. J., & Hatcher, R. P. (1983). Use
    of oscillating waterbeds and rhythmic sounds for preterm infant
    stimulation. Developmental Psychology, 19, 746-751.

Capute, A. J., Palmer, F. B., Shapiro, B. K., Wachtel, R. C., Ross, A., &
    Accardo, P. J. (1984). Primitive reflex profile: A quantification
    of primitive reflexes in infancy. Developmental Medicine and Child
    Neurology, 26, 375-383.

Chee, F. K. W., Kreutzberg, J. R., & Clark, D. L. (1978). Semicircular canal stimulation in cerebral palsied children. Physical Therapy, 58, 1071-1075.

Clark, D. L., Chee, F. K. W., Kanter, R. M., & Kreutzberg, J. R. (1980). Evaluation of motor skills in the preambulatory child. Unpublished manuscript, Ohio State University, Columbus, OH.

Clark, D. L., Kreutzberg, J. R., & Chee, F. K. W. (1977). Vestibular stimulation influence on motor development in infants. Science, 196, 1228-1229.

Cratty, B. J. (1970). Perceptual and motor development in infants and young children. New York: MacMillan.

Crome, T. D., Cowie, V., & Slater, E. (1966). A statistical note on cerebellar and brain-stem weight in mongolism. Journal of Mental Deficiency Research, 10, 69-72.

de Lissovoy, V. (1962). Headbanging in early childhood: A suggested cause. Journal of Genetic Psychology, 102, 109-114.

DiVitto, B., & Goldberg, S. (1979). The effects of newborn medical status on early parent-infant interactions. In T. Field, A. Sosteck, S. Goldberg, & H. H. Shuman (Eds.), Infants born at-risk (pp. 331-332). New York: Spectrum.

Donoghue, E. C., Kirman, B. H., Bullmore, G. H. C., Laban, D., & Abbas, K. A. (1970). Some factors affecting age of walking in a mentally retarded population. Developmental Medicine and Child Neurology, 12, 781-792.

Eastham, R. D., & Jancar, J. (1968). Clinical pathology in mental retardation. Bristol: Wright.

Fiorentino, M. R. (1981). A basis for sensorimotor development - Normal and abnormal. Springfield, IL: Thomas.

Flavell, J. H. (1963). The developmental psychology of Jean Piaget. New York: Van Nostrand Reinhold.

Field, T. (1977a). Effects of early separation, interactive deficits, and experimental manipulations on infant-mother face-to-face interaction. Child Development, 48, 763-771.

Field, T. (1977b). Maternal stimulation during infant feeding. Developmental Psychology, 13, 539-540.

Field, T. (1979). Interaction patterns of preterm and term infants. In T. Fields, A. Sostek, S. Goldberg, & H. H. Shuman (Eds.), Infants born at-risk (pp. 333-3546). New York: Spectrum.

Folio, M. R., & Fewell, R. R. (1983). Peabody developmental motor scales and activity cards. Allen, TX: DLM Teaching Resources.

Gesell, A. (1939). Reciprocal interweaving in neuromotor development: A principle of spiral organization shown in the patterning of infant behavior. Journal of Comparative Neurology, 70, 161-180.

Gibson, J. J. (1966). The senses considered as perceptual systems. Boston: Houghton-Mifflin.

Gibson, J. J. (1979). An ecological approach to visual perception. Boston: Houghton-Mifflin.

Goldberg, S. (1978). Prematurity: Effects on parent-infant interaction. Journal of Pediatric Psychology, 3, 137-144.

Gregg, C. L. , Haffner, M. E., & Korner, A. E. (1976). The relative efficacy of vestibular-proprioceptive stimulation and the upright position in enhancing visual pursuit in neonates. Child Development, 47, 309-314.

Griffiths, R. (1976). The abilities of babies. Amersham, Bucks, England: Association for Research in Infant and Child Development.

Holmes, D. L., Nagy Reich, J., & Pasternak, J. F. (1984). The development of infants born at-risk. Hillsdale, NJ: Erlbaum.

Howe, C. E. (1959). A comparison of motor skills of mentally retarded and normal children. Exceptional Children, 25, 352-354.

Huttenlocher, R. P. (1975). Synaptic and dendritic development and mental defect. In N. A. Buchwald & M. A. B. Brazier (Eds.), Brain mechanisms in mental retardation (pp. 123-140). New York: Academic Press.

Kandel, E. R., & Schwartz, J. H. (1981). Principles of neural science. New York: Elsevier North Holland.

Kantner, R. M., Clark, D. L., Allen, L. C., & Chase, M. F. (1976). Effects of vestibular stimulation on nystagmus response and motor performance in the developmentally delayed infant. Physical Therapy, 56, 414-421.

Kelso, J. A. S. (1982). The process approach to understanding human motor behavior: An introduction. In J. A. S. Kelso (Ed.), Human motor behavior: An introduction (pp. 3-19). Hillsdale, NJ: Erlbaum.

Kelso, J. A. S., & Stelmach, G. E. (1976). Central and peripheral mechanisms in motor control. In G. E. Stelmach (Ed.), Motor control: Issues and trends (pp. 1-40). New York: Academic Press.

Klaus, M. H., Kennell, J. H., Plumb, N., & Zuehlke, S. (1970). Human maternal behavior at the first contact with her young. Pediatrics, 46, 187-192.

Knobloch, H., Stevens, F., & Malone, A. F. (1980). Manual of developmental diagnosis. Hagerstown, MD: Harper & Row.

Kopp, C. B. (1975). Development of fine motor behaviors: Issues and research. In N. R. Ellis (Ed.), Aberrant development in infancy (pp. 149-160). Hillsdale, NJ: Erlbaum.

Korner. (1979). Maternal rhythms and waterbeds: A form of intervention with premature infants. In E. B. Thoman (Ed.), Origins of the infant's social responsiveness (pp. 95-124). Hillsdale, NJ: Erlbaum.

Korner, A. F., Schneider, P., & Forrest, T. (1983). Effects of vestibular-proprioceptive stimulation on the neurobehavioral development of preterm infants: A pilot study. Neuropediatrics, 14, 170-175.

Korner, A. F., & Thoman, E. B. (1972). Relative efficacy of contact and vestibular stimulation in soothing neonates. Child Development, 43, 443-453.

Kravitz, H., & Boehm, J. (1971). Rhythmic habit patterns in infancy: Their sequences, age of onset, and frequency. Child Development, 42, 399-413.

Kravitz, H., Rosenthal, V., Teplitz, Z., Murphy, J., & Lesser, R. (1960). A study of headbanging in infants and children. Diseases of the Nervous System, 21, 203-208.

Kreutzberg, J. R. (1976). Effects of vestibular stimulation on the reflex and motor development in normal infants. Dissertation Abstracts International, 37, 2013B. (University Microfilms No. 76-24, 631.)

Kris, E. (1954). Problems of infantile neurosis: A discussion. Psychoanalytic Study of the Child, 9, 16-71.

Kubie, L. S. (1941). The repetitive core of neurosis. Psychoanalytic Quarterly, 10, 123-143.

Kugler, P. N., Kelso, J. A. S., & Turvey, M. T. (1982). On the control and co-ordination of naturally developing systems. In J. A. S. Kelso & J. E. Clark (Eds.), The development of movement control and co-ordination (pp. 5-78). New York: John Wiley.

Leifer, A. D., Leiderman, P. H., Barnett, C. R., & Williams, J. A. (1972). Effects of mother-infant separation on maternal attachment behavior. Child Development, 43, 1203-1218.

Levine, S. (1960). Stimulation in infancy. Scientific American, 214, 80.

Lipsitt, L. P. (1979). Critical conditions in infancy. Child Development, 48, 1633-1639.

Lloyd, K. G., Hornykiewicz, O., Davidson, L., Shannak, K., Farley, I., Goldstein, M., Shibuya, M., Kelly, W. N., & Fox, I. H. (1981). Biochemical evidence of dysfunction of brain neurotransmitters in the Lesch-Nyhan syndrome. The New England Journal of Medicine, 305, 1106-1111.

MacLean, W. E., Jr., & Baumeister, A. A. (1982). Effects of vestibular stimulation on motor development and stereotyped behavior of developmentally delayed children. Journal of Abnormal Child Psychology, 10(2), 229-245.

Mason, W. A., & Berkson, G. (1975). Effects of maternal mobility on the development of rocking and other behaviors in rhesus monkeys: A study with artificial mothers. Developmental Psychobiology, 8, 197-211.

McGraw, M. B. (1943). The neuromuscular maturation of the human infant. New York: Hafner.

Molnar, G. E. (1974). Motor deficit of retarded infants and children. Archives of Physical Medicine and Rehabilitation, 55, 393-398.

Neal, M. V. (1968). Vestibular stimulation and developmental behavior of the small preterm infant. Nursing Research Report, 3, 2-5.

Parker, D. E. (1980). The vestibular apparatus. Scientific American, 243(5), 118-135.

Parmelee, A. H., Jr., & Sigman, M. D. (1983). Perinatal brain development and behavior. In P. M. Mussen (Ed.), Handbook of child psychology: Vol. 2. Infancy and developmental psychobiology (pp. 95-155). New York: Wiley.

Piaget, J. (1952). The origins of intelligence in children (M. Cook, Trans.). New York: Norton.

Piaget, J. (1970). Piaget's theory. In P. H. Mussen (Ed.), Carmichael's manual of child psychology (Vol. 1, pp. 733-772). New York: Wiley.

Purpura, D. P. (1974). Dendritic spine "dysgenesis" and mental retardation. Science, 186, 1126-1128.

Purpura, D. P. (1975). Normal and aberrant neuronal development in the cerebral cortex of human fetus and young infant. In N. A. Buchwald & M. A. B. Brazier (Eds.), Brain mechanisms in mental retardation (pp. 141-169). New York: Academic Press.

Rosenfeld, A. G. (1980). Visiting in the intensive care nursery. Child Development, 52, 939-941.

Rosenzweig, M. R., Bennett, E. L., & Diamond, M. C. (1972). Brain changes in response to experience. Scientific American, 226, 22-29.

Sallustro, F., & Atwell, C. W. (1978). Body rocking, head-banging, and head-rolling in normal children. Journal of Pediatrics, 93, 704-708.

Sameroff, A. J. (1978). Organization and stability of newborn behavior: A commentary on the Brazelton Neonatal Behavior Assessment Scale. Monographs of the Society for Research in Child Development, 43, (5-6, Serial No. 177).

Scherzer, A. L. & Tscharnuter, I. (1982). Early diagnosis and therapy in cerebral palsy. New York: Dekker.

Scola, P. S. (1982). Neurology. In S. M. Pueschel & J. E. Rynders (Eds.), Down's syndrome (pp. 219-225). Cambridge, MA: Academic Guild.

Sellick, K. J., & Over, R. (1980). Effects of vestibular stimulation on motor development of cerebral-palsied children. Developmental Medicine and Child Neurology, 22, 476-483.

Spitz, R., & Wolf, K. (1949). Autoerotism: Some empirical findings and hypotheses on three of its manifestation in the first year of life. Psychoanalytic Study of the Child, 3, 85-120.

Solkoff, N., Yaffe, S., Weintraub, D., & Blase, B. (1969). Effects of handling on the subsequent developments of premature infants. Developmental Psychology, 1, 765-768.

Thelen, E. (1979). Rhythmical stereotypies in normal human infants. Animal Behavior, 27, 699-715.

Thelen, E. (1980). Determinants of amounts of stereotyped behavior in normal human infants. Ethology and Sociobiology, 1, 141-150.

Thelen, E. (1981). Rhythmical behavior in infancy: An ethological perspective. Developmental Psychology, 17, 237-257.

Thelen, E. (1984). Learning to walk: Ecological demands and phylogenetic constraints. In L. P. Lipsitt & C. Rovee-Collier (Eds.), Advances in infancy research (Vol. 3, pp. 215-250). Norwood, NJ: Ablex.

Thelen, E. (1985). Developmental origins of motor coordination: Leg movement in human infants. Developmental Psychobiology, 18, 1-22.

Tibbling, L. (1969). The rotatory nystagmus response in children. Acta Oto-Laryngologica, 68, 459-467.

Turvey, M. T. (1977). Preliminaries to a theory of action with a reference to vision. In R. Shaw & J. Bransford (Eds.), Perceiving, acting, and knowing: Toward an ecological psychology (pp. 211-265). Hillsdale, NJ: Erlbaum.

Turvey, M. T., Fitch, H. L., & Tuller, B. (1982). The Bernstein principle: I. The problems of degrees of freedom and context-conditioned variability. In J. A. S. Kelso (Ed.), Human motor behavior: An introduction (pp. 239-252). Hillsdale, NJ: Erlbaum.

VonWendt, L., Makinen, H., & Rantakallio, P. (1984). Psychomotor
    development in the first year and mental retardation - A prospective
    study. Journal of Mental Deficiency Research, 28, 219-225.

Wachs, T. D., & Gruen, G. E. (1982). Early experience and human
    development. New York: Plenum Press.

Wolff, P. H. (1967). The role of biological rhythms in early
    psychological development. Bulletin of the Menninger Clinic, 31,
    197-218.

Zelazo, P. R. (1983). The development of walking: New findings and old
    assumptions. Journal of Motor Behavior, 15, 99-137.

Zelazo, P. R. (1976). From reflexive to instrumental behavior. In L. P.
    Lipsitt (Ed.), Developmental psychobiology: The significance of
    infancy (pp. 87-104). Hillsdale, NJ: Erlbaum.

Motor Skill Acquisition of the Mentally Handicapped:
Issues in Research and Training
M.G. Wade (editor)
© *Elsevier Science Publishers B.V. (North-Holland), 1986*

COMMENTS ON COORDINATION, CONTROL AND SKILL PAPERS

K. M. Newell

Institute for Child Behavior and Development
University of Illinois at Urbana-Champaign

The papers that I have been asked to comment on reflect a relatively
diverse set of issues and problems with respect to the coordination,
control, and skill exhibited by mentally retarded persons engaged in
action. Moreover, all the papers are outside the traditional approaches of
the motor skill and mental retardation literature, which has been dominated
heretofore by what I have labelled elsewhere as the physical fitness and
information processing approaches (Newell, 1985). The papers to be discussed, however, are not reflective of a unifying theoretical position,
although they are all consonant with a psychobiological approach to action
and mental retardation. In light of the diverse nature of the issues
raised in this set of papers, it seems most appropriate to discuss each
paper independently rather than attempt to weave unifying theoretical
threads where none might exist.

SHUMWAY-COOK AND WOOLLACOTT

The Shumway-Cook and Woollacott experiments examine the development of
neural control processes underlying balance and preparation for movement in
both normal and Down's syndrome children. Posture control is often viewed
as a problem of statics and divorced from the dynamic and general problem
of movement control. However, postural control of one body configuration
or another is required in most actions and recent analyses indicate postural control to be a complex dynamic process (Gurfinkel, Kots, Paltsev, &
Feldman, 1971; Nashner & McCollum, 1985). The distinction between posture
and movement, therefore, can be viewed as a relative one based on the
degree of motion rather than a qualitative categorization.

Although the development of prone progression forms the backbone of much of
the early motor development research (e.g., Gesell, McGraw, & Shirley),
very little is known about the neural control processes underlying the
development of natural upright posture. Shumway-Cook and Woollacott (1985)
have initiated a research program to fill this void and to allow comparisons to Down's syndrome children (15 months - 6 years) as provided in their
contribution here. Using a platform perturbation protocol pioneered by
Nashner, they are attempting to understand the delays in postural control
typically exhibited by Down's syndrome children. A particular focus is the
use of EMG techniques to distinguish between the myotatic stretch reflex
and long loop contributions in postural responses to perturbations. The
manipulation of the informational support for posture is also employed to
examine the sensory integration mechanisms underlying the organization of
postural control.

The data from the platform perturbation studies reveal that older children (7-10 years) and adults exhibit a stereotypic and short latency (approximately 100 ms) proximal and distal muscle organization. Normal children under 6 years produce a structural organization of muscle activity similar to that of the adult but with greater variability in the timing and amplitude relationships of the muscle activity. Similarly, the Down's syndrome children tend to produce the appropriate direction specific postural synergies in response to the perturbations although with a longer latency and with greater variability than that of their so-called counterparts.

The reduction of the latency and variability of responses is a typical reflection of practice effects. That is, practice speeds up all elements of a response and leads to reduced variability in response outcome. In light of these well known findings in the motor skill literature, I believe it is premature for Shumway-Cook and Woollacott to infer that age or population differences are developmental differences, given only a cross-sectional comparison. The response differences between the age and population groups reflect all the symptoms of learning. Undoubtedly, the older the individual, the more practice that person has engaged in for upright postural control. Similar expectations may be placed on young normal children in contrast to their chronological peers with Down's syndrome. The failure to distinguish between state transitions that reflect learning on the one hand and development on the other is a problem pervading much of the motor development literature. In short, an age trend cannot be taken to be a developmental trend in a cross-sectional experimental design (Wohlwill, 1973), and the influence of practice per se on performance may account for much of what often passes as an age or developmental trend.

The aging child is also typically a growing child. The influence of the changing mechanical constraints to action that accompany the growth and form transitions of the aging child is often a forgotten factor in developmental accounts of motor control (see Newell, 1984, for a review). In the platform perturbation protocol of Shumway-Cook and Woollacott, the amount of torque required in the respective muscle groups by children of varying ages is most likely very different. There is a considerable literature documenting the fact that response variability changes systematically as a function of the force requirements of the task (see Newell, Carlton, & Hancock, 1984). Typically, the more force required in response output, the greater the response variability. This variability in response output appears to be coherent across kinematic and EMG measures (Carlton, Robertson, Carlton, & Newell, in press). Thus, the failure to body scale the perturbations in the platform protocol may contribute to the differences in response variability observed by Shumway-Cook and Woollacott between age and population groups. The older and larger individual has to produce a smaller percentage of muscular output in reacting to the platform perturbations than a younger and smaller individual. Consideration of these growth related factors in age group assessments also opens the question of whether the adult is the 'norm' for so-called developmental comparisons.

An additional problem is that the actual movement pattern that emerges from coordinated action may hold a number of significant differences between individuals even though the populations under consideration are performing the same act. For example, the natural standing posture of the growing child changes (Sinclair, 1978). Eighteen month old children tend to stand upright with legs bowed, 3 year old children tend to exhibit knocked knees while 6 year old children tend to stand with straight legs. These postural differences could, in and of themselves, contribute to the variations in latency and amplitude of the muscular responses of children in the perturbation protocol employed by Shumway-Cook and Woollacott.

The significance of the above comments for the Shumway-Cook and Woollacott studies is that the differences in postural variability observed may be due to a number of factors that typically <u>covary</u> with age and population differences. Thus, it is too early to assess the theoretical significance of the age and Down's syndrome differences reported by Shumway-Cook and Woollacott in postural responses to perturbation. However, the ongoing systematic work of this group with the platform protocol provides a foundation for understanding the development of neural control processes underlying posture and preparation for movement in both normal and Down's syndrome children.

BERKSON AND GALLAGHER

Stereotyped behaviors appear to reflect an important transition period in the development of the fundamental movement patterns, although exactly what role these behaviors play remains an open question. These stereotypic behaviors, however, can extend beyond the 'normal' period of development and become a dominating element in the life of a number of population groups including those exhibiting severe mental retardation. Berkson has been studying these superfluous patterns of coordination in the mentally retarded for some 20 years. This paper with Gallagher provides a more refined description of the stereotypic activities of the mentally retarded and attempts to understand the role of feedback as self-stimulation in the maintenance of these stereotypic activities. I will limit this commentary to the measurement of 'form' in physical activities and the self-stimulation hypothesis for abnormal stereotypic activities proposed by Berkson and Gallagher.

Traditional characterizations of stereotypic behaviors have been qualitative and relied primarily on the checklist categorization of activities such as hand-gazing, body-rocking, head-banging and so on. There have been few kinematic analyses of the movement patterns produced in stereotypic activities (although see Gardos, Cole, & LaBrie, 1977). Thus, the issue of whether the form of abnormal and normal stereotyped behaviors is the same or different remains an empirical question with interesting and important theoretical consequences. Berkson and Gallagher (with Schwartz) attempt a direct answer to this question by conducting a topographic analysis of the videotapes of hand-gazing and body-rocking of severely retarded and normal infants. The findings showed that on a number of dimensions of the movement analysis (duration, body position, and repetition) the population groups differed, and these differences provided the basis for the proposal that the form of the stereotypic behaviors for the two population groups was different.

A topographic analysis of movement documents the absolute physical configuration (in space-time) of the body parts during an activity. In many respects, a topographic analysis of human movement is similar to a geographical map that represents all features of the physical configuration of a land surface area but without time varying constraints. Repeated engagements in the same activity by an individual, however, always exhibit

response variability (see Newell et al., 1984), or, in the terms of a
topographic analysis, changes in the response configuration. Similarly,
the exact configuration of the movement will also vary between individuals
engaged in the same act due to the naturally varying organismic constraints. Thus, there will inevitably be absolute motion differences in
the physical configuration of any two movement sequences, even in those of
the same individual performing the same movement sequence.

In light of the above, it would appear that the form of a movement sequence
is more appropriately characterized by an analysis of the relative motion
of the body parts (Newell, in press). The relative motion refers to the
motion of one body part with respect to another from the perspective of the
observer, rather than with respect to absolute body configuration in
Euclidean 3-dimensional space. These relative body motions seem more
appropriately analyzed by a topological analysis than a topographical
approach (McGinnis & Newell, 1982). A topological kinematic property is a
kinematic parameter that remains invariant under metrical transformations
of scale. This measurement approach allows one to distinguish between the
topological and metrical properties of kinematics that may reflect the
concepts of coordination and control, respectively (Kugler, Kelso, &
Turvey, 1980; Newell, in press). For example, changes of velocity within a
given gait pattern typically leave a number of kinematic properties
invariant in spite of the metrical or absolute changes in the kinematics.

A topological kinematic analysis of movement provides a direct means to
characterizing and comparing the form of different movement activities. On
this view, the form of a given activity may be defined by a unique set of
topological kinematic properties. The question is still open, therefore,
as to whether the form of abnormal and normal stereotyped behaviors is the
same or different. A systematic topological analysis of the stereotypic
behaviors may not only provide a more veridical description of the movement
sequence but a firmer basis from which to infer explanatory principles
regarding the coordination and control of these rhythmical and stereotypic
movement sequences.

The series of experiments represent a systematic line of enquiry into the
role of feedback in stereotyped behaviors. Two basic points emerge from
the data: a) that a specific pattern of feedback is maintaining the
stereotypic behavior; and b) that stimulation and control may be two
separate processes in the maintenance of stereotypic behaviors through
feedback. Control in this view involves the regulation of feedback by the
individual whereas stimulation may occur through passive movement.

The Morton study showed a clear reduction of body-rocking as a consequence
of the specific feedback from the intervention activity. This confirms
previous findings that maintenance of stereotypic behaviors is not likely
to be a consequence of a general stimulation hypothesis. It is possible
that the head rolling data were less clear cut due to the difficulty of
matching kinematically the head rolling movement sequence. An interesting
feature of the body-rocking experiment is that the feedback specificity
effects emerge in spite of the fact that the feedback received by the
subject will differ between the voluntary and passive intervention situation. That is, the active/passive manipulation is not as clear cut as it
appears at first sight because even active and passive movements that
exhibit the same topological and metrical kinematic properties, will
provide different feedback. This ambiguity in the active/passive manipula-

tion may also have contributed to masking the effects of the chair manipulation study conducted by Buyer.

The link between developmental level and preference for self control in the chair study was apparently stronger than the general preference for the type of chair. This finding points up the limitation that can occur in studies that fail to consider individual differences. Berkson and Gallagher provide another example of the effect of individual differences in discussing the consequences of the presence or absence of eyeglasses on the maintenance of stereotypic behaviors on a visual severely retarded child. The intertwining of a traditional group approach to research with a consideration of individual differences is another strength of the studies reported in this paper. This orientation also seems to hold promise with respect to its significance for clinical practice in preventing or eliminating abnormal stereotypies. Furthermore, the reasoned plea for a commitment to an early intervention program to eliminate stereotypic behaviors should be acted upon because the evidence suggests that these abnormal stereotypic behaviors are difficult if not impossible to eliminate once developed. Whether abnormal stereotypics reflect irreversible states is an interesting theoretical question with obvious practical implications.

Although the series of studies reported by Berkson and Gallagher reveal the significance of information picked up by the sensory receptors in the maintenance of stereotypic behaviors, the experimental findings do not relate directly to the traditional debate about the central-peripheral control of such behaviors (Wolff, 1968). The central-peripheral debate in motor control has waned in recent years and it has even been asked whether this type of issue is a relevant question for understanding problems of coordination and control (Kugler & Turvey, 1979). Regardless, investigators of abnormal stereotypic behaviors always seem to come down on one side or the other of the central-peripheral debate in approaching solutions to the elimination of stereotypic behaviors. Within this orientation, Berkson and Gallagher have provided systematic evidence that feedback may play a self stimulation role in the maintenance of stereotypic behaviors.

MACLEAN, ARENDT AND BAUMEISTER

The focus of this paper is the effect of vestibular stimulation on early motor development and stereotyped behavior. Although it has long been accepted in child rearing circles that vestibular stimulation has a soothing effect on a distressed infant, it is only recently that the effect of systematic manipulation of vestibular stimulation on the motor development of normal and developmentally delayed infants has been studied. Part of the reason for this situation relates to the emphasis given to vision as the 'Queen of the Senses' and the fact that controlled manipulation of vestibular input requires a certain sophistication of technology. Thus, although Sherrington gave a place for vestibular stimulation within the general category of proprioception, it is the muscle spindles, golgi tendon organs and joint receptors that have dominated the proprioception literature. General theoretical and practical interest in the vestibular system has been heightened by the demands of the space program which requires an understanding of man's capabilities in a gravity free environment.

The vestibular apparatus, unlike the other proprioceptors listed above, provides information about the position and movement of the body with

respect to the environment. Thus, as MacLean and colleagues have docu-
mented, the vestibular apparatus provides information about the position of
the head relative to gravity and it also responds to changes in the rotational acceleration of the head in the three dimensions of Euclidean space.
This category of information has been called exproprioception by Lee (1978)
as a way to distinguish it from the body relative information (proprioception) that is provided by the other receptors. Thus, the Lee categorization is based upon types of information rather than receptor categories.

Developmental interest in the vestibular system has been sparked by the
studies of Clark and colleagues (Clark, Kreutzberg, & Chee, 1997; Chee,
Kreutzberg, & Clark, 1978) and these experiments also provide the starting
point for the empirical work reported from the laboratory of MacLean and
colleagues. The Clark experiments showed that systematic semicircular
canal stimulation of preambulatory normal infants and children with cerebral palsy over a 4 week period resulted in improvements on reflex and
motor ability tests. Some studies have failed to replicate these findings
with a cerebral palsy population and MacLean and colleagues list several
important methodological differences between the vestibular stimulation
experiments which may have contributed to the discrepant findings.

The experiments of MacLean and colleagues seem to reflect an improved
methodology over the Clark vestibular stimulation protocol in that tighter
controls were employed in the rotation manipulation and a broader range of
behavior assessment methods were used to measure behavioral change. The
published and ongoing experiments of this group show that rotational
vestibular stimulation of both normal and developmentally delayed infants
advances the time-course of the onset of the various motor milestones and,
also possibly, the development of other skills. Why these effects occur,
and the potential that these manipulations hold as an early intervention
strategy for the prevention of abnormal stereotypies, are the challenging
questions that emerge from the paper offered by MacLean and colleagues.

It is always tempting and comforting (to some) to invoke the argument of
physiological changes to account for the behavioral differences between
experimental conditions, such as the vestibular stimulation groups.
MacLean and colleagues recognize, however, that the necessary experiments
have not been conducted to force a sufficiently direct link between the
differing levels of analysis. Even if such links could be advanced, the
changes in physiological structure may more appropriately be regarded as a
change in constraint to action rather than a causal agent in the
perception-action cycle.

It is sobering to note that the facilitation effects of the vestibular
stimulation arise from a passive and very artificial set of circumstances.
In the experiments reported, the infant does not pick up information from
the environment in relation to voluntary motion but rather from a passive
manipulation in which a person or machine moves the child's head with
respect to the environment. Research on vision and proprioception has
consistently revealed the advantage of active over passive manipulations
(e.g., Held, 1965; Kelso, & Wallace, 1978) in a variety of movement proto-
cols. Indeed, the Held studies suggest that visual stimulation induced by
passive movement may even be detrimental to performance, although the
nonmovement controls were not examined. Thus, the vestibular stimulation
experiments pose the additional challenge of why the effects appear even
with passive movement in a darkened room.

It is likely that a considerable time will pass before we understand why vestibular stimulation facilitates motor development. However, this lack of theoretical knowledge will not, in all likelihood, preclude the use of vestibular stimulation as an intervention technique with the developmentally delayed infant. Indeed, it may well be that the practical use of this augmented strategy can provide insight into the nature of the vestibular stimulation effect.

DAVIS

An important focus of the motor skills and mental retardation literature is the trainability of mentally retarded persons (Wade, Hoover, & Newell, 1983). The experiments reported by Davis are on this general theme and ask whether manipulation of visual information and instructional cues can facilitate the ball throwing accuracy of 14-15 year-old mentally handicapped subjects (IQ approximately 40), some of whom have Down's syndrome. Previous work by Davis had revealed some advantage of the visual information manipulation with university students in learning the same ball throwing task.

The visual manipulation in the ball throwing experiments was the inclusion or exclusion of a small red dot (20 mm in diameter) in the center of the larger circular target (245 cm in diameter). The results of the two experiments suggest that the inclusion of the dot only facilitates performance of the mentally retarded adolescents when some prior instruction regarding the relevance of the red target is provided. This finding is consistent with many previous studies that show mentally retarded subjects do not spontaneously generate the appropriate strategy for the task at hand.

Given that the findings of the Davis experiments are robust, the question remains as to why the effects emerge. The target manipulation is a rather different visual information manipulation than typically occurs in motor skill experiments and it is worth trying to unpack the information that this target provides. Before attempting such an analysis, it is appropriate to emphasize that the task employed by Davis almost certainly required the subjects to refine the scaling of an already established pattern of coordination rather than develop the form or structure of the throwing action itself (Newell, in press). Thus, we need to ask why the information from the target should facilitate the refinement of the scaling of the throwing action?

One interpretation is that the augmented small dot in the center of the large target focuses the subject's attention on the target center, and this in turn leads to an improved performance. On this view, the target dot does not provide any additional information to the subject. A related but alternative interpretation is that the augmented target dot actually informs the subject that this is the center of the target and the goal of the task. It is possible that without this aid, the mentally retarded subjects do not understand the task as established by the experimental instructions and, as a consequence, the subjects erroneously believe that they can hit the large target anywhere. On this view, the augmented target dot may actually change the subject's perception of the task constraints.

Davis provides another interpretation of the data by suggesting that the small target dot was used as a reference to provide the subject more precise knowledge of results (KR), of the outcome of each throw. This is a very plausible interpretation given the KR literature (see Newell, 1976) which has shown consistent effects of information precision on performance outcome. However, this information feedback account of the target manipulation needs to be isolated from the other prior to action information accounts raised above.

Thus, the theoretical significance of the visual information manipulation in the throwing experiments is not apparent. Davis needs to tease apart the possible theoretical interpretations of the data. A stronger approach is to manipulate the information based upon some apriori line of theoretical reasoning regarding augmented information and skill learning. The link that Davis builds between the vision manipulation of the experiments and the vision literature quoted in the introduction to the paper, is tenuous at best.

CONCLUDING COMMENTS

Although the papers that I have commented on are largely disparate in their theoretical orientation, I believe they are representative of what I hope will be a continuing trend in future mental retardation and motor skills research. That is, the papers all focus on problems of coordination, control, and skill in the mentally retarded rather than merely using a motor skill as a means to the end of studying retardation per se. This latter perspective has dominated too much of the recent information processing orientation to mental retardation and motor skills and has resulted in a failure to understand the impact of specific constraints on coordination, control, and skill. Action needs to be studied as an end in itself with mentally retarded populations if fruitful links are to be made between the concepts of intelligence, cognition, and movement.

REFERENCES

Berkson, G., & Gallagher, R. P. (1985). Control of feedback from abnormal stereotyped behaviors 1. In M. G. Wade (Ed.), Motor skill acquisition of the mentally handicapped. Amsterdam: North Holland.

Carlton, M. J., Robertson, R. N., Carlton, L. G., & Newell, K. M. (in press). Response timing variability: Coherence of kinematic and EMG parameters. Journal of Motor Behavior.

Chee, F. K. W., Kreutzberg, J. R., & Clark, D. L. (1978). Semicircular canal stimulation in cerebral palsied children. Physical Therapy, 58, 1071-1075.

Clark, D. L., Kreutzberg, J. R., & Chee, F. K. W. (1977). Vestibular stimulation influences on motor development in infants. Sciences, 196, 1228-1229.

Davis, W. E. (1985). Precise visual information and throwing accuracy. In M. G. Wade (Ed.), Motor skill acquisition of the mentally handicapped. Amsterdam: North Holland.

Gardos, G., Cole, J. O., & LaBrie, R. L. (1977). The assessment of tardive dyskinesia. Archives of General Psychiatry, 34, 1206-1212.

Gurfinkel, V. S., Kots, Y. M., Paltsev, Y. I., & Feldman, A. G. (1971). The compensation of respiratory disturbances of the erect posture of man as an example of organization of interarticular interaction. In I. M. Gelfand, V. S. Gurfinkel, S. V. Fomin, & M. L. Tsetlin (Eds.), Models of the structural functional organization of certain biological systems (pp. 382-395). Cambridge, MA: MIT Press.

Held, R. (1965). Plasticity in sensory-motor systems. Scientific American, 213, 84-93.

Kelso, J. A. S., & Wallace, S. A. (1978). Conscious mechanisms in movement. In G. E. Stelmach (Ed.), Information processing in motor control and learning (pp. 79-116). New York: Academic Press.

Kugler, P. N., & Turvey, M. T. (1979). Two metaphors for neural afference and efference. Brain and Behavioral Sciences 2, 305-307.

Kugler, P. N., Kelso, J.A.S., & Turvey, M. T. (1980). On the concept of coordinative structures as dissipative structures: I. Theoretical lines on convergence. In G. E. Stelmach & J. Requin (Eds.), Tutorials in motor behavior (pp. 3-48). Amsterdam: North Holland.

Lee, D. N. (1978). The functions of vision. In H. Pick & E. Saltzman (Eds.), Modes of perceiving and processing information (pp. 159-170). Hillsdale, NY: Erlbaum.

MacLean, W. E., Jr., Arendt, R. E., & Baumeister, A. A. (1984). Early motor development and stereotyped behavior: The effects of semi-circular canal stimulation. In M. G. Wade (Ed.), Motor skill acquisition of the mentally handicapped. Amsterdam: North Holland.

McGinnis, P. M., & Newell, K. M. (1982). Topological dynamics: A framework for describing movement and its constraints. Human Movement Science, 1, 289-305.

Nashner, L. M., & McCollum, G. (1985). The organization of human postural movements: A formal basis and experimental synthesis. Behavioral and Brain Sciences, 8, 135-172.

Newell, K. M. (1976). Knowledge of results and motor learning. In J. Keogh & R. S. Hutton (Eds.), Exercise and sport reviews (Vol. IV) (pp. 195-228).

Newell, K. M. (1984). Physical constraints to development of motor skills. In J. R. Thomas (Eds.), Motor development during childhood and adolescence (pp. 105-120). Minneapolis: Burgess.

Newell, K. M. (1985). Motor skill acquisition and mental retardation: Overview of traditional and current orientations. In J. E. Clark & J. H. Humphrey (Eds.), Motor development: Current selected research (Vol. 1) (pp. 183-192). Princeton: Princeton Book Co.

Newell, K. M. (in press). Coordination, control and skill. In D. Goodman, I. Franks, & R. Wilberg (Eds.), Differing perspectives on motor control. Amsterdam: North Holland.

Newell, K. M., Carlton, L. G., & Hancock, P. A. (1984). A kinetic analysis of response variability. Psychological Bulletin, 96, 133-151.

Shumway-Cook, A., & Woollacott, M. H. (1985). The growth of stability: Postural control from a developmental perspective. Journal of Motor Behavior, 17, 131-147.

Sinclair, D. (1978). Human growth after birth. 3rd Edition. London: Oxford University Press.

Wade, M. G., Hoover, J. H., & Newell, K. M. (1983). Training and trainability in motor skills performance of mentally retarded persons. In J. Hogg & P. J. Mittler (Eds.), Advances in mental handicap research (Vol. 2) (pp. 175-202). New York: Wiley.

Wohlwill, J. F. (1973). The study of behavioral development. New York: Academic Press.

Wolff, P. H. (1968). Stereotypic behavior and development. Canadian Journal of Psychology, 9, 474-484.

Section II
Response Timing and Motor Behavior: A

Motor Skill Acquisition of the Mentally Handicapped:
Issues in Research and Training
M.G. Wade (editor)
© *Elsevier Science Publishers B.V. (North-Holland), 1986*

SPEED OF INFORMATION-PROCESSING, INTELLIGENCE, AND MENTAL RETARDATION

Philip A. Vernon

Department of Psychology
University of Western Ontario

INTRODUCTION

In a recent article, Campione and Brown (1978) described a number of ways in which research with the mentally retarded might provide information about the nature of human intelligence. They summarized their rationale for this approach as follows:

> If it is possible to identify characteristics which are lacking or reduced in retarded individuals relative to nonretarded individuals, and which are wholly or in part responsible for observed performance differences in a class of cognitive tasks, we will have identified some important components of intelligence. Essentially, a partial defini- tion of intelligence, and one which is at least implicit in our work, is that it consists of processes which are lacking or reduced in effectiveness in the population of retarded children (p. 280).

In this chapter, the topics of intelligence and mental retardation are approached from the other direction than that adopted by Campione and Brown. Rather than discussing the implications that research with the retarded may have to theories of intelligence, the chapter will focus on studies of information-processing correlates of intelligence and will draw some conclusions as to how the results of such studies might pertain to mental retardation. The rationale for this approach is that the identifi- cation of correlates or components of intelligence in non-retarded popula- tions may at least provide some directions which researchers who are primarily interested in mental retardation might find fruitful to pursue.

SPEED-OF-PROCESSING AND INTELLIGENCE

In the past few years, considerable interest has been generated by research investigating the relationship between intelligence and speed of information-processing. In the context of this research, "speed of information-processing" refers to the speed with which persons can execute a number of basic cognitive processes, such as encoding information, scanning or processing information in short-term or working-memory, and retrieving information from long-term memory, while performing relatively simple reaction time tasks which typically do not demand the knowledge or problem-solving skills assessed by standard psychometric tests of intelli- gence.

As is described in more detail below, a number of recent studies have reported moderate to fairly high correlations between reaction times -- or speed-of-processing -- and performance on tests of intelligence; the relationship holding both with timed and untimed measures of intelligence (Vernon, 1983a; Vernon, Nador & Kantor, 1984a); with measures of both fluid and crystallized intellectual abilities (Jenkinson, 1983; Smith & Stanley, 1983); among school-aged children and adults (Hunt, 1976; Keating & Bobbitt, 1978; Vernon, 1983a; Vernon & Jensen, 1984); across groups of a wide range of mental ability (Baumeister & Kellas, 1968; Jensen, 1979; Vernon, 1981); and in studies employing diverse measures of speed-of-processing.

Several reviews of the research in this area have appeared elsewhere (e.g., Jensen, 1982; Vernon, 1983b, 1985a, 1985b), so it will be described only briefly here. Following is a summary of some of the major findings that have been reported, organized around the various tests of reaction times and speed-of-processing which have most frequently been employed.

Simple and Choice Reaction Time. Several varieties of tests and types of equipment or apparatus have been used to measure simple and choice reaction times (RTs), which have a long history in individual differences research. Typically, subjects respond or react to visual or auditory stimuli (e.g., the appearance of a light or the sounding of a tone) by pressing or releasing a button or a telegraph key. In the simple RT condition, subjects are entirely aware of the nature of the stimulus that will be presented and of the response that they will be required to make: no uncertainty or decision-making is involved. For choice RTs, either the stimulus, the response, or both may vary from trial to trial, such that subjects are in a state of uncertainty and must make a decision about what response to make to a given stimulus.

Jensen (e.g., 1979) has conducted numerous studies of the relationship between measures of intelligence and various parameters derived from a simple-choice RT test. The apparatus he uses requires subjects to respond to visual stimuli (lights) under one of four conditions, involving either 0, 1, 2, or 3 bits of decision-making information-processing. The 0-bit condition corresponds to simple RT; the remaining choice conditions involve increasing amounts of uncertainty.

In diverse samples, varying in age from 6th graders to university students and in intelligence from severely retarded to highly gifted, RTs on this test consistently increase as a linear function of the degree of uncertainty. The only exception was a sample of severely retarded young adults, for whom RTs increased from 0 bits to 1 bit but remained constant at the other conditions (Jensen, 1979). The degree to which RTs increase as a function of bits (i.e., the slope of the regression of RTs on bits) is negatively correlated with intelligence within groups and is significantly different for groups of different levels of mental ability: higher ability groups having flatter slopes. On average, RTs on this test correlate about -.30 with measures of intelligence (Jensen, 1982), and higher ability groups obtain markedly and significantly faster mean RTs than do lower ability groups (Vernon, 1981). A third parameter, subjects' intraindividual standard deviations (intra-SDs) -- a measure of the consistency with which a person can maintain a given speed of reaction across trials -- shows a similar pattern. Within groups, intra-SDs correlate about -.35 with intelligence, and higher ability groups show less variability than do lower ability groups.

Elsewhere, this test has been referred to as providing an essentially "content-free" measure of speed of information-processing (Vernon, 1985a). Subjects' RTs depend negligibly, if at all, on prior learning, knowledge, problem-solving skills, or strategy-use. The fact that their RTs nonetheless correlate with complex measures of mental ability has important implications to understanding the nature of intelligence, which will be addressed in greater detail in a later section.

Short-Term Memory Information-Processing. S. Sternberg (1966) developed a measure of the speed with which persons could scan or process certain kinds of information in short-term memory (STM). Typically, subjects are presented with a string of one to seven digits which they are instructed to rehearse for later recall. Subsequently, the digits are removed and are replaced by a single "probe" digit. The subjects are then required to indicate whether or not the probe was a member of the initial string of digits. A number of variations of this basic paradigm have used letters, shapes, or colors instead of digits.

This test may be described as being somewhat more "content-loaded" than the simple and choice RT tests discussed previously. At the very least, subjects must be familiar with alphanumeric stimuli and they must engage in some form of rehearsal to retain the stimulus-set in STM. Error rates, however, are typically very low, suggesting that individual differences in RTs on this test are more a function of differences in the speed with which subjects can perform the necessary information-processes of scanning, comparing, and decision-making than they are of differences in knowledge (stimulus-familiarity) or strategy-use. Again, despite its apparent simplicity, RTs on the Sternberg test are negatively correlated with measures of intelligence (Jenkinson, 1983; Snow, Marshalek, & Lohman, 1976; Vernon, 1983a; Vernon & Jensen, 1984) and higher ability groups perform faster and more consistently than do lower ability groups (Dugas & Kellas, 1974; Harris & Fleer, 1974; Keating & Bobbitt, 1978; McCauley, Dugas, Kellas, & DeVellis, 1976; Vernon & Jensen, 1984).

Another STM processing task, based on the sentence-verification test developed by Clark and Chase (1972), has recently been investigated as a correlate of intelligence by Jenkinson (1983) and by Vernon et al. (1984a). In the latter study, subjects were presented with statements of the form "A BEFORE B", "A AFTER B", "A NOT BEFORE B", and variations of these, on the screen of a computer monitor. After a brief interval, the statements were replaced by a test-stimulus of the form "AB" or "BA" and the subjects' task was to indicate as quickly as possible whether or not the test-stimulus conformed to the previous statement.

Rather than involving the scanning of information -- as in the Sternberg test -- it was hypothesized that a primary cognitive operation underlying this test would be the recoding of the initial statement into the format of the to-be-presented test-stimulus. That is, subjects might be presented with "A NOT AFTER B" and recode this as "AB". Subsequently, when the test-stimulus was presented, they could make a direct comparison between it and the recoded statement and decide whether or not the two matched.

RTs on this test correlated .68 with RTs on the Sternberg test and both

correlated negatively with intelligence (-.38 and -.39, respectively) in
Vernon et al.'s (1984a) study. Other versions of the sentence-
verification test have also shown moderate negative correlations with
measures of intelligence (Baddeley, 1968; Jenkinson, 1983; Jensen, 1985).

Speed of retrieval of information from long-term memory. Posner (Posner,
Boies, Eichelman, & Taylor, 1969) developed a letter-comparison test to
measure the speed with which persons could access and retrieve information
from long-term memory (LTM). Subjects are presented with pairs of letters
which are either physically identical -- e.g., AA or aa -- or which share
the same name -- e.g., Aa. The difference between RTs to the two types of
stimuli provides a measure of speed of retrieval of information from LTM.

Hunt (1976), and his colleagues (Hunt, Frost, & Lunneborg, 1973; Hunt,
Lunneborg & Lewis, 1975) reported that groups of university students who
differed in average level of verbal ability also differed in their performance on the letter-comparison test: higher ability subjects being
able to access and retrieve information from LTM more quickly than lower
ability subjects. The results of these studies have since been replicated
with samples of school-children (Keating & Bobbitt, 1978), mentally
retarded subjects (Hunt, 1978), and subjects over the age of 60 (Hunt,
1978).

Following Goldberg, Schwartz, and Stewart (1977), Vernon (1983a) and
Vernon and Jensen (1984) used a modification of the Posner test which
involved pairs of words rather than letters. In their tests, subjects
were presented with word-pairs which were either physically same or
different (e.g., DOG - DOG or DOG - LOG) or which were synonyms or
antonyms. Reaction times on both tests correlated negatively with measures of intelligence, as did the difference between RTs on both types of
word-pairs -- the latter providing a measure of LTM retrieval. In
addition, between-group comparisons again showed that higher ability
subjects performed more quickly and more consistently that did lower
ability subjects.

Vernon et al. (1984a) employed another modification of these LTM retrieval
tasks, which they referred to as a category-matching test. In this test,
subjects were presented with pairs of words, the first of which was the
name of one of five categories (Animals, Clothing, Fruits, Furniture, and
Sports), and the second of which was either a member of that category or
of one of the other categories. Subjects were instructed to indicate as
quickly as possible whether or not the second word in each pair was a
member of the category identified by the first word. RTs on this test
proved to be moderately highly related to performance on a mental ability
test, correlating -.34 and -.44 with untimed and timed intelligence test
scores, respectively.

Multiple correlations between RTs and intelligence. Many of the studies
cited above investigated the relationship between intelligence and one or
another speed-of-processing variable individually. In this section, four
studies will be described which have obtained multiple measures of speed
of information-processing from the same samples of subjects, thereby
allowing an investigation of the extent to which they measures correlate
with each other and the extent to they collectively correlate with intelligence.

First, Keating and Bobbitt (1978) regressed Raven Matrices scores on measures derived from a simple-choice RT test, and from the Sternberg and Posner tests. In samples of 20 children in each of grades 3, 7, and 11, they reported multiple correlations of .59, .57, and .60, respectively. In the total sample ($\underline{n}$ = 60), a multiple $\underline{R}$ of .72 was obtained. This is substantially higher than the zero-order correlations between any single speed-of-processing variable and intelligence, indicating that the information-processes Keating and Bobbitt measured are sufficiently independent of one another to make a unique contribution to the prediction of intelligence.

Second, Vernon (1983a) gave a sample of 100 above-average ability university students a battery of speed-of-processing tests, including measures of simple and choice RT, STM processing, LTM retrieval, and STM storage-processing trade-off. Tests of the latter required subjects to perform the Sternberg STM test while simultaneously making same-different judgments about pairs of words. When full-scale WAIS IQs were regressed on subjects' RTs and intra-$\underline{SD}$s on these tests, the shrunken multiple $\underline{R}$ obtained was .464. Corrected for restriction of range in IQ, this correlation was boosted to .688 -- comparable to the values reported by Keating and Bobbitt.

In a third study, Vernon and Jensen (1984) sought to replicate Vernon's (1983a) results in a sample of subjects of the same age level but of lower average mental ability than university students. They administered the same, or shortened versions of the same speed-of-processing tests used by Vernon (1983a) to 106 male vocational college students and obtained these subjects' scores on the Armed Services Vocational Aptitude Battery (ASVAB). When ASVAB factor scores were regressed on RTs and intra-$\underline{SD}$s on the several tests, a shrunken multiple $\underline{R}$ of .465 was obtained. This is virtually identical to the correlation of .464 reported by Vernon (1983a).

The results of a fourth study involving multiple measures of speed-of-processing will be described in some detail. Vernon et al. (1984a) tested 81 university students, obtaining two measures of STM processing, two measures of LTM retrieval, and three measures of storage-processing trade-off. Subjects were also administered the Multidimensional Aptitude Battery (MAB; Jackson, 1984), a multiple-choice test of mental ability patterned closely after, and highly correlated with the WAIS-R.

One of the issues Vernon et al. (1984a) planned to address was the influence that a timed test of mental ability might have on the relationship between intelligence and speed-of-processing. A number of writers have suggested that correlations between RTs and intelligence may at least in part be attributable to the fact that many psychometric tests of ability are timed (e.g., Carroll, 1981; Schwartz, Griffin, & Brown, 1983; Sternberg, 1984). Vernon (1983a) performed a series of analyses which indicated that the timed nature of the intelligence test he used (the WAIS) was not responsible for its correlation with speed-of-processing measures, but Vernon et al. (1984a) made a more direct test by obtaining timed and untimed intelligence test scores from each subject.

Like the WAIS-R, the MAB has two subscales, Verbal and Performance, each containing five subtests. For each subtest, which contains between 20 to 50 items arranged in order of increasing difficulty, subjects were provided with an answer sheet and were instructed to circle the letter (A

to E) corresponding to their answers. Subjects were instructed to work as
quickly and accurately as they could for the first five minutes on each
subtest, circling their answers with a blue pen. After five minutes,
subjects were told to put down their blue pens but to continue working for
as long as they required, now circling their answers with a red pen.
After completing all five subtests within each scale in this manner,
subjects were allowed additional items, using the red pens. Each subject
was subsequently assigned a <u>timed</u> score, computed as the number of correct
responses circled with the blue pen, and an <u>untimed</u> score, computed as the
total number of correct answers circled in blue or red.

A number of multiple regression analyses were performed, using timed and
untimed MAB scores and g factor scores derived from these (referred to
subsequently as g-timed and g-untimed, respectively) as the dependent
variables. Independent variables consisted of subjects' RTs and intra-SDs
on the several reaction times tests, and their scores on the three speed-
of-processing variables and factors (STM processing, LTM retrieval, and
STM storage-processing trade-off) derived from and hypothesized to underlie the RT tests.

The main results are summarized in Table 1. As can be seen, all the
multiple R's are of moderate to high magnitude, indicating a fairly
pronounced relationship between the independent and dependent variables.
Comparing the timed MAB and g-timed with the untimed MAB and g-untimed
reveals that the timed measures of mental ability are slightly more highly
correlated with the RT and speed-of-processing variables than are the
untimed measures. The differences are small, however, and none is significant, indicating that it is not merely the timed nature of the test that
is responsible for their relationship with reaction times. Even when
subjects were allowed as much time as they required to work on the MAB,
the scores they obtained are still quite highly correlated with their
performance on the RT tests.

Some further analyses of these data reveal other interesting results.
Certain subtests of the MAB -- for example, Information, Vocabulary, and,
perhaps to a somewhat lesser extent, Comprehension and Similarities -- are
primarily tests of how much information or knowledge a subject has
acquired. To answer the items on these subtests, subjects have to access
and retrieve relevant information from LTM. Other subtests, such as the
Spatial subtest or the Performance subtests generally, place fewer demands
on subjects' ability to retrieve information from LTM and greater demands
on their capacity to store and process information in short-term or
working memory. To the extent that these subtests require different
cognitive processes to be performed, correlations between them and the
different speed-of-processing variables should vary in a predictable
manner. Specifically, high information-loaded subtests should correlate
most highly with LTM retrieval RTs, while subtests which require the
simultaneous storage and mental manipulation or processing of information
in working-memory should correlate more highly with the storage-processing
trade-off measures.

Correlations relevant to these hypotheses are presented in Table 2. Quite
consistently, the information-loaded and Verbal subtests correlate more
highly with LTM retrieval than they do with storage-processing trade-off.
In fact, with the exception of Comprehension, the information-loaded
subtests have low or negligible correlations with storage-processing

Table 1

Summary of Shrunken Multiple Correlations
Obtained in Regression Analysis

Independent Variables	Dependent Variables			
	Timed MAB	Untimed MAB	g-Timed	g-Untimed
RTs	.605	.504	.621	.533
SDs[a]	.625	.612	.642	.622
RTs & SDs	.687	.645	.695	.655
Speed-of-Processing Variables	.546	.493	.563	.531
Speed-of-Processing Factors	.515	.460	.531	.471

[a]SDs refer to subjects' intraindividual standard deviations on the reaction time tests.

trade-off. The reverse pattern is evident for the Spatial and Performance subtests, which correlate more highly with storage-processing trade-off than they do with LTM retrieval. In addition, these patterns and the magnitude of the correlations are very similar for both the timed and the untimed scores, suggesting again that the timed nature of some intelligence test items may exert only a small influence on the relationship between these tests and RTs. More generally, the results of these analyses indicate that it is possible to identify specific cognitive processes whose speed of execution is related to performance on tests requiring quite different kinds of mental abilities.

Group differences in intelligence and speed-of-processing. The results of the several studies described above indicate that, within a variety of different samples, significant and moderately high correlations exist between measures of intelligence and measures of speed of information-processing. Mention has also been made of a number of comparisons between subjects of different levels of ability: the results consistently indicating that higher ability groups process information more quickly and with less variability in processing-speed than do lower ability groups. In this section, two recent studies of group differences in intelligence and speed-of-processing will be described in more detail.

Vernon and Jensen (1984) compared the RTs and intra-SDs of university and vocational college students on tests of STM processing, LTM retrieval, and STM storage-processing trade-off. They also compared subsamples of whites and blacks which composed the vocational college sample. Briefly, univer-

Table 2

Correlations Between LTM and Storage-Processing Trade-Off RTs
and Selected Timed and Untimed Verbal and Performance MAB Subtests

		Information	Vocabulary	Similarities	Comprehension
LTM[a]	Timed	-.29	-.49	-.46	-.44
	Untimed	-.31	-.46	-.48	-.31
SPTO[b]	Timed	-.07	-.05	-.18	-.21
	Untimed	-.02	.007	-.03	-.13
		Verbal	Spatial	Performance
LTM[a]	Timed	-.49	-.10	-.20
	Untimed	-.46	-.07	-.19
SPTO[b]	Timed	-.15	-.34	-.35
	Untimed	-.07	-.45	-.38

[a]LTM refers to speed of retrieval of information from long-term memory.

[b]SPTO refers to short-term memory storage-processing trade-off.

sity students and whites obtained shorter RTs and smaller intra-SDs, on
average, than did vocational college students and blacks, respectively.
Whites also obtained higher average ASVAB scores than did blacks.

Vernon, Nador, and Kantor (1984b) extended Vernon and Jensen's study by
including a third sample, which was intermediate in intelligence between
the previous university and vocational college samples, in their comparisons of RT.performance. It was predicted that RTs and intra-SDs should
increase as the average level of mental ability of the groups decreased
and, by and large, this prediction was borne out. Tables 3 and 4 show the
mean RTs and intra-SDs, respectively, obtained by the three samples.
Group 1 is the high ability sample tested by Vernon (1983a); Group 2 is
the intermediate ability sample tested by Vernon et al. (1984a); and Group
3 is the lower ability vocational college sample tested by Vernon and
Jensen (1984). As can be seen, Group 1 obtained significantly faster mean
RTs than Group 2 on 5 of 7 RT tests, and Group 2 was significantly faster
than Group 3 also on 5 of the 7 tests, and Group 2 shows significantly

Table 3

Mean Reaction Times[a] on Reaction Time Tests
Obtained in Three Groups[b]

RT Tests[c]	Group 1 (n = 100)		Group 2 (n = 81)		Group 3 (n = 106)
1.	746.17 (146.88)	<	794.86 (149.15)	<	951.77 (213.41)
2.	553.01 (153.14)	<	649.52 (141.81)	=	637.17 (174.07)
3.	741.12 (127.91)	<	776.69 (156.52)	<	1005.28 (244.86)
4.	597.27 (147.72)	<	670.53 (260.12)	=	723.80 (212.07)
5.	1006.01 (185.13)	=	955.96 (230.41)	<	1366.87 (358.25)
6.	886.01 (154.61)	=	902.33 (203.05)	<	1327.55 (355.84)
7.	561.71 (133.23)	<	674.37 (259.98)	<	749.62 (244.81)

[a]Mean RTs appear with sample standard deviations in parentheses beneath them.

[b] < symbols indicate a significant difference (p < ,05, 1-tailed).
= symbols indicate no significant difference (p > ,05, 1-tailed).

[c]RT tests are: 1. Same-different word-pairs; 2. Sternberg STM test; 3. and 4. Storage-processing trade-off tests; 5. Synonyms and antonyms; 6. and 7. Storage-processing trade-off tests.

smaller intra-SDs than Group 3 on all 7 tests.

Interestingly, comparisons between Groups 1 and 3 and between Groups 2 and 3 -- the groups which differed the most in intelligence -- revealed that these groups differed to the greatest extent on the relatively more complex RT tests. Complexity was operationally defined in terms of the groups' mean RTs on the tests: tests with longer mean latencies being presumed to require more, and more complex information-processing to be performed than tests with shorter mean latencies. In contrast, Groups 1 and 2, which were both of relatively high intelligence and which did not differ in intelligence to the same extent as each differed from Group 3,

Table 4

Mean Intraindividual Standard Deviations[a] on Reaction Time Tests
Obtained in Three Groups[b]

RT Tests[c]	Group 1 (n = 100)		Group 2 (n = 81)		Group 3 (n = 106)
1.	165.50 (62.77)	=	174.42 (71.43)	<	245.37 (111.63)
2.	158.45 (83.17)	=	157.16 (68.65)	<	223.63 (154.17)
3.	132.94 (44.89)	<	148.66 (72.62)	<	257.50 (123.93)
4.	193.92 (92.55)	<	232.91 (136.68)	<	289.84 (155.14)
5.	247.58 (90.66)	<	284.68 (101.35)	<	406.81 (203.38)
6.	108.60 (85.17)	<	202.74 (92.68)	<	392.02 (214.81)
7.	183.30 (85.31)	=	176.06 (120.52)	<	321.98 (191.32)

[a]Mean intraindividual standard deviations appear with sample standard deviations in parentheses beneath them.

[b] < symbols indicate a significant difference ($p < .05$, 1-tailed).
= symbols indicate no significant difference ($p > .05$, 1-tailed).

[c]RT tests are as defined in Table 3.

showed relatively small differences on the more complex RT tests and relatively larger differences on the less complex RT tests. Typically, the more complex RT tests have shown higher correlations with intelligence within groups and the largest differences between groups of different levels of mental ability (Vernon & Jensen, 1984). This was only partially replicated in Vernon et al.'s (1984b) study. It should perhaps be not surprising that two high ability groups would not differ to a very large extent in their speed-of-processing of complex information. Further investigation is required, however, before a satisfactory explanation can be proposed as to why these groups would differ on the less complex RT tests.

The Basis of the Relationship between Speed-of-Processing and Intelli-

gence. In the previous section, some of the tests of speed of
information-processing were referred to as being relatively more complex
than others: the distinction being based on the mean latencies associated
with various tests. To some extent, the distinction can also be made in
terms of the "content-loadedness" of the tests, or the extent to which
they require subjects to access, retrieve, and process information which
must be available to them in order for them to perform successfully.
Thus, Jensen's simple-choice RT test was described as being relatively
content-free, and mean latencies on this test are always considerably
shorter than they are on the other RT measures. Sternberg's memory-
scanning test was referred to as being somewhat more content-loaded, and
the test requiring subjects to decide whether a pair of words are synonyms
or antonyms could be considered relatively highly content- or information-
loaded.

Although the content-loadedness of the speed-of-processing measures
appears to be correlated with their mean latencies, it is important to
point out that the relative complexity of these measures is more a function of the amount or types of information-processing they require than it
is of their difficulty per se. All of the tests have very low or nonexis-
tent error rates in the samples I have studied, indicating that individual
differences in acquired knowledge or information-availability do not
account for a large amount of the variance in subjects' RTs. In addition,
the relationship between the relative complexity of the tests and their
correlations with measures of intelligence is due less to the fact that
the more complex tests are also more content-loaded and is more likely
attributable to the fact that tests with longer latencies require a
greater amount of information-processing to be performed, thus more
closely approximating the cognitive activity required by a test of intelligence.

Four propositions will be offered as a possible explanation for the
finding that RTs even on a relatively content-free test such as Jensen's
are correlated with performance on tests of intelligence and mental
ability:

1. Intelligence tests come in a variety of forms and require subjects to
draw on varying amounts of previously-acquired knowledge, strategies, and
problem-solving skills. At another level, however, regardless of their
specific nature, all intelligence tests require subjects to encode and
store information in STM and to retrieve information from LTM. If not
all, many also require information to be stored and processed in STM
simultaneously.

2. The activities of the human short-term or working-memory system are
constrained by at least three limiting properties. The system has a
limited capacity; the small amount of information it can hold is subject
to very rapid decay or loss in the absence of rehearsal; and there is a
trade-off between the amount of information that it can store and process
simultaneously.

3. Without the existence of a fourth property, even what might appear to
be a relatively simple problem-solving item could involve sufficient
storage, retrieval, and processing of information for its solution for the
limited capacity STM system to reach its threshold. If this occurred, the
system would be unable to perform all the component operations required by

the problem and the subject would either have to start again or would be
unable to solve the problem.

4. The fourth property of the information-processing system, which allows
it to cope despite its limitations, is speed. The more quickly that
incoming information can be recoded into a small number of chunks, the
less likely is the system to reach the threshold of its storage-capacity
or to overload. Chunking information also reduces the storage demands on
the system and allows more processing to be carried on simultaneously.
The more quickly that information needed to solve the problem can be
retrieved from LTM, the less likely is earlier-encoded information to
decay or to become inaccessible. At each step, the more quickly the
requisite cognitive operations can be performed, the less likely the
system is to fail, and the greater is the probability that the problem
will be solved.

Jensen's simple-choice RT test provides a very basic measure of speed of
information-processing. Its correlation with tests of intelligence may be
attributed to the fact that, at a very basic level, the latter involve a
general speed component which is required for their solution as a function
of the four propositions outlined above. More complex RT measures require
more information-processing to be performed, thereby coming close to
tapping the same sorts of cognitive activities that are required during
intelligence test performance. As a result, these RT tests correlate more
highly with intelligence. As was described in a previous section, it is
also possible to perform what may be described as an information-
processing task-analysis of different subtests of intelligence tests (see
also Carroll, 1976; Sternberg, 1977, 1979, 1980) and predict which cognitive activities are most likely to be required by the different subtests.
The more closely the RT tests come to tapping the same cognitive processes
as the subtests, the higher is the correlation between the two (see Table
2).

Speed-Of-Processing and Timed vs. Untimed Intelligence Test Scores. As
reported previously, Vernon et al. (1984a) found correlations of approximately the same magnitude between RTs and performance on timed and untimed
measures of intelligence. To the extent that speed-of-processing is a
factor underlying intelligence, it would be expected that persons who can
process information quickly (as evidenced by their RTs) should -- assuming
they are motivated to work as quickly as they can -- be able to answer
more questions correctly during a timed intelligence test. At first,
during the 5-minute timed testing period in Vernon et al. (1984a), most of
the items subjects encountered would be relatively simple (recall that
items on the MAB are arranged in order of increasing difficulty), but more
intelligent subjects would be expected to be able to retrieve the information and/or perform the component processes required to answer these items
more quickly than would subjects of lower intelligence. Hence, the
correlation between RTs and timed intelligence tests scores is quite
predictable.

During the untimed period of testing, subjects would begin to encounter
more difficult items and problems, which would place greater demands on
their information-processing capabilities. As the items become progressively harder, imposing increasing information-processing demands, speed-
of-processing continues to be an asset by preventing the items' demands
from overburdening the limited capacity system in which the processing is

being performed. In fact, barring a ceiling effect, it is the untimed items -- by nature of their greater difficulty -- that might be expected to correlate most highly with speed of information-processing. This is not borne out by the multiple correlations reported in Table 1, but a number of the correlations in Table 2 are higher for untimed subtest scores than they are for timed scores.

In sum, faster speed-of-processing provides two distinct advantages. First, on relatively simple intelligence test items, it allows relevant information to be accessed and retrieved quickly. Persons of higher intelligence would therefore be expected to be able to solve a larger number of simple items correctly in a given period of time than would persons of lower intelligence. Second, on more difficult items, persons who can process information quickly have a higher probability of not reaching or exceeding the threshold of their working-memory capacity. This, in turn, affords them a higher probability of solving these items correctly.

SPEED-OF-PROCESSING AND MENTAL RETARDATION

How might the results discussed in the previous sections be applied to the field and study of mental retardation? Clearly, to the extent that speed of information-processing is a correlate of intelligence, it would be expected that a defining feature of mental retardation would be slower processing speed. In itself, this may not sound unreasonable, and there is considerable evidence that mentally retarded subjects do perform more slowly on several of the different types of RT tests discussed above (e.g., Baumeister & Kellas, 1968; Dugas & Kellas, 1974; Harris & Fleer, 1974; Vernon, 1981). Of more interest and potential theoretical importance is the implication that performance differences between retarded and nonretarded populations on a variety of cognitive or intellectual tasks may be attributable less to knowledge-differences or to differences in problem-solving skills and strategies than to differences in the speed of execution of a number of basic information-processes. In computers, the differences may lie more in the hardware of the information-processing system and less in the software.

This should not be taken to imply that knowledge and strategy-use differences between retarded and nonretarded groups do not exist; there is ample evidence that they do. However, the acquisition and subsequent availability of knowledge and strategies may themselves be partly or even largely attributable to more fundamental differences in information-processing. Faster speed-of-processing, implying a more efficient use of limited short-term storage and processing capacities may, over a period of time, be in part responsible for the amount and types of information which an individual acquires. If a person cannot process new incoming information quickly -- that is, if previously-acquired information is not quickly scanned and selected on the basis of its relationship or similarity to the new information, thereby allowing a bond or association to be formed between the two -- this might be expected to impede the person's acquisition of the information.

One of the most striking features of studies which have sought to train mentally retarded persons in the use of certain learning strategies -- for example, the use of clustering in the free recall of categorized lists of words -- is that, while the retarded typically fail to use the strategy spontaneously before training, often only rather minimal instruction or coaching is required for them to learn to use the strategy and to improve their performance. In this instance, it appears that the strategy may already have been available to them but that they were unaware that its use would enhance their recall (Campione & Brown, 1978). Unfortunately, another salient feature of such training studies is the limited general-izability or transfer that retarded subjects demonstrate when their ability to use a strategy taught in the context of one task is tested in a different context. Neither of these features -- the relative ease with which mildly retarded subjects can be trained to use certain strategies and their lack of transfer after training -- is incompatible with a model that views speed-of-processing as an important determinant of intellectual behaviors. In the first case, the learning strategy (e.g., clustering or rehearsal) reduces the information-processing demands of the task, thereby allowing persons with a less efficient information-processing system to cope more adequately. In the second case, lack of transfer may be indica-tive of slower forming of associations between knowledge and skills learned in different contexts, which hinders or prevents the recognition (or metacognition) of the applicability of a strategy to a variety of different but related tasks.

In conclusion, research on the relationship between speed of information-processing and intelligence provides another perspective on behavioral and learning differences between mentally retarded and nonretarded persons. At this point, it is simply unknown to what extent -- if at all -- the speed with which mentally retarded individuals or persons of any level of intellectual ability process information might be amenable to external manipulation or change. In addition, it remains to be seen whether changes in processing speed -- assuming these could be effected in the first place -- would result in improved capabilities for acquiring and using information. Conjectures regarding potential practical applications of speed-of-processing research are, at present, premature but continued studies of the underlying cognitive and neural bases of intelligence -- of which speed-of-processing appears to form a not insubstantial part -- may provide an increased understanding of the nature of mental ability which in turn could be of value from a theoretical and from a practical point of view.

REFERENCES

Baddeley, A. D. (1968). A 3 min reasoning test based on grammatical transformation. Psychonomic Science, 10, 341-342.

Baumeister, A. A., & Kellas, G. (1968). Reaction time and mental retard-ation. In N. R. Ellis (Ed.), International review of research in mental retardation. New York: Academic Press.

Campione, J. C., & Brown, A. L. (1978). Toward a theory of intelligence: Contributions from research with retarded children. Intelligence, 2, 279-304.

Carroll, J. B. (1976). Psychometric tests as cognitive tasks: A new "Structure of Intellect". In L. B. Resnick (Ed.), The nature of Intelligence. Hillsdale, NJ: Erlbaum.

Carroll, J. B. (1981). Ability and task difficulty in cognitive psychology. Educational Researcher, 10, 11-21.

Clark, H. H., & Chase, W. G. (1972). On the process of comparing sentences against pictures. Cognitive Psychology, 3, 472-517.

Dugas, J. L., & Kellas, G. (1974). Encoding and retrieval processes in normal children and retarded adolescents. Journal of Experimental Child Psychology, 17, 177-185.

Goldberg, R. A., Schwartz, S., & Stewart, M. (1977). Individual differences in cognitive processes. Journal of Educational Psychology, 69, 9-14.

Harris, G. J., & Fleer, R. E. (1974). High speed memory scanning in mental retardates: Evidence for a central processing deficit. Journal of Experimental Child Psychology, 17, 452-459.

Hunt, E. (1976). Varieties of cognitive power. In L. B. Resnick (Ed.), The nature of intelligence. Hillsdale, NJ: Erlbaum.

Hunt, E. (1978). Mechanics of verbal ability. Psychology Review, 85, 109-130.

Hunt, E., Frost, N., & Lunneborg, D. (1973). Individual differences in cognition: A new approach to intelligence. In G. Bower (Ed.), The psychology of learning and motivation (Vol. 7). New York: Academic Press.

Hunt, E., Lunneborg, C., & Lewis, J. (1975). What does it mean to be high verbal? Cognitive Psychology, 7, 194-227.

Jackson, D. N. (1984). Multidimensional aptitude battery. Port Huron, Michigan: Research Psychologists Press, Inc.

Jenkinson, J. C. (1983). Is speed of information processing related to fluid or to crystallized intelligence? Intelligence, 7, 91-106.

Jensen, A. R. (1979). g: Outmoded theory or unconquered frontier? Creative Science & Technology, 2, 16-29.

Jensen, A. R. (1982). Reaction time and psychometric g. In H. J. Eysenck (Ed.), A model for intelligence. Berlin: Springer-Verlag.

Jensen, A. R. (1985, in press). Speed of information processing and population differences. In S. H. Irvine & Jr. Berry (Ed.), Human abilities in cultural context. London: Wiley.

Keating, D. P., & Bobbitt, B. (1978). Individual and developmental differences in cognitive processing components of mental ability. Child Development, 49, 155-169.

McCauley, C., Dugas, J., Kellas, G., & DeVellis, R. F. (1976). Effects of serial rehearsal training on memory search. Journal of Educational Psychology, 68, 474-481.

Posner, M., Boies, S., Eichelman, W., & Taylor, R. (1969). Retention of visual and name codes of single letters. Journal of Experimental Psychology, 81, 10-15.

Schwartz, S., Griffin, T. M., & Brown, J. (1983). Power and speed components of individual differences in letter matching. Intelligence, 7, 369-378.

Smith, G. A., & Stanley, G. (1983). Clocking g: Relating intelligence and measures of timed performance. Intelligence, 7, 353-368.

Snow, R. E., Marshalek, B., & Lohman, D. F. (1976). Correlation of selected cognitive abilities and cognitive processing parameters: An exploratory study (Technical Report 3). Palo Alto, California: Stanford University, School of Education.

Sternberg, R. J. (1977). Intelligence, information processing, and analogical reasoning: The componential analysis of human abilities. Hillsdale, NJ: Erlbaum.

Sternberg, R. J. (1979). The nature of mental abilities. American Psychologist, 34, 214-230.

Sternberg, R. J. (1980). Sketch of a componential subtheory of human intelligence. The Behavioral and Brain Sciences, 3, 573-614

Sternberg, R. J. (1984). Toward a triarchic theory of human intelligence. The Behavioral and Brain Sciences, 7, 269-315.

Sternberg, S. (1966). High-speed memory scanning in human memory. Science, 153, 652-654.

Vernon, P. A. (1981). Reaction time and intelligence in the mentally retarded. Intelligence, 5, 345-355.

Vernon, P. A. (1983a). Speed of information processing and general intelligence. Intelligence, 7, 53-70.

Vernon, P. A. (1983b). Recent findings on the nature of g. Journal of Special Education, 17, 389-400.

Vernon, P. A. (1985a, in press). Relationships between speed-of-processing, personality, and intelligence. In C. Bagley & G. Verma (Eds.), Personality, cognition, and values. London: McMillan.

Vernon, P. A. (1985b, in press). Individual differences in general cognitive ability. In L. C. Hartlage & C. F. Telzrow (Eds.), The neuropsychology of individual differences: A developmental perspective. New York: Plenum Press.

Vernon, P. A., & Jensen, A. R. (1984). Individual and group differences in intelligence and speed of information-processing. Personality and Individual Differences, 5, 411-423.

Vernon, P. A., Nador, S., & Kantor, L. (1984a). Reaction times and speed-of-processing: Their relationship to timed and untimed measures of intelligence. Manuscript submitted for publication.

Vernon, P. A., Nador, S., & Kantor, L. (1984b, in press). Group differences in intelligence and speed of information-processing. Intelligence.

Motor Skill Acquisition of the Mentally Handicapped:
Issues in Research and Training
M.G. Wade (editor)
© *Elsevier Science Publishers B.V. (North-Holland), 1986*

ATTENTIONAL AND REACTION TIME ANALYSIS OF PERFORMANCE:
IMPLICATIONS FOR RESEARCH WITH MENTALLY HANDICAPPED INDIVIDUALS

Howard N. Zelaznik and Susan K. Aufderheide

Department of Physical Education
Health and Recreation Studies
Purdue University

Howard Zelaznik is affiliated with the Department of Psychological Sciences, Purdue University. Susan Aufderheide was
supported by the U.S. Department of Education, Office of Special
Education and Rehabilitative Services, Grant 84.128. Please
address all correspondence to H. N. Zelaznik, Motor Behavior
Laboratory, Purdue University, Lambert 119, West Lafayette,
Indiana, 47907.

Since the pioneering work of Donders (1969), the interval of time following the onset of an imperative stimulus and the initiation of a response,
commonly called reaction time (RT), has served as an important tool in the
study of elementary information-processing events. Donders believed that
the processes associated with stimulus identification, decision, and
response selection occurred in a serial order. He stated that one could
"delete" a stage in this processing chain by varying the number of stimuli
to identify and the number of possible responses to select from, prior to
the arrival of the imperative stimulus. Thus, the use of choice, simple
and c-reactions, allowed the research to make inferences concerning the
durations of these elementary processes.

While much has been gained concerning the organization of mental events by
the use of reaction-time analysis, there are still no clear-cut concep-
tualizations about the way these processes are structured. For example,
the additive-factors method developed by Sternberg (1969), while not
assuming that stages can be added or deleted, does assume that many stages
are discrete processes in which information is passed to the next stage in
the information-processing stream of events. Extensions of these methods
by Schwieckert (1978) have allowed one to determine the network of
processes. In these extensions of the original conceptions of Donders,
information processing is thought to consist of a set of discrete stages,
in which each stage provides output only after completely processing the
input. Recently, work by McClelland (1979) and Miller (1982) has questioned the necessity for the discrete stages assumptions and has suggested
that stages might be organized in a cascade fashion, in which stages are
continually passing partial output to other stages. Figure 1, illustrates
the difference between these two conceptions.

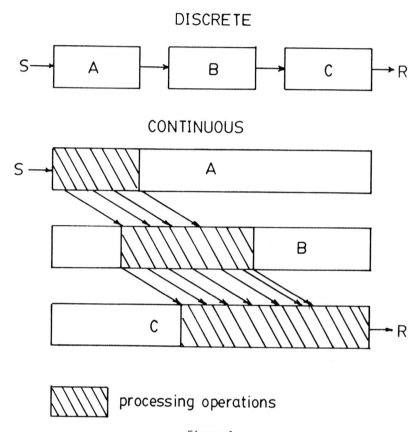

Figure 1

Schematic diagrams of discrete and continuous models of reaction time
performance. Note in the discrete model a stage does not begin
operations until processing from the previous stage has been completed.
In the continuous model output from a stage is continuously
being fed into the subsequent stages.

During the time that a large amount of basic research was being conducted
to begin to understand the elementary information-processing events (see
Posner, 1978; Posner & McLeod, 1982), there was a growing body of literature that had begun to apply some of the reaction time analyses to special
populations (see Baumeister & Kellas, 1968). We would like to focus our
efforts on the relationship between these reaction time analyses and the
performance of mildly retarded individuals. We then would like to present
and discuss some of the newer methodologies and questions from the study
of attention, and of motor behavior, and suggest how they might be applied
to work with mildly
retarded individuals.

REACTION TIME OF MILDLY RETARDED INDIVIDUALS

Studies of reaction time in which retarded subjects are compared with normal subjects have continually demonstrated that retarded individuals have slower reaction times than do nonretarded individuals (Baumeister, Hawkins, & Kellas, 1965; Baumeister & Kellas, 1968; Berkson, 1960; Berkson & Baumeister, 1967; Brewer & Nettelbeck, 1979; Ellis & Sloan, 1957; Nettelbeck & Brewer, 1981). While there has been little disagreement over this finding, it has been tempting to attempt to ascertain "where" in the information-processing chain of events lies the locus of this reaction time difference. We will present evidence to implicate several of the information-processing stages in the performance of midly mentally retarded individuals.

A prevailing attitude is that reaction time is composed of discrete stages, and therefore, it seems reasonable to assume that mildly retarded individuals might exhibit inefficient processing in one stage. In the search for this stage it has been demonstrated that there are perceptual, decision, and motoric deficits in reaction time performance of retarded individuals (Baumeister & Kellas, 1968; Berkson, 1960; Nettelbeck & Brewer, 1981; Wade, Newell, & Wallace, 1978).

Stimulus Processing Effects. Holden (1965) attributed the increased RT of retarded individuals to a prestimulus arousal defect. Brewer and Nettelbeck (1977), Nettelbeck and Brewer (1976), and Brewer (1978) proposed that the slower reaction times of mentally retarded subjects could be due to a slower rate of accumulating relevant information for discriminating the stimulus and its associated response (translation). Nettelbeck and Lally (1976), and Lally and Nettelbeck (1977) used a limited exposure stimulus discrimination task, in which inspection time was independent of reaction time, to demonstrate that reaction time performance difficulties are a result of slower perceptual processes.

Maistro (Maistro & Jerome, 1977; Maistro & Sipe, 1980) demonstrated that the difference in reaction time performance of mentally retarded subjects could be due, in part, to less efficient encoding of information on their part. Maistro and Sipe found that retarded subjects were less sensitive to stimulus-probability information than nonretarded subjects when they performed a choice reaction time task in which stimulus probability and probe stimulus quality were varied.

Saccuzzo, Kerr, Marcus, and Brown (1979) used a tachistoscope task to examine input capability and speed processing of mentally retarded subjects. They found that nonretarded chronological and mental age controls required less time to process the same amount of information and shorter stimulus duration requirements to meet criterion accuracy than did the retarded subjects. These results suggest that retarded individuals have deficiencies in both iconic storage and speed of information processing. The Saccuzzo et al. (1979) data are supportive of the inspection time work in which retardates require more time to make comparison judgments.

Response process limitations. Berkson (1960) proposed that the retarded subject's initiation of performance of a response rather than the sensory phase of the reaction time was affected. Berkson compared five distinct intelligence groups (ranging from nonretarded to individuals with Down's

syndrome) on four reaction time tasks. After 20 trials it was reported
that intelligence is related to functions involved in the speed of performance. It was also reported that speed of performance is positively
related to intelligence in the lower half of the IQ range. Dingman and
Silverstein (1964) felt that the poorer performance of the mentally
retarded subjects could be due to factors associated with motor disability. They found when a control was made for the effects of perceptual
and motor disabilities that the relationship between intelligence and
reaction time disappeared.

Wade, Newell, and Wallace (1978) concluded that reaction time performance
differences between retarded and nonretarded subjects could be, at least
partially, attributed to response patterns or organization. They used
both simple and choice reaction time paradigms to examine reaction time
and movement time of retarded and nonretarded subjects. They found that
the reaction time of the retarded individuals was both longer and more
variable than that of the nonretarded and that movement difficulty in the
choice reaction time tasks served to increase the reaction times of both
retarded and nonretarded subjects. However, the movement time of the
retarded population was significantly slower than that of the nonretarded
group.

Kirby, Nettelbeck, and Western (1982) attempted to locate the information-processing deficit of mildly mentally retarded subjects by trying to
determine if retarded subjects are more dependent on the structure of a
response display than nonretarded subjects and by examining the effects of
changing stimulus and response displays. Eight mentally retarded subjects
and eight nonretarded subjects participated in four 4-choice reaction time
tasks. Findings of the study indicated that the reaction times of both
subject groups were increased to about the same extent by the addition of
nonoperative lights to the stimulus display. The reaction times of the
retarded subjects were slower than that of the nonretarded subjects when
nonoperative keys were added to the response display. These results
suggest that retarded subjects have a response-processing deficit, not a
stimulus-processing deficit. The results of all of the conditions in this
study infer that stimulus-display and response-display effects are due not
only to difficulty with identification of the correct stimulus or
response, but also to problems of translating the stimulus-display and the
response-display. Kirby et al. (1982) proposed that the results of this
investigation provided evidence for a central translation deficit as well
as a response-processing deficit.

As can be seen from the preceding studies, the controversy of why there
are differences in the reaction time performance of mentally retarded
subjects compared to that of nonretarded subjects has not been resolved.
Research appears to suggest that there is not any one locus. Hindsight
makes this easy to see. Most, if not all, of the subjects used in these
experiments were classified as mildly retarded by the use of one of the
general IQ tests, and as such specific differences in individuals were not
controlled for. Furthermore, since IQ at best, in our opinion is a
measure of some general capacity g, (see Vernon, Chapter X), it is hard to
hypothesize why the deficit in RT should be located in a specific stage.

Strategic Limitations. There is one kind of explanation for these general
deficits in reaction time, which we shall call strategic. Basically this
idea postulates that the differences in RT for mildly retarded individuals

might be due not to some deficiency in their elementary information processing, but to some global strategic, and/or capacity limitation that prevents them from maximizing their capabilities. One way to infer strategic differences, especially changing strategies over trials, is to examine the distribution of reaction time scores between different populations. One should expect that the variabilities between these populations be different. In particular, if the retarded subjects cannot settle in one the proper strategy, there should be large increases in variability in RT compared to normal controls.

In support of this strategic notion, Berkson and Baumeister (1967) found that there was more heterogenity among retarded subject reaction times than among normal subjects. The retarded group exhibited greater variability within-subjects as well as between-subjects. Baumeister and Kellas (1968) suggested that the behavior of retarded subjects is, in some instances, characterized as much by a lack of consistency as by a generally low level of responding. They conceptualized that normals not only have different limits of performance from retarded subjects but seem to be able to work nearer their optimal level more consistently.

Baumeister and Kellas (1968) compared normal and mentally retarded subjects in reaction time. They found that not only were the retarded subjects slower than the normal ones, but that the pattern of their responses was also quite different. The distribution for the mentally retarded group tended to be more variable, platykurtic and symmetrical, while the normal subject distribution displayed a leptokurtic distribution skewed to the right. Perhaps it was the skill to stay near their optimal level of performance that produced the increased reaction time for retarded subjects.

Two additional studies (Caffrey, Jones, & Hinkle, 1971; Dugas & Baumeister, 1968) also found that mentally retarded subjects were generally slower in reaction time than their nonretarded controls, and that retarded subjects demonstrated a higher degree of between-subject and within-subject variability than did nonretarded subjects. Weaver and Raveris (1970) compared reaction times of mild, moderate, and severely retarded subjects. They found less variability in the mildly retarded group while the severely retarded group exhibited the greatest amount of variability. This finding is consistent with others, which compared the reaction time of nonretarded and retarded subjects.

Baumeister (1968) hypothesized that mentally retarded subjects were capable of a level of performance equivalent to that of normal children but that their depressed level of performance was largely a result of their inability to perform consistently close to their performance limit. Kellas (1969) supported Baumeister's hypothesis. He found that within-subject variability in reaction time contributed more to the average performance of the mentally retarded group than to the average performance of the nonretarded group. Thus, it can be suggested that variability contributes more to the general level of performance of the retarded subjects. Their lower levels of performance seem to rely, in part, on their failure to perform consistently close to their optimal level of performance.

Based on Baumeister's hypothesis that retarded subjects are capable of a level of reaction time performance that is equivalent to that of nonretarded individuals, Aufderheide (1984) conducted a reaction time study where the fastest reaction time trials of 15 educable mentally retarded males were compared to the fastest reaction time trials of 15 intellectually normal males. It was reported that there was no significant difference in the fastest reaction time trials of the two groups. This kind of finding suggests that some of the RT difference might be attributable to the mentally retarded subjects not being capable of maintaining proper motivation, and/or preparatory set throughout an experimental session.

Krupski (1976) examined heart rate changes of normal and retarded subjects during reaction time trials of varying preparatory intervals. When group data were analyzed, she found that the group of retarded subjects had significantly slower reaction time scores than did those in the nonretarded group. She also found that, for both groups, reaction time increased as the preparatory interval increased in length. However, they fail to maintain the rapid, correct responding level. They suggest that the retarded subjects recognize most of their errors, but are less efficient than nonretarded subjects at using the information obtained to sustain their high level of performance.

It is clear that optimal reaction-time performance depends upon the subject maintaining proper set, which some people have called attention. Therefore, a frequent interpretation of poor reaction time performance is related to an inability to sustain attention, or to maintain an appropriate preparatory set. In support of this hypothesis, Krupski (1977, Krupski & Boyle, 1978) found significantly more off-task glancing in a group of mentally retarded subjects and in a group of nonretarded slow responders than in a group of nonretarded fast responding subjects. In both studies, the subjects with the slower reaction time trials looked away from the task during the preparatory interval significantly more often than those with faster responses. Most of the off-task glances occurred during the middle portion and/or the end of the preparatory interval. Under those conditions in which demands for sustained attention were the greatest group differences were the most pronounced. It appeared that the subjects began each trial in an attentive state but failed to maintain an adequate preparatory set for the duration of the preparatory interval. In addition, Krupski and Boyle (1978) found that the performance of those in the slow group tended to deteriorate over trials while the performance of the faster responders tended to remain fairly consistent.

LIMITED CAPACITY ATTENTION AND PERFORMANCE

A fruitful avenue that could be traveled in understanding the poorer performance of mildly retarded subjects is that of limited capacity attention (Kahneman, 1973; Keele, 1973; McLeod, 1978; Norman & Bobrow; 1975; Posner, 1978). Figure 2 presents an older, simpler view of limited capacity attention as it applied to information-processing tasks.

CAPACITY

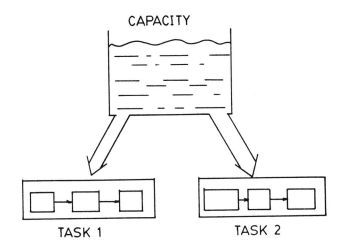

TASK 1   TASK 2

Figure 2
Conceptual diagram of a limited capacity attentional model for
performance. Capacity is viewed as a reservoir of fluid,
utilized to drive the operations of tasks. In this figure,
two tasks are being performed, each receiving capacity.

In this framework the energy source that is driving the information-
processing stages is thought to have a finite amount of fuel, and that
this source of energy is distributed to the information-processing stages.
While this simple view of limited capacity attention has been supplanted
by more recent ideas about multiple sources of resources (Kantowitz &
Knight, 1978; Navon & Gopher, 1979; Wickens, 1976; see Navon, 1984, for a
good discussion of the drawbacks of a capacity approach), much work in the
attention demands of information-processing stages can still be explained
by the limited capacity notion (see Posner, 1978).

The procedure necessary for the examination of the capacity requirements
of information-processing tasks involves having subjects perform two tasks
at the same time (see Kantowitz, 1974). It is assumed that the combined
capacity demands of the two tasks is greater than the amount of mental
resources at the person's disposal. The manner in which this methodology
can be utilized to study capacity demands of various information-
processing tasks is straightforward. The experimenter manipulates the
emphasis of one of the two tasks, either by instructions, and/or differential pay-off schemas and then observes the joint performance of the two
tasks. In addition to the dual task condition, one must employ single
task controls to serve as baseline comparison conditions.

Norman and Bobrow (1975) make the distinction between resource-limited and
data-limited processes. A resource-limited process is one in which
performance depends upon the amount of resources (capacity) allocated to
it, while a data-limited process is independent of processing resources.
Norman and Bobrow dichotomize data-limited processes into signal-limited

and memory-limited. Signal-limited is where processing would depend upon the signal-to-noise ratio of the stimulus to its background, whereas memory-data limited is in the quality of the memorial representation of the stimulus, such as in absolute pitch discrimination.

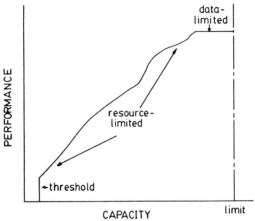

Figure 3
A hypothetical Performance Resource Function illustrating the relationship between capacity supplied and performance of a task. Notice that there is a minimum amount of capacity required (threshold) before any performance is obtained. (Adapted from Norman & Bobrow, 1975.)

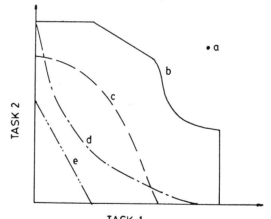

TASK 1
Figure 4
A hypothetical set of Performance Operating Characteristics (POC), which depicts performances on two tasks, performed within that same time frame. a demonstrates a case where both tasks are data limited, b shows that both tasks have data-limited regions and resource-limited regions, c illustrates a case where small changes in Task 1 performance produce large changes in Task 2 performance, d illustrates the converse --small changes in Task 2 produce large changes in Task 1, and e illustrates a linear trade-off. (Adapted from Norman & Bobrow, 1975.)

The curves in Figure 4 are called performance-operating characteristics, or POCs. If the experimenter can cause a subject to operate along a wide range of the POC, good inferences can be made concerning the nature of the limitation in the information-processing requirements of the task. For example, suppose that two tasks did not demand resources from the same source, but that there was a constant overhead cost in time-sharing the tasks. In this instance, one would observe joint performance to be inferior to the single-task control conditions. However, the tasks might appear as data-limited throughout the POC.

The effects of practice upon resource utilization can be examined through a POC analysis. One view of practice is that fewer resources are required as the task becomes learned better. This would show up on a POC as an increased data limited-region, in which the POC would become steeper. However, for mildly retarded individuals there has been the suggestion that they need to learn to supply the proper resources to the task at hand. If such were the case and, in fact, training produced better resource allocation policies, one would observe increased resource limited regions for a period of practice.

Furthermore, this methodology can be utilized to ascertain whether mildly retarded individuals can allocate the appropriate attentional strategies to the task at hand. This could be studied with this dual task methodology in that it would be predicted that if mildly retarded subjects cannot allocate their attention on the demand of the task, one should not see POC functions that show resource limited regions, whereas normal subjects in the same task will show these resource limited regions. It is important to note that this approach seems to be fundamentally different from the approach taken by many studies that examine group differences between normal and mildly retarded subjects. In the POC approach, you are interested in the quality of the POC curve, not on some absolute level of performance. Furthermore, if some strategic explanation was not at the cause of the differences between mildly retarded and normal subjects, the POC functions would look identical in shape, but different in scale.

This approach is sympathetic to the approach taken by Brewer and Smith (1984). In these experiments, they are concerned with understanding the relationships between speed and accuracy in RT tasks, in which it has been shown that mildly retarded subjects do not appear to be as adept at choosing the proper RT bandwidth in which to operate (Brewer & Smith, 1984). We believe that approaches such as these will further the understanding of the information-processing procedures in mildly retarded subjects. The hope that much of the difference between mildly retarded subjects and normals resides in strategies and/or processes outside of the elementary mental operations of RT tasks, can mean that the proper training procedures mildly retarded individuals can function close to normal IQ individuals.

REACTION TIME ANALYSIS OF MOTOR PROGRAMMING

Several researchers have implicated limitations in the processing of response information as a major source of the limitation in the reaction time performance of mildly retarded individuals (Berkson, 1960; Wade, Newell, & Wallace, 1978). Being motor behavior researchers, we are not about to claim that all of the RT effects can reside in the response end

of the information-processing procedures. Instead we shall provide a
tutorial about some of the newer procedures that utilize reaction time to
study motor programming, and hope to show how this kind of research might
be useful in studying the motor processes of mildly retarded individuals
in a RT setting.

RESPONSE COMPLEXITY AND RT

Franklin Henry (1960) popularized the complexity method for the investigation of response programming. Henry's notions were straightforward.
If subjects were asked to complete a movement at maximal speed, the simple
RT to initiate a movement should be related to the complexity of the
movement. Henry (1960, 1980) defined complexity as the number of
elements. While Henry's methods generated a wealth of research in RT and
response programming, there were some empirical and conceptual difficulties with the complexity paradigm.

First, Klapp and colleagues (Klapp, 1977a,b, Klapp & Wyatt, 1976;
Klapp, Wyatt, & Lingo, 1974) argued that in simple reaction time, since
the movement is known ahead of time, the subject, if properly motivated,
can pre-program the movement during the foreperiod, and thus, reaction
time would be insensitive to the complexity variable. In fact, Klapp
demonstrates that a Morse code dit and dah key press exhibit identical
reaction time values in simple RT, but in choice RT the dah key press
possesses a longer RT than a dit. A similar effect is observed for the
production of speech. One-syllable words possess a smaller choice RT than
two-syllable words; this effect is not observed in simple RT.

How might this paradigm be useful in understanding the nature of the
information-processing procedures of mildly retarded individuals? There
is some suggestion in the literature that mildly retarded individuals have
a difficult time predicting the temporal structure of the foreperiod. In
other words, they do not take advantage of environmental information. For
example, Gosling and Jenness (1974) looked at the effects of specific
temporal factors in simple reaction times of retarded and nonretarded
subjects. By examining the foreperiod length of the target trial and of
the preceding trial, and intertrial interval it was shown that reaction
times were fastest when the preliminary interval was the same as or larger
than the period preliminary interval. While this was true for both groups
of subjects the effect was significantly greater for the retarded group.
It was also demonstrated that while increasing the intertrial interval had
very little effect on the nonretarded subjects it had a significant impact
on the performance of the retarded subjects.

Distefano and Brunt (1982) found that reaction times of mildly mentally
retarded eight and ten year old children increased as a result of the
uncertainty of movement within the task. The uncertainty of movement did
not affect the motor performance of the nonretarded subjects. Thus, it is
possible that some of the difficulties in anticipation might reside in the
lack of skill in preprogramming responses. If such were the case, one
might see consistent effects of complexity in both simple and choice RT
situations for mildly retarded subjects, but under certain conditions
observe the lack of RT differences for normal subjects in simple RT but
never in choice.

Table 1

Reaction Time (MS) for Speech and Key-Press Responses
in Simple and Choice Reaction Time Conditions
(Adapted from Klapp et al., 1974)

Speech

		Number of Syllables	
		1	2
	Simple	311	313
	Choice	518	533

Key-Press

		"dit"	"dah"
	Simple	246	245
	Choice	358	382

Before jumping on the complexity bandwagon, it is necessary to mention
that the complexity effect is not as robust as one might believe. First,
Kerr (1979), and Zelaznik and Hahn (1984) do not show reliable reaction
time differences between long and short key press responses. Second,
there is support for the notion that some, if not all, of the effects on
reaction time can be explained by a confounding of responses duration
(Quinn, Schmidt, Zelaznik, Hawkins, & McFarquhar, 1980), or some biomechanical differences in response initiation as a function of complexity
(Anson, 1982).

Sternberg and colleagues, well aware of some of the problems with the
complexity paradigm, and problems in interpreting choice RT differences,
developed a variation of the complexity paradigm in which subjects are
primed to speak a word, known in advance, as quickly as possible following
a go signal (Sternberg, Monsell, Knoll, & Wright, 1978). This paradigm
controls for the differences in biomechanical initiation properties by
having the same syllable be used as the first sound regardless of the
length of the string of words to be produced. Furthermore, from an
analysis of the slope and intercepts of the RT, and MT functions as
related to the number of spoken elements, Sternberg, et al. have developed
a precise model of rapid speech production. Since verbal skills are
usually one of the deficient cognitive processes of the mildly retarded,
it would be interesting to examine their speech production control
strategies.

PRECUING AND RESPONSE PROGRAMMING

The precuing approach is concerned with discovering the nature of the
cognitive (not necessarily conscious) processes and decisions that are
believed to precede the execution of a skilled act. For example, the
organization of the processes responsible for the selection of such
response parameters as side of body, duration, and direction can be
examined. The major concern centers around whether dimensions of movement
are selected in a specific order (Rosenbaum, 1980), in parallel, as a
whole (Goodman & Kelso, 1980), or whether there is a hierarchy in the
selection of movement dimensions (Rosenbaum, 1983; Rosenbaum & Kornblum,
1982; Zelaznik, 1981). To answer questions such as these, chronometric
methods have been utilized extensively (Posner, 1978).

In the precuing method, prior to the arrival of the imperative stimulus,
the subject receives a cue, which conveys information concerning the
to-be-produced response [the reader is referred to Rosenbaum (1982), and
Goodman & Kelso (1980) for a more thorough discussion of precuing issues].
This cue can provide partial or full advance information about the
upcoming motor act. Of course full information makes the upcoming
response completely certain, and is a simple reaction time task. The
theoretically interesting situations are when certain features of the
movement are known in advance, but others must be specified after the
imperative stimulus. These processes associated with these motor
dimensions can be made from an examination of patterns of reaction time as
a function of which features are cued and not cued prior to the arrival of
the imperative stimulus.

Rosenbaum (1980) utilized this paradigm to ascertain whether in an aiming
task, the selection of limb, direction and extent occurred in parallel, or
in a specific order. In this experiment there were two levels of each of
these dimensions, right/left, toward/away, and near/far, for the limb,
direction and extent dimensions, respectively. Rosenbaum showed that the
programming of arm, direction and extent could be conceptualized as a
flexible-ordered serial process with the arm decision requiring the most
time to be completed. However, Goodman and Kelso (1980) criticized the
Rosenbaum paradigm in that the mapping of stimuli to responses was not
"natural" and that the pattern of results could be attributable to
stimulus-response translation processes (Teichner & Krebs, 1972). They
report precuing experiments that they interpret as support for the idea
that movements are organized holistically. While the failure to support
the Rosenbaum data is problematic to the organization of these three
dimensions, as studied by Rosenbaum, the Goodman and Kelso argument does
not de facto rule out all other kinds of precuing data.

Klapp (1977a) utilized the precuing technique to examine the organization
of the digit selection and response timing processes in a key press task.
In this experiment the duration of the upcoming key press (a Morse-code
dit or dah response) always was not-cued, and, on one-half of the trials
the digit to be utilized was cued. First, the dah key press exhibited a
longer RT than the dit. Second, when digit was not-cued, RT was longer
than when digit was cued, and these two factors interacted in an underadditive fashion. The RT for a dah response when the digit was not-cued

Table 2

Reaction Time (MS) as a Function of Advance Information
and Key-Press Duration (Dit Versus Dah)
(from Klapp, 1977a)

Advance Information			
	"dit"	"dah"	"dit - dah"
Digit	299	352	53
None	559	591	32

was less than predicted by the additive effects of digit uncertainty and level of key press duration (see Table 2). Klapp, based upon this result, and the converging results of his Experiments 2 and 3 concluded that the response timing and digit selection processes were organized in parallel. [See Stanovich & Pachella (1977) for a discussion of the interpretation of underadditivity.]

The interpretations of the Klapp (1977a) and the Rosenbaum (1980) experiments both are weakened by a methodological difficulty. Since in the Rosenbaum precuing technique, each additional cued dimension reduces the stimulus-response set by a factor of two, the comparison in precue conditions between different numbers of dimensions cued confounds the number of stimulus-response pairs with the uncertainties of the motor dimensions. Suppose that the time to specify arm requires more time than to specify the digit to be utilized. According to Rosenbaum, if arm and digit are specified serially then the difference in reaction time for specifying duration and arm compared to duration and digit should be equal to the difference in reaction time for specifying arm alone compared to specifying digit alone. This test for a serial-independent ordering a motoric processes rests upon the assumption that when the number of stimulus-response pairs increases from two (specify one dimension during reaction time) to four (specify two dimensions during reaction) the increases attributable to increased nonmotoric processing add a constant to the overall reaction time. However, it is possible that when the durations of these nonmotoric processes are prolonged, certain aspects of the stimulus are processed relatively faster than when these processes are shortened. Such a result would result in an underadditive interaction between the specify two dimensions versus specify one and, of course, would render inferences concerning the order of motoric processes problematic. Thus, additivity between motoric factors might be interpretable in terms of serial order of motoric decision processes, lack of additivity is not interpretable with respect to the motoric processes under investigation.

Zelaznik (1978) and Zelaznik, Shapiro, and Carter (1982), cognizant of the problems associated with the previously developed precuing paradigm, attempted to devise a somewhat better method of precuing. In this method, precues were manipulated by changing the S-R mapping in a two-choice reaction time paradigm. Specifically, subjects produced a key press response with a digit from either the left or right hand (the hand in this experiment, was not cued). For one set of subjects the identical digit was utilized on both hands -- thus, digit was defined as cued. For other sets of subjects, the duration could be common between the two hands, although the digit was not common -- thus, the duration was defined as cued. When there was both, a common finger and common duration across both hands, both dimensions were defined as cued. Finally, when a unique duration and digit were associated the with hand, neither dimension was cued. Each of these four conditions involved different subjects.

This method was able to maintain an invariant number of S-R alternatives (two), but manipulated the underlying motor dimension uncertainty. When the duration was cued, there were no differences between 300 and 150 msec key press responses. However, when the duration was not cued, there were significant reaction time differences between these key press durations. Furthermore, the RT difference between long and short key press responses increased when both digit and duration were not cued, compared to only duration not cued.

These results support Klapp (1977a) in that the duration of the response behaves as though it can be programmed in advance, when it is cued, independently of whether the digit is cued or not cued. When the duration was not cued, it cannot be programmed in advance, and thus one obtains the relatively reliable "dit-dah" effect (Kerr, 1979; Klapp, Wyatt, & Lingo, 1974; Klapp & Wyatt, 1976). However, the overadditive interaction between digit and duration uncertainty, and level of duration (short versus long) supported the notion that a single set of processes, commonly called a stage (see Sanders, 1980) was responsible for the selection and programming of digits and durations rather than a set of parallel processes proposed by Klapp (1977a).

While the results of the Zelaznik et al. (1982) paper were promising in the development of a better method of precuing, this method produced a qualitative change in the nature of the task. The conditions which involved different levels of response uncertainty were between subjects and one set of subjects performed under one level of digit and/or duration uncertainty. This is a serious drawback. Since the same two S-R pairs were presented for blocks of trials, the subject need not have selected any dimensions in advance, rather subjects could have established a "Gestalt", a specific strategy, to perform in their specific S-R mapping condition. Thus, differences in RT observed in Zelaznik et al. could have been the result of condition-specific strategies, and not the result of selecting dimensions in advance [see Rosenbaum, 1983, for a discussion of these issues].

To examine these precuing issues we (Zelaznik & Hahn, 1984) examined the precuing of hand, digit and duration of a key press task under both the normal precuing paradigm, and the newer procedure developed by Zelaznik and colleagues. In the normal precuing procedure, to be called Variable an alphanumeric precue appeared on a CRT screen that informed the subject as to none, one, two, or three dimensions of the upcoming key press response. Thus, this method confounded the number of remaining stimulus-response pairs with the number of type of precue. In the Fixed method, two sets of alphanumeric strings that informed the subject which two possible response would be required. On some trials the two pairs shared the same hand, digit or duration or combinations of two or three of these features. Figure 5 presents the major results of this experiment.

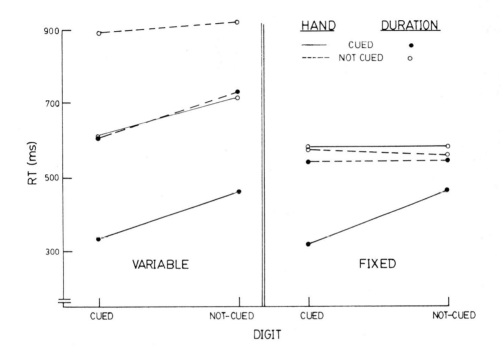

Figure 5
RT (ms) as a function of method of precuing, hand, digit and duration uncertainty, (From Zelaznik & Hahn, 1984.)

The right hand side of the figure is for the Fixed S-R Pairs method, and the left side depicts the Variable S-R Pairs method. First, due to the increased time for identification of the alphanumeric stimuli there is a general increase in reaction time compared to the first two experiments. There was a four way interaction between precuing method and the movement dimension uncertainty variables. This was due to the confounding of S-R information in the Variable method which produced increases in RT as more dimensions had to be selected. Therefore, we conducted separate analysis on each method of precuing.

For the Fixed S-R Pairs method, there was a triple interaction between hand, digit, and duration uncertainty. This is the result of the differ-ence in RT between the simple RT conditions and the other uncertainty conditions. Additional post-hoc analysis revealed that the digit no-cued condition to possessed a smaller RT than any of the older not-cued condi-tions. In the hand not-cued conditions, there was no effect of digit and duration uncertainty upon RT.

In the Variable method, there was a triple interaction between hand, digit, and duration uncertainty. As seen in the figure, this appears to be the result not attributable to the simple-RT situation, but rather the smaller increase in reaction time when all dimensions were not-cued (eight S-R alternatives) compared to when only the digit was cued (four S-R alternatives), versus the larger increases in reaction time when digit was not cued in the simple to two-choice, and the two-choice to four-choice conditions. Thus, the effect of digit being not-cued was less when the number of alternatives was increased from four to eight, compared to one to two, and two to four. This underadditive interaction between digit and duration uncertainty is reminiscent of the underadditive interaction found between level of duration and digit uncertainty by Klapp (1977a).

In addition this underadditive interaction means that in this experiment Hick's (1952) law was not confirmed. The increase from one to two bits of information (2 to 4 choices) was greater than the increase from two to three bits of information (4 to 8 choices).

There are some other interesting observations from these data. First, RTs in the all-cued conditions (simple-RT) were similar for both methods of precuing. The same was true for all of the two S-R pair conditions in both methods of precuing. Since the imperative stimuli were identical in both methods, but the precues differed, it seems safe to conclude that subjects utilized the different kinds of precues with the same degree of effectiveness.

In this experiment there appears to be a very simple explanation for the different pattern of results across the two methods of precuing. When there are only two stimulus response alternatives, and thus the perceptual processes and decisional processes require relatively smaller amounts of time the identification of the stimulus is completed prior to any motor preparation during reaction time.

Thus, we can see evidence for a response execution hierarchy. However, when perceptual processing is increased in time, due to an increase in the number of S-R pairs, the subject might attempt to identify what hand is required (the "L" or "R" stimulus) prior to identifying the digit and/or duration. Thus, when there are four stimulus response pairs, and overall reaction time is longer, the preparation of hand might be occurring in the same time frame as the digit and duration stimuli are being identified. This interpretation is similar to a partial output model of reaction time advocated by McClelland (1979), and Miller (1982). An alternative interpretation utilizes the notion of critical path analysis (Schweickert, 1978), in which the processes of identifying, and programming the appropriate dimension occur in parallel, but when processing is slowed down by an increase in the number of S-R alternatives the hand decisions no longer lie along the "critical path", and thus one observes facilitation in RT when duration is cued compared to when digit is cued.

Thus, the present experiment suggests that the human information processing system is not comprised of discrete stages in which output is sent from a stage after processing has been completed. Instead, it seems as though if the perceptual aspects of a task are made difficult enough, these processes will send partial information to the response selection processes. Miller (1982) has developed a more formal method to examine this kind of question.

Miller first finds that it is easier to select one of two digits on the same hand then identical digits on different hands. Thus, a response preparation effect is established. The ingenious part of Miller's method is that he creates multifeatured stimuli, in which one feature is easier to process than the other. Thus, if the easier feature signals one of two digits on the same hand, can the subject take advantage of this situation. If they can, it suggests that partial output is sent to response processes, even though the entire stimulus has not been processed fully.

How can these precuing methods be utilized to help us understand the reaction time performance of mildly retarded individuals? First, it is not conceivable to us that mildly retarded persons will perform in these tasks in a qualitatively different fashion than their normal counterparts. Rather, there might be difference in strategy. For example, mildly retarded subjects might not begin response preparation until the entire stimulus has been processed, and thus, although partial information is available it is not utilized. Another likely possibility is that mildly retarded subjects will not take advantage of precue information and as such will not show benefits in RT to precues. This kind of finding can be illustrated by conducting the type of experiment that manipulates both types of precuing methods. One can compare the reductions in RT between traditional Hick's law experiments and those of the Variable precuing procedure. If advance information cannot be utilized effectively, then the reductions in RT as a function of stimulus-response alternatives should be much less in precuing than in the Hick procedure.

The reaction time approach described in this chapter leads to one major prediction. Peripheral motor difficulties of mildly retarded subjects should produce additive effects upon RT, while the precuing variables should cause interactive effects. One might even want to consider that additive effects implies more peripheral difficulties.

CONCLUSIONS

It is clear that reaction time performance of mildly retarded individuals is inferior to that of normal individuals. The reasons for this differ-

ence remain an important research area. We suggest that the understanding
of limited resources and response selection in reaction time performance
should produce a better understanding of the general deficits in information processing mechanisms in reaction time performance of mildly retarded
individuals.

REFERENCES

Anson, J. G. (1982). Memory drum theory: Alternative tests and explana-
    tions for the complexity effects on simple reaction time. Journal of
    Motor Behavior, 14, 228-246.

Aufderheide, S. K. (1984). A sequential comparison of the simple
    reaction time of educable mental retardates and intellectually normal
    children. Manuscript under review.

Baumeister, A. A. (1968). Behavioral inadequacy and variability of
    performance. American Journal of Mental Deficiency, 73, 477-483.

Baumeister, A. A., Hawkins, W. F., & Kellas, G. (1965). Reaction speed
    as a function of stimulus intensity in normals and retardates.
    Perceptual and Motor Skills, 20, 649-652.

Baumeister, A. A., & Kellas, G. (1968). Reaction time and mental retard-
    ation. In N. R. Ellis (Ed.), International review of research in
    mental retardation (Vol. 3, pp. 163-193). London: Academic Press.

Berkson, G. (1960). An analysis of reaction time in normal and mentally
    deficient young men. III. Variation of stimulus and or response complexit
    Journal of Mental Deficiency Research, 4, 69-77.

Berkson, G., & Baumeister, A. A. (1967). Reaction time variability of
    mental defectives and normals. American Journal of Mental Defi-
    ciency. 72, 262-266.

Brewer, N. (1978). Motor components in the choice reaction time of
    mildly retarded adults. American Journal of Mental Deficiency, 82,
    565-572.

Brewer, N., & Nettelbeck, T. (1977). The influence of contextual cues on
    the choice reaction time of mildly retarded adults. American Journal
    of Mental Deficiency, 82, 37-43.

Brewer, N., & Nettelbeck, T. (1979). Discrimination, translation, or
    response organization: A clarification of factors underlying slower
    responding among mentally retarded persons. American Journal of
    Mental Deficiency, 84, 195-199.

Brewer, N., & Smith, G. A. (1984). How normal and retarded individuals
    monitor and regulate speed and accuracy of responding in serial
    choice tasks. Journal of Experimental Psychology: General, 113,
    71-93.

Caffrey, B., Jones, J. D., & Hinkle, B. R. (1971). Variability in reaction times of normal and educable mentally retarded children. Perceptual and Motor Skills, 32, 255-258.

Dingman, H. F., & Silverstein, A. B. (1964). Intelligence, motor disabilities, and reaction time in the mentally retarded. Perceptual and Motor Skills, 19, 791-794.

Distefano, E. A., & Brunt, D. (1982). Mentally retarded and normal children's performance on gross motor reaction- and movement-time tasks with varying degrees of uncertainty of movement. Perceptual and Motor Skills, 55, 1235-1238.

Donders, F. C. (1969). On the speed of mental processes. Translated by W. G. Koster. Attention and Performance II: Acta Psychologica, 30, 412-431.

Dugas, J. L., & Baumeister, A. A. (1968). A comparison of intrasubject variability in auditory difference limens of normals and retardates. American Journal of Mental Deficiency, 73, 500-504.

Ellis, N. R., & Sloan, W. (1957). Relationship between intelligence and simple reaction time in mental defectives. Perceptual and Motor Skills, 7, 65-67.

Goodman, D., & Kelso, J. A. S. (1980). Are movements prepared in parts? Not under compatible (naturalized) conditions. Journal of Experimental Psychology: General, 109, 475-495.

Gosling, H., & Jenness, D. (1974). Temporal variables in simple reaction times of mentally retarded boys. American Journal of Mental Deficiency, 79, 214-224.

Henry, F. M. (1960). Increased response latency for complicated movements and a "memory drum" theory of neuromotor reaction. Research Quarterly, 31, 448-458.

Henry, F. M. (1980). Use of simple reaction time in motor programming studies: A reply to Klapp, Wyatt, and Lingo. Journal of Motor Behavior, 12, 163-168.

Hick, W. E. (1952). On the rate of gain of information. Quarterly Journal of Experimental Psychology, 4, 11-26.

Holden, E. A. (1965). Reaction time during unimodal and trimodal stimulation in educable retardates. Journal of Mental Deficiency Research, 9, 183-190.

Jensen, A. R. (1982). Reaction time and psychometric g. In H. J. Eysenck (Ed.), A model of intelligence (pp. 93-132). New York: Springer-Verlag.

Kahneman, D. (1973). Attention and effort. Englewood Cliffs, NJ: Prentice-Hall.

Kantowitz, B. H. (1974). Double stimulation. In B. H. Kantowitz (Ed.), Human information processing: Tutorials in performance and cognition. New York: Erlbaum.

Keele, S. W. (1973). Attention and Human Performance. Pacific Palisades, CA: Goodyear.

Kellas, S. W. (1973). Reaction-time and response variability of normal and retarded individuals. American Journal of Mental Deficiency, 74, 409-414.

Kerr, B. (1979). Is reaction time different for long and short response duration in simple and choice conditions? Journal of Motor Behavior, 11, 269-274.

Kirby, N. H., Nettelbeck, T., & Western P. (1982). Locating information-processing deficits of mildly mentally retarded young adults. American Journal of Mental Deficiency, 87, 338-343.

Klapp, S. T. (1977a). Response programming as assessed by reaction time, does not establish commands for particular muscles. Journal of Motor Behavior, 9, 301-312.

Klapp, S. T. (1977b). Reaction time analysis of programmed control. Exercise and Sport Sciences Reviews, 5, 231-253.

Klapp, S. T., & Wyatt, E. P. (1976). Motor programming within a sequence of responses. Journal of Motor Behavior, 8, 19-26.

Klapp, S. T., Wyatt, E. P., & Lingo, W. M. (1974). Response programming in simple and choice reactions. Journal of Motor Behavior, 5, 263-271.

Kornblum, S. (1965). Response competition and/or inhibition in two-choice reaction time. Psychonomic Science, 2, 55-56.

Krupski, A. (1976). Heart rate changes during reaction time: An approach for understanding deficient attention in retarded individuals. In R. Karrer (Ed.), Developmental psychophysiology of mental retardation (pp. 92-118). Springfield, IL: Charles C. Thomas.

Krupski, A. (1977). Role of attention in the reaction-time performance of mentally retarded adolescents. American Journal of Mental Deficiency, 82, 79-83.

Krupski, A. (1980). Attention processes: Research, theory, and implications for special education. In B. K. Keogh (Ed.), Advances in special education (pp. 101-140). Greenwich, CN: JAI Press.

Krupski, A., & Boyle, P. R. (1978). An observational analysis of children's behavior during a simple reaction-time task: The role of attention. Child Development, 49, 340-347.

Lally, M., & Nettelbeck, T. (1977). Intelligence, reaction time, and inspection time. American Journal of Mental Deficiency, 82, 273-281.

Maisto, A. A., & Jerome, M. A. (1977). Encoding and high-speed memory scanning of retarded and nonretarded adolescents. American Journal of Mental Deficiency, 82, 282-286.

Maisto, A. A., & Sipe, S. (1980). Effects of stimulus probability on encoding by mentally retarded and nonretarded persons. American Journal of Mental Deficiency, 84, 577-581.

McClelland, J. L. (1979). On the time relations of mental processes: An examination of systems of processes in cascade. Psychological Review, 86, 287-330.

McLeod, P. (1978). Does probe RT measure central processing demand? Quarterly Journal of Experimental Psychology, 29, 651-668.

Miller, J. (1982). Discrete versus continuous stage models of human information processing: In search of partial output. Journal of Experimental Psychology: Human Perception and Performance, 8, 273-296.

Navon, D. (1984). Resources: A theoretical soup stone. Psychological Review, 91, 216-234.

Navon, D., & Gopher, D. (1979). On the economy of the human information processing system. Psychological Review, 86, 214-255.

Nettelbeck, T., & Brewer, N. (1976). Effects of stimulus response variables on the choice reaction time of mildly retarded adults. American Journal of Mental Deficiency, 81, 85-92.

Nettelbeck, T., & Brewer, N. (1981). Studies of mild mental retardation and timed performance. In N. R. Ellis (Ed.), International review of research in mental retardation, 9, (Vol. 10, pp. 61-106). New York: Academic Press.

Nettelbeck, T., & Lally, M. (1976). Inspection time and measured intelligence. British Journal of Psychology, 67, 17-22.

Norman, D. A., & Bobrow. (1975). On data-limited and resource-limited processes. Cognitive Psychology, 7, 44-64.

Posner, M. I. (1978). Chronometric explorations of mind. Hillsdale, NJ: Lawrence Erlbaum.

Posner, M. I., & McLeod, P. (1982). Information processing models -- In search of elementary operations. Annual Review of Psychology, 33, 477-514.

Quinn, J. T., Schmidt, R. A., Zelaznik, H. N., Hawkins, B., & McFarquhar, R. (1980). Target-size influences on reaction time with movement time controlled. Journal of Motor Behavior, 12, 239-261.

Rosenbaum, D. A. (1980). Human movement initiation: Specification of arm, direction and extent. Journal of Experimental Psychology: General, 109, 444-474.

Rosenbaum, D. A. (1983). The movement precuing technique: Assumptions, applications, and extensions. In R. A. Magill (Ed.), Memory and control in motor behavior (pp. 231-274). Amsterdam: North Holland.

Rosenbaum, D. A., & Kornblum, S. (1982). A priming method for investigating the selection of motor responses. Acta Psychologica, 51, 223-243.

Saccuzzo, D. P., Kerr, M., Marcus, A., & Brown, R. (1979). Input capability and speed of processing in mental retardation. Journal of Abnormal Psychology, 4, 341-345.

Sanders, A. F. (1977). Structural and functional aspects of the reaction process. In S. Dornic (Ed.), Attention and Performance. Hillsdale, NJ: Erlbaum.

Sanders, A. F. (1980). Stage analysis of reaction processes. In G. E. Stelmach & J. Requin (Eds.), Tutorials in motor behavior (pp. 331-354). Amsterdam: North Holland.

Schweickert, R. (1978). A critical path generalization of the additive factor method: Analysis of the stroop task. Journal of Mathematical Psychology, 18, 105-139.

Sroufe, L. A. (1971). Age changes in cardiac deceleration within a fixed foreperiod reaction-time task: An index of attention. Developmental Psychology, 5, 338-343.

Stanovich, K. E., & Pachella, R. G. (1977). Encoding, stimulus-response compatibility and stages of processing. Journal of Experimental Psychology: Human Perception and Performance, 3, 411-421.

Sternberg, S. (1969). The discovery of processing stages: Extensions of Donders method. Acta Psychologica, 30, 276-315.

Sternberg, S., Monsell, S., Knoll, R. L., & Wright, C. E. (1978). The latency and duration of rapid movement sequences: Comparisons of speech and typewriting. In G. E. Stelmach (Ed.), Information processing in motor control and learning (pp. 118-152). New York: Academic Press.

Teichner, W. H., & Krebs, M. J. (1972). Laws of simple reaction time. Psychological Review, 79, 344-358.

Wade, M. G., Newell, K. M., & Wallace, S. A. (1978). Decision time and movement time as a function of response complexity in the motor performance of retarded persons. American Journal of Mental Deficiency, 83, 135-144.

Weaver, L. A., & Ravaria, C. (1970). The distribution of reaction times in mental retardates. Journal of Mental Deficiency Research, 14, 295-304.

Wickens, C. D. (1976). The effects of divided attention on information processing in manual tracking. Journal of Experimental Psychology: Human Perception and Performance, 2, 1-13.

Zelaznik, H. N. (1978). Precueing response factors in choice reaction time: A word of caution. Journal of Motor Behavior, 10, 77-79.

Zelaznik, H. N. (1981). The effects of force and direction uncertainty on choice reaction time in an isometric production task. Journal of Motor Behavior, 13, 18-32.

Zelaznik, H. N., & Hahn, R. Reaction time methods in the study of motor programming: The precuing of hand, digit and duration. Manuscript under review.

Zelaznik, H. N., Shapiro, D. C., & Carter, M. C. (1982). The specification of digit and duration during motor programming: A new method of precuing. Journal of Motor Behavior, 14, 57-68.

Motor Skill Acquisition of the Mentally Handicapped:
Issues in Research and Training
M.G. Wade (editor)
© Elsevier Science Publishers B.V. (North-Holland), 1986

REACTION TIME AND THE STUDY OF INTELLIGENCE

Joseph C. Campione

University of Illinois

Preparation of this manuscript was supported in part by
Grants HD-05951 and HD-15808 from the National Institute of
Child Health and Human Development.

In my role as discussant, I will try to present some general observations
on the papers presented by Vernon, and Zelaznik and Aufderheide, place
their approach in an overall context of theories of intelligence and
mental retardation, and indicate some of my enthusiasms and concerns about
those approaches. Of course, commentators bring with them a set of biases
and attitudes that influence their evaluation. My own perspective is that
of a cognitive developmental psychologist whose interests are in the
diagnosis and remediation of students, including the retarded, experiencing academic problem. My reactions, then, are based on the implications
of the research findings for both theoretical and practical issues.

THEORETICAL ISSUES

In several papers, my colleagues and I (Campione & Brown, 1977, 1978;
Campione, Brown, & Ferrara, 1982) have taken a modal information processing model and asked where, in that model, important sources of individual
differences in intellectual functioning are likely to be found. Specifically, we have considered that variation among individuals may be attributable to: (a) differences in knowledge -- individuals who score higher on
IQ tests and on school tasks may simply know more, or have their knowledge
better organized, than those whom they outperform; (b) varying tendencies
to bring to bear a variety of task-appropriate strategies that are essential for optimal performance; (c) differential understanding and control
of one's own cognitive resources and processes -- the area referred to as
metacognition -- that allow the efficient and flexible use of those
resources; and (d) variations in the speed of mental processing. Needless
to say, the interactions among these sources must also be understood
before we can hope to have anything approaching a complete theory of
intelligence. In our own reviews, we have emphasized aspects (b) and (c)
as most directly relatable to differences in assessed intelligence.

In their papers, Vernon, and Zelaznik and Aufderheide review two quite
different approaches (see Cronbach, 1957), based on analyses of subjects'
reaction times, to understanding human performance in general, and
intelligence in particular. Although both use reaction time methodologies, their emphases are quite different from each other, stemming from

different intellectual traditions. Vernon's approach, as he notes, dates
back to Galton, who included measures of reaction time in a battery he
developed to assess individual differences in intelligence. As is clear
from Vernon's paper, this particular indicator variable has survived the
test of time, whereas many of Galton's other items have not (e.g., head
circumference). Vernon also attempts to use reaction time measures quite
directly to provide information about the speed with which specific mental
operations are carried out. That is, in terms of our list of potential
sources of individual differences in intelligence, Vernon believes the
speed of processing aspect may be of paramount interest, that it is in
this domain that important information about the nature of intelligence
can be gleaned. This position is similar to those outlined recently by
Hunt (1978), Jensen (1982), and others, and earlier by several investigators interested in mental retardation per se (see Maisto & Baumeister,
1984, for a review).

In contrast, Zelaznik and Aufderheide, following a different research
tradition, use reaction time measurements as a way to evaluate alternative
hypotheses about the ways in which subjects approach different kinds of
motor tasks, a method dating back at least to Donders. They are less
concerned with inferences about mental processing capabilities based
directly on the reaction times than they are with using those times to
evaluate different hypotheses about the organization of behavior, or about
the kinds of approaches subjects take in dealing with particular tasks.
This approach has been used successfully in the retardation area. For
example, a number of investigators (e.g., Belmont and Butterfield, 1969;
Brown, Campione, Bray, & Wilcox, 1973) have used patterns of reaction
times to make inferences about the use of mnemonic strategies by retarded
and nonretarded children. Again, the data of principal interest were not
the absolute magnitudes of response times, but the patterns and the
information those patterns held regarding strategy use. Thus, while the
two papers share an interest in the analysis of reaction times, they use
them in different ways, to assess different types of questions. I will
try to indicate what I see as the strengths and weaknesses of these
alternatives approaches.

In his paper, Vernon provides a brief review of ideas about "mental
speed," dating back to Galton and extending to the more recent studies by,
among others, Hunt (1978), Jensen (1982), Keating and Bobbitt (1978), and
some work from his own laboratory. He points out that there has been a
clear shift in the weight of the evidence concerning speed-intelligence
relations.

Although the early studies failed to produce much impressive confirmatory
evidence relating mental speed and intelligence, most recent studies have
ben much more successful. This shift is no doubt due to the increasing
sophistication, both theoretical and methodological, underlying the
research; and herein, in my view, lies the major strength of this
approach. The development of specific and powerful theories of the mental
operations involved in some simple laboratory tasks has allowed investigators to obtain estimates of the facility with which specific elementary
mental operations are carried out by individual subjects. Rather than
measuring a global reaction time (RT) involving a number of distinct
components, it has become possible (at least within the confines of some
specific theory) to estimate the speed with which theoretically more
interesting components are carried out. With this change in measurement

precision came an acceleration of successful demonstrations of speed-ability relations, in the form of either differences between groups of subjects varying in assessed ability or correlations between intelligence scores and speed estimates.

Investigators have looked at the speed with which subjects can access long-term memory codes, scan short-term memory, generate simple and choice reaction times, conduct logical operations such as negation, etc.; they have been able to document differences in these speed scores between high and low verbal ability college students, retarded and nonretarded children, and children of different ages. There is no paucity of such demonstrations, although the consistency and magnitude of these differences, particularly in the case of simple and choice reaction times has been challenged (e.g., Longstreth, 1984). But even granting the correlations, the important question remains: how are these differences to be interpreted; and it is here that this approach seems to run into problems.

After reviewing some of the basic data on the mental speed-ability relation, Vernon makes two points, one empirical and the other more theoretical. The first concerns the possibility that many of the relations found between processing speed and intelligence scores may reflect nothing more than the fact that some of the performance tests are given under time pressure. That is, the "faster" subjects are better able to deal with the requirement of answering as many questions as possible in a limited time. This would lead one to believe that relations involving mental speed and performance would be diminished if the criterion test were given in an untimed format. Vernon provides data indicating that the magnitude of the multiple correlation between several speed of processing indices and WAIS performance is approximately the same when the test is administered in either timed or untimed versions. Hence we need to look farther for the mechanism involved in the relations.

Vernon's second main point, regarding the reason why speed differences might be important even when the performance task is not timed, is more speculative. It is based on the notion of a limited capacity information processing system. The argument is that capacity is "used up" by both the contents of working memory and the operations employed to access and work on those contents. To the extent that the retrieval/operation components are done effortlessly and quickly, there is more "space" for maintenance and chunking operations. Vernon processes the possibility that "... performance differences between retarded and nonretarded populations may be attributable less to knowledge differences or to differences in skills or problem solving strategies than to differences in the speed or efficiency with which a number of basic cognitive processes are executed." While conceding that population differences in knowledge and strategic expertise exist, Vernon would like to suggest that those differences are secondary symptoms of the more basic, speed of processing, differences. The slower speed of information-processing is what has limited the acquisition of these cognitive resources. While the argument is not unreasonable, the problem is to bring those ideas to an experimental test. It would be nice to, for example, somehow intervene and increase the processing speed of some individuals and then determine the effect such as increase had on overall ability. However, that experiment remains to be done.

The issues here are highly reminiscent of those that have been addressed

in some detail in the more specific area of memory span performance.
Review, empirical papers, and theoretical analyses by Chi (1976), Dempster
(1981), and Huttenlocher and Burke (1977), among others, have followed
this line extensively. The problem is that it is difficult to obtain
direct evidence supporting the position that speed factors are paramount.
While Dempster (1981) concludes in his review that speed of processing
(encoding time) variations are in good part responsible for differences in
memory spans, the evidence tends to be indirect; because it is difficult
to find positive evidence for strategy- or knowledge-based differences in
some tasks and under some circumstances, Dempster argued by default that
speed factors must be important.

To cite one example, Huttenlocher and Burke (1977) were unable to find
positive evidence for the influence of rehearsal or chunking strategies as
determinants of developmental differences. More specifically while they
did find that altering the presentation method to facilitate chunking did
improve performance, it did so in all cases, leaving developmental differences unaffected; they concluded that efficiency of item identification
represented the most likely source of developmental differences.

It is important to notice the nature of the evidence here. There is no
dispute about the importance of strategies in influencing overall performance levels. Subjects who employ task-appropriate strategies outperform
those who do not. The problem is that it is not clear that the use of
"the same" strategies eliminates individual differences; if it does not,
there must be additional factors involved in producing individual or
developmental differences. Unfortunately, it is not clear that the
manipulations involved in most studies do result in all subjects using the
"same" strategies with the "same" proficiency. Nor is it possible to know
if other strategies might have been involved. If that is not guaranteed,
the inference that speed factors must be involved is considerably
weakened. In any event, we certainly need more intensive analyses of the
extent to which individual differences are altered or maintained following
various types of intervention before we can make any strong statements.
Thus, while there is certainly some indirect evidence available, it would
be nice to have more direct evidence before we jump confidently onto the
speed bandwagon.

There are, of course, other factors that have pronounced effects on
performance. We know that knowledge factors and extended practice in the
use of specific strategies can result in dramatic improvements in performance. An excellent demonstration of the effects of knowledge and practice on memory performance comes from research reported by Ericsson and
Chase (1982), working with an individual subject. That subject, a track
buff, recoded series of digits, e.g., 359, into meaningful times for some
event, in this case a 3.59 mile. With (to say the least) extensive
practice, the subject was able to work up to a digit span of over 80.
This change was not accompanied by any change in his span for letter
series. Therefore, it is difficult to argue that the change was accompanied by any general increase in mental processing efficiency. It may
well have been the case that, as his knowledge of various track standards
increased and with increasing practice, he became better able to identify
chunks and even to build larger ones, but such changes would have to be
extremely specific to the domain in question. I assume that a speed view
of the kind favored by Vernon would have to explain the original improvement in terms of increases in mental speed; further, I would expect that

such a view would also predict more general benefits from the practice than actually exist. If these are, in fact, the predictions that Vernon would make, clearly the data provide no comfort.

There are, in addition, other kinds of evidence indicating that "capacity limitations" are affected by practice. Consider the work of Spelke, Hirst, and Neisser (1976) having to do with performance on concurrent tasks. They have shown that, with considerable practice, individuals who initially suffered considerable interference on the primary task of reading a text for comprehension while engaging in a secondary task, shadowing a tape playing a list of words while being required to make semantic judgments about them, were eventually able to perform as well on the primary reading task when it was presented alone or in combination with the secondary task. Another relevant case is the work of Shiffrin and Schneider (Shiffrin & Schneider, 1977; Schneider & Shiffrin, 1977) on the development of automaticity. It may be the case that there are important individual differences in the rate at which, or extent to which, such automaticity can be developed, and that these differences are themselves attributable to speed variations; however, I know of no evidence indicating that such is (or is not) the case. And it is this issue which we are beginning to investigate in our own laboratory.

INTERACTIONS BETWEEN THEORY AND PRACTICE

There is another consideration I would like to introduce. From my perspective, the most useful theories of intelligence, mental retardation, or academic functioning are those that lead to prescriptions regarding remediation. My concern about the speed view in this context is that it seems to fail this particular test. It is not clear that we know how to proceed to increase mental speed, even assuming that is possible; and fact can be interpreted as indicating a structural limitation on information processing, i.e., one that cannot be influenced. In contrast, views stressing the role of strategic and metacognitive factors do lead nicely to prescriptions for remediation. We do know that teaching retarded children to use a variety of mnemonic strategies can promote large improvements in their ability to learn and retain new material; we also know that teaching academically weak students a variety of comprehension-fostering and monitoring strategies increases their reading and listening comprehension dramatically (e.g., see Brown & Campione, this volume).

In one sense, this argument has little to say about the theoretical importance of the results Vernon has stressed. Those results are quite relevant to a scientific theory of intelligence, and the fact that they say little about remediation can be regarded as quite irrelevant. However, I would argue that the training results do speak to the possible centrality of speed factors as determinants of g, or as underlying performance in a variety of intellective domains. It seems unlikely, for example, that the training efforts that have been obtained (and there have been many) involved an increase in the mental speed of the learners. If this is true, the results indicate that strategic factors play a greater role in determining performance than do speed factors.

This brief review is meant to indicate only that the issues here are complex ones and that, while there has been a considerable amount of effort expended on trying to sort out the various contributions of

strategies, knowledge, and speed, the picture is still not a clear one.
Considerably more work will have to be done before we can come to any
strong conclusions.

The paper by Zelaznik and Aufderheide takes a somewhat different track,
both in method and in the areas they target as important sources of individual differences. They are interested in the kinds of strategies for
resource allocation that subjects might bring to bear on simple motor
tasks, more specifically in motor programming as indicated by a variety of
precuing manipulations. Their paper represents a case study of research
in this area, and they point out some of the developments that have
occurred during the last ten or so years. While I am impressed with the
treatment, the problem I have is that it is difficult to see how these
developments will help us deal with the problem of individual differences.
The stumbling block is that there are a variety of different theoretical
interpretations of the same general patterns, certainly not a problem
unique to this area of research. The result, however, is that the interpretation of the reaction times depends upon the theory's being correct.
If this analysis is less than impeccable, it is hard to know what the
individual difference assessments mean.

To consider a concrete example, MacLeod, Hunt, and Mathews (1978) have
used the Clark and Chase (1972) sentence/picture comparison task to obtain
estimates of the speed of carrying out mental operations such as negation.
They found that different subjects used different strategies to approach
the task, globally a verbal vs. a visual strategy. The result was that
the patterns of reaction times were quite different for the two "groups."
Although this is not necessarily a problem, unless one knows that these
strategic variations exist, and can discover who is using which, the
overall set of reaction times cannot provide useful information. Even if
the investigator can identify who is doing what, there remains the question of whether reaction times obtained from subjects using different
strategic approaches to the task are comparable. This is not to say that
these approaches are not useful, rather that they are difficult to imple-
ment. Detailed theoretical analyses are required before the individual
difference estimates are in any way interpretable, and as Zelaznik and
Aufderheide show, that process can be an extremely time-consuming one.

I would like to offer one final comment about the analysis of intelligence
into sets of component cognitive operations based on breakdowns of
reaction times. Once the theoretical analysis of a specific set of
experimental operations is complete, there is still the question of the
"quality" of the individual difference estimates. Specifically, I am
referring to questions about reliability and what I might call representativeness. The reliability issue is straight-forward. By representativeness, I am referring to the fact that some component processes (e.g.,
encoding or identification time, speed of negating, etc.) might be esti-
mated in more than one way, or via more than one paradigm. Would the
estimates obtained in the different settings themselves correlate?
Negative answers to either the reliability or representativeness questions
lessen the attractiveness of the overall approach. Unfortunately, in his
review of much of the extant developmental literature, Keating (1983) does
not paint a very optimistic picture; many of the parameters investigated
appear very task-specific. Work in our laboratory (Campione & Kurland,
unpublished) also failed to find substantially greater relations between
information processing parameters expected theoretically to be similar

than between those presumed to reflect different sets of mental operations.

Finally, we have argued before (Campione, Brown, & Ferrara, 1982), unless the molecular operations being assessed can be related theoretically to a class of interesting more molar behaviors, we will not go any farther toward "explaining" intelligence than to conclude that people of lower ability have more sluggish systems. While that is no doubt a contribution to the problem, it is less than completely satisfying.

SUMMARY

First, regarding Vernon's paper, advances have been made, and data indicating relations between reaction time measurements and ability have been found. It may, in fact, be possible to build an intelligence test based in good part on the analysis of a variety of reaction time measures. Despite this advance, and an advance it is, I am not convinced that we have learned as much about the nature of intelligence as the early results had promised. Second, the analysis presented by Zelaznik and Aufderheide indicates that analysis of reaction times of performance in sets of motor tasks. This is again an important contribution, and one that meshes nicely with research conducted in other areas of retardation. The difficulty here is that we appear to be a long way from using that research to do the kinds of analyses of individual differences necessary to further our understanding of variations in intellectual capabilities.

PRACTICAL ISSUES

My final comments concern the role of theories of intelligence in the design of remediation programs. As Binet argued, identification without diagnosis leading to potential remediation is not the name of the game. While discovering correlates of intellectual variation can and does advance our theoretical understanding of the nature of intelligence, it seems less likely to lead to the kinds of diagnoses to which Binet was referring. His own theorizing was on a more global level, and he did use that emerging theory to derive suggestions about the kinds of remedial activities likely to facilitate the academic performance of children identified as likely to experience difficulties (Binet, 1909; also see Brown, in press). In this case, it would seem that we would make faster progress by understanding the components of academic performance and using that understanding to build the kinds of intervention programs that are needed.

REFERENCES

Belmont, J. M., & Butterfield, E. C. (1969). The relation of short-term memory to development and intelligence. In L. P. Lipsitt & H. W. Reese (Eds.), Advances in child development and behavior (Vol. 4). New York: Academic Press.

Binet, A. (1909). Les idees modernes sur les infants. Paris: Ernest Flammarion.

Brown, A. L. (in press). Mental orthopedics: A conversation with Alfred Binet. In S. S. Chipman, J. W. Segal, & R. Glaser (Eds.), Thinking and learning skills: Current research and open questions (Vol. 2). Hillsdale, NJ: Erlbaum.

Brown A. L., Campione, J. C., Bray, N. W., & Wilcox, B. L. (1973). Keeping track of changing variables: Effects of rehearsal training and rehearsal prevention in normal and retarded adolescents. Journal of Experimental Psychology, 101, 123-131.

Campione, J. C., & Brown, A. L. (1977). Memory and metamemory development in educable retarded children. In R. V. Kail, Jr. & J. W. Hagen (Eds.), Perspectives on the development of memory and cognition. Hillsdale, NJ: Erlbaum.

Campione, J. C., & Brown, A. L. (1978). Toward a theory of intelligence: Contributions from research with retarded children. Intelligence, 2, 279-304.

Campione, J. C., & Brown, A. L., & Ferrara, R. A. (1982). Mental retardation and intelligence. In R. J. Sternberg (Ed.), Handbook of human intelligence. New York: Cambridge University Press.

Clark, H. H., & Chase, W. G. (1972). On the process of comparing sentences against pictures. Cognitive Psychology, 3, 472-517.

Chi, M. T. H. (1976). Short-term memory limitations in children: Capacity or processing deficits? Memory and Cognition, 4, 559-572.

Cronbach, L. J. (1957). The two disciplines of scientific psychology. American Psychologist, 12, 671-684.

Dempster, F. N. (1981). Memory span: Sources of individual and developmental differences. Psychological Bulletin, 89, 63-100.

Ericsson, K. A., & Chase, W. G. (1982). Exceptional memory. American Scientist, 70, 607-615.

Hunt, E. B. (1978). Mechanics of verbal ability. Psychological Review, 85, 109-130.

Huttenlocher, J., & Burke, D. (1977). Why does memory span increase with age? Cognitive Psychology, 8, 1-31.

Jensen, A. R. (1982). Reaction time and psychometric g. In H. J. Eysenck (Ed.), A model for intelligence. Pringer-Verlag.

Keating, D. P. (1983). The emporer's new clothes: The "new look" in intelligence research. In R. J. Sternberg (Ed.), Advances in the psychology of human intelligence (Vol. 2). Hillsdale, NJ: Erlbaum.

Keating, D. P., & Bobbitt, B. L. (1978). Individual and developmental differences in cognitive processing components of ability. Child Development, 49, 155-167.

Longstreth, L. E. (1984). Jensen's reaction-time investigations of intelligence: A critique. Intelligence, 8, 139-160.

Maisto, A. A., & Baumeister, A. A. (1984). Dissection of component processes in rapid information processing tasks: Comparison of retarded and nonretarded people. In P. H. Brooks, R. Sperber, & C. McCauley (Eds.), Learning and cognition in the mentally retarded. Hillsdale, NJ: Erlbaum.

MacLeod, C. M., Hunt, E. B., & Mathews, N. N. (1978). Individual differences in the verification of sentence-picture relationships. Journal of Verbal Learning and Verbal Behavior, 17, 493-507.

Schneider, W., & Shiffrin, R. M. (1977). Controlled and automatic human information processing: I. Direction, search, and attention. Psychological Review, 84, 1-66.

Shiffrin, R. M., & Schneider, W. (1977). Controlled and automatic human information processing: II. Perceptual learning, automatic attending, and a general theory. Psychological Review, 84, 127-190.

Spelke, E., Hirst, W., & Neisser, U. (1976). Skills of divided attention. Cognition, 4, 215-230.

Section III
Response Timing and Motor Behavior: B

Motor Skill Acquisition of the Mentally Handicapped:
Issues in Research and Training
M.G. Wade (editor)
© *Elsevier Science Publishers B.V. (North-Holland), 1986*

INPUT, CENTRAL AND MOTOR SEGMENTS OF RESPONSE TIME
IN MENTALLY RETARDED AND NORMAL CHILDREN

Rathe Karrer

Institute for the Study of Developmental Disabilities and
Department of Psychology
University of Illinois at Chicago

Paper to: Conference on the Development of Control, Coordination and Skill in the Mentally Handicapped, NICHD, Washington,
D.C., September 28-29, 1984. This paper was supported by the
NICHD Grant # HD 08365. The work supported here was the result
of collaboration with many people over the last ten years. I
specifically wish to thank Dr. Charles Warren for his role in
the initial implementation of the project and many analyses and
discussions; Dr. Jorge Daruna and Bruce McDonough for analysis
and discussion of the results; and Randall Cone for keeping our
instrumentation functional and for much of the software for
computer control and analysis.

Motor performance in individuals with mild mental retardation has been
repeatedly demonstrated as slower than that of nonretarded peers
(Baumeister & Kellas, 1968; Berkson, 1960; Clausen, 1966; Karrer & Ivins,
1976). There have been various explanations advanced for this slowness
that focuses on arousal, attention, response initiation, and preparatory
set. These processes have been inferred from various manipulations of
task requirements that are presumed to affect the process in question.
Therefore, the evidence is at best indirect. It is possible, however, to
obtain convergent evidence from the direct measurement of specific physiological events. The general question is: can the slowness of the moderate to mild mentally retarded be more explicitly localized to some segment
of the chain of processes from stimulus to response? By independently
manipulating the various temporal components that make up the stimulus-to-
response chain, the contribution of each component to slowness can be
determined and the processes within each component can be inferred and
elaborated.

With the use of physiological events, one can partition the stimulus to
response time into the various processes making up the chain: (1) preparation time; (2) stimulus registration or input time (IT); (3) central
processing or cortico-muscular (CT); and (4) muscle movement or motor
execution time (MT). The physiological markers for the last three segments were an evoked potential (EP) from primary cortex and the muscle
activity (EMG) of the responding digit. The physiological marker for
preparation was the contingent negative variation. ·

RT ANALYSIS STRATEGY

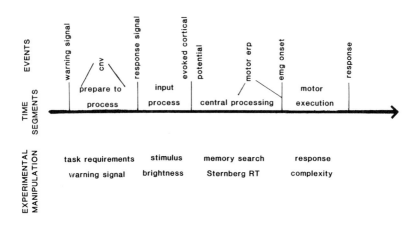

Figure 1
Schematic representation of the overall response speed project.

Figure 1 show a diagram of the research plan and the various manipulations
used to answer the general question posed above. The four segments have
specific events that define them and different tasks to experimentally
manipulate them. The preparatory interval was the time between the onset
of a warning signal and a response signal. This was 1.5 sec in the
present studies. The Input Time (IT) segment of reaction time was the
latency of an evoked potential (EP) to a visual stimulus. The Central
Time (CT) segment extended from this evoked potential to the onset of the
EMG in the thumb. The Motor Execution Time (MT) was the latency between
EMG and the completion of the appropriate movement. These last three
segments (IT, CT, MT) are ipsative with respect to RT. That is, any one
is determined when RT and two others are known.

The four components were systematically varied as follows. The presence
or absence of a warning signal allowed the study of the effects of prior
preparation on the three subsequent segments. The intensity of the
response signal manipulated input time. Different numbers of items held
in memory allowed variation of central processing time, while the complexity of the response varied motor execution time.

The results from five studies will be briefly reported to demonstrate the
major findings pertinent to motor performance of the moderate and mildly
mentally retarded. These are as follows:

1.   The first study demonstrates the developmental trends of the
      segments of IT, CT, and MT during a simple non-warned
      reaction time task and shows the involvement of response
      initiation (Footnote #1).

2.   The second shows the effects of different levels of motor
      complexity on reaction time and the temporal segments.

3. The third shows the effects of cognitive activity in a memory search reaction time task.

4. The fourth demonstrates the developmental and MR differences in movement-related potentials and the relationship of these potentials to motor control.

5. Lastly, a study of the neural organization accompanying simple-motor tasks will present the role of development and MR for neural organization.

The overall design was one that used four groups of male subjects: children (6-8 yrs.), preadolescents (10-12 yrs.), young adults (16-18 yrs.), and a group of mentally retarded young adults (16-18 yrs.). The IQ's of the first three groups were in the normal range, while that of the MR had a mean of 65. The MR. therefore, were matched in chronological age to the young adults but in mental age to the preadolescents. It should be noted that the MR had no diagnosed neurological or organic impairment and were students at special education facilities. There were no serious impairments in any of the subjects.

A schematic of how the data were collected can be seen in Figure 2.

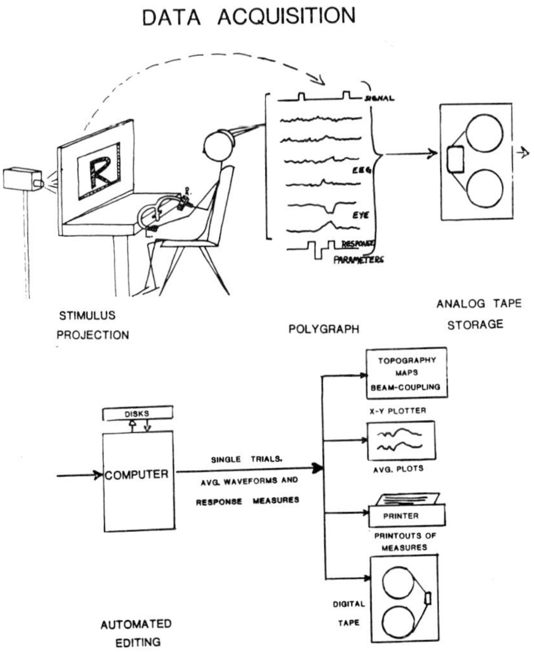

Figure 2
Schematic representation of data collection.

SIMPLE NON-WARNED RT

Subjects were instructed to respond as fast as possible to a light flash
by pressing a button switch in a hand-held cylinder. Event-related
potentials were recorded from the scalp, muscle potentials from the
responding thumb as well as the reaction time in pressing the button.
From these recordings the segments IT, CT, and MT during reaction time
were calculated. Input Time (IT) was the peak latency of the second
positive EP component after stimulus onset (P2), Cortico-muscle time (CT)
was the difference between the evoked potential latency and the beginning
of muscle activity in the thumb, and muscle execution time (MT) was the
difference between the onset of muscle activity and the closure of the
button switch. The data for each group are presented in Figure 3.

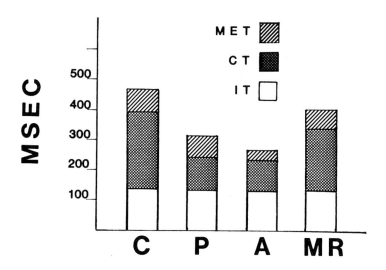

Figure 3
Non-warned reaction time task: Mean reaction times, input times,
central times, and motor execution times for the four groups.

It can be seen that RT decreased with age. The MR were significantly
slower than either the CA or MA matched non-retarded. It can also be seen
that CT and MT decreased with development but that IT remained the same
across the groups. The MR had significantly longer CT and MT than their
age-matched peers. Note that the MR were not different on IT indicating
that input processes, and attention to the response signal, were not
responsible for their slower RT.

To further determine the role of these segments to RT, the ten fastest and
slowest trials for each subject were selected and similar analyses done.
This can be seen in Figure 4.

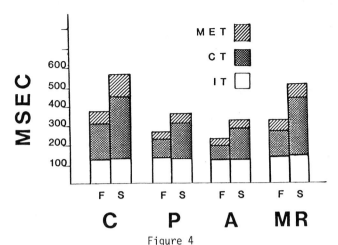

Figure 4
Non-warned reaction time task: Mean values (in Msec) for segments
and RT on each subject's fastest and slowest RT trials.

Again, there was no contribution of IT to slowness or fastness within a
subject. Central time, however, shows a significant effect with longer CT
on slow trials. There is also an interaction with groups: the CT of the
children and MR became relatively longer on slow trials than that of the
preadolescents or adults. Motor time also changed significantly from fast
to slow trials but there was no interaction with groups (p > 0.06).

In summary, this study demonstrated that the three segments were relatively independent. Input time was independent of age, speed, and retardation. Central time and MT decreased with age and speed. The MR were
particularly slow on both CT and MT (and this was true especially of CT on
slow trials, in similarity to the children). The slowness of the MR,
therefore, was primarily due to central processes with some contribution
from peripheral motor processes. This was also true for the non-retarded,
e.g., the children. The same processes had effects within the individual
as well as between the groups. It should be remembered that the CT
segment includes everything between stimulus registration and the beginning of the response in the peripheral muscle. Stimulus classification
and evaluation, response selection and response initiation would all be
included depending on the task requirements. The only requirement in this
task, however, was to initiate a known response whenever there was the
flash "go" signal. There was on stimulus evaluation or classification,
and no response selection requirement. Consequently, CT in this task
reflects response initiation.

While it is true that the same factors make for slowness in all groups,
the processes underlying response initiation are probably not the same
across the groups. This point will be returned to with evidence from the
neuro-electric data below.

If response initiation is a problem for responding quickly, along with
motor execution time, then these factors should be made more explicit by
manipulating the complexity of the response.

RESPONSE COMPLEXITY

Response complexity was manipulated by using the morse code responses "DIT/DAH" from the motor literature (Klapp, Wyatt, & MacLingo, 1974). The RT to perform a "DAH" is longer than the RT to perform a "DIT". Consequently, it is reasoned that the performance of a "DAH" requires more "programming" and is more complex than performance of a "DIT". The task entails a brief button press or a long button press. The subject sat with his thumb holding down the central button of three buttons in a row. When a letter appeared on the screen, the subject lifted his thumb from the central home button, traveled to an adjacent left target button, pressed a "DIT" (or a "DAH") and then returned to the home button. All this was done as fast as possible. There were no cognitive requirements of stimulus evaluation or decision involved. Thus, this was still a simple RT task. The motor programming for "DIT" or "DAH" could now be done prior to making the response because there was a warning signal that allowed the subject time to prepare to move. Blocks of fifty DIT and fifty DAH trials were obtained separately. In addition to recording initial RT and its segments, also collected were travel time from the central home key to the adjacent target key, the pause duration on the target key, and the return time to the home key. Subjects were instructed to complete the total sequence as fast as possible.

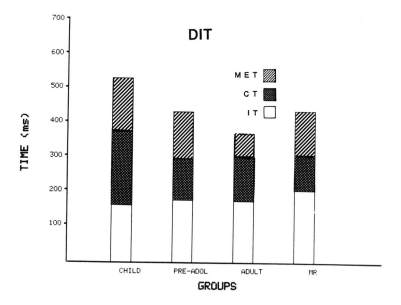

Figure 5
DIT task: Mean RT and segment values for the four groups.

The data are presented in Figure 5 for "DITS" -- the simpler response. As before, there was a developmental decrease in RT with the retarded as fast as the MA matched preadolescents but slower than their CA peers. Input time did not change across groups. Central time was slower only for the children. Motor time showed the main effect between groups and the MR were again similar to the preadolescents. The data are presented in Figure 6 for the more complex DAH response. It is again clear that the groups differed as before in RT. Interestingly, they again did not differ on CT (although there was a non-significant developmental decrease.) The

DAH

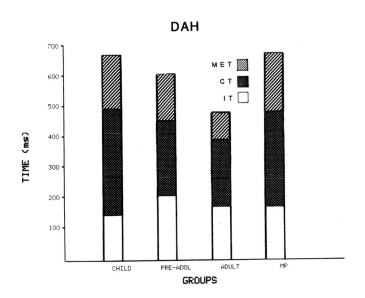

Figure 6
Figure 6. DAH task: Mean RT and segment values for the four groups.

IT was again not different across groups. Motor time was the main segment discriminating the groups. The MR had more than twice the MT of the adults while their RT was only about one third slower. This proportion was about the same as for the children. When the within-subject analysis of fast trials vs. slow trials was done, however, a different picture emerged (Figure 7). It is the CT segment that was responsible for slow trials within subjects rather than the MT segment that discriminated groups. The same effects occurred on the fast vs. slow DIT trials. Thus, this data shows the MR to be slower in the MT segment than the adults, but they were also slower in the CT segment on slow trials. The performance of the retarded approximated their MR peers.

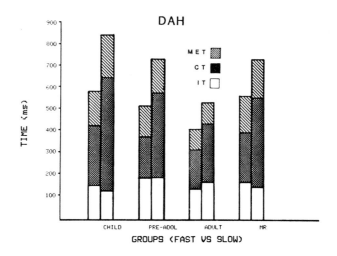

Figure 7
DAH task: Mean RT and segment values on each subject's
fast and slow RT trials.

As in the first study, response initiation and muscle activation were the
underlying processes. And these same factors held for the non-retarded.
The differences between CT in the non-warned RT task and in the DIT/DAH
task supports the interpretation of CT as response initiation. Both tasks
required no cognitive processing or response selection, only a known
response to any signal. Since the DIT/DAH task had a warning signal, the
preparation for response initiation was available prior to the "go" signal
and CT was not affected by response initiation (when considering mean
performance). In the non-warned RT task, the response initiation must
occur after the go signal within the CT segment resulting in large developmental trends and MR slowness. On the other hand, when subjects do not
utilize the preparation period during the DIT/DAH either to program the
DIT/DAH or to prepare to initiate, they exhibit a slow trial and increased
CT times. Therefore, on slow trials CT reflects the programming for
response duration as well as response initiation.

MEMORY SEARCH

If central processing is the most important factor that changes with
development and MR, then varying the central processing necessary for
responding should differentially affect the MR and the child who show
larger contributions of CT. The manipulation of specific central
processes should also give information on the nature of the CT measure.

The response stimuli and the motor response were identical to the response
complexity task. The only difference between tasks was that sets of 1, 3,
or 5 letters were memorized by the subject prior to blocks of 15 trials
for each set size. Set sizes were counterbalanced in a fixed-set procedure. There was a 50% probability of the stimulus letters being in-set or
out-of-set. After deciding whether the flashed letter was in-set or

out-of-set, the subject lifted his thumb off the home button and pressed the left target button (in-set) or right target button (out-of-set) and then returned to press down the central home button (side of target button was counterbalanced).

In contrast to the response complexity task, there was a specific cognitive load in this memory task. The subjects must decide after the response signal whether the letter was in-set or out-of-set. There was an additional motor process also: response selection; to go to the right or left target button depending on whether the stimulus letter was in or out of set. After decision and response selection, the initiation of the appropriate movement was needed as in the other tasks. The data for the initial RT (lifting off the home button) as a function of set size is in Figure 8.

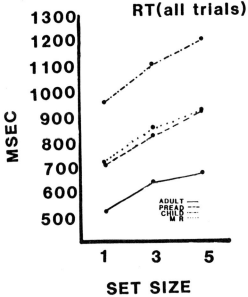

Figure 8
Sternberg task: Mean RT as a function of set-size for four groups.

It is clear that RT was a function of set-size for all four groups. There was significant group differences and set size effects, but there was no interaction of set-size with age or MR. Children were slower than preadolescents or the adults but not slower than the MR. This latter result was just beyond significance (p = .058) due to the variability of the children. The adults were significantly faster than the preadolescents and MR. The equivalent MA groups, preadolescents and MR, did not differ in speed. There, was no slope difference between groups, Thus, the time to search through the items in memory was the same for the MR and the other groups. The groups did not differ in number of errors because all were essentially at the ceiling. Figure 9 shows the segments of IT, CT, and MT as a function of set size.

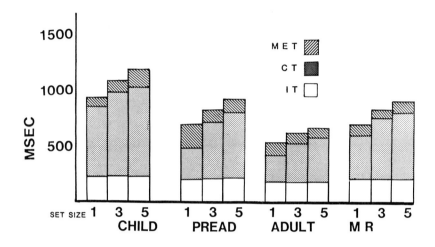

Figure 9
Sternberg task:　Mean values for segments and RT as a function
of set-size for each group.

Groups differ on CT but not on MT.　The preadolescents and MR again had
equivalent CT as they did for RT.　There was also a significant small
effect of IT.　Children were slower in IT than the other groups and the
adults were faster than the preadolescents and MR.　This IT difference is
on the order of 30 to 50 msec between MR and adults and between children
and adults respectively -- less than 5% of the total RT.

In sum, the MR again differed most on the CT segment that now included a
cognitive factor, decision, and an additional motor factor, response
selection.　They again matched their MR peers in CT and IT.　Response
initiation and response selection were the key processes in CT.　Input
time probably reflected decision time in this task because the EP latency
was longer than for comparable stimuli in the DIT/DAH.　Task that required
no decision and since the error rate indicated no lapse in attention.

TASK DIFFERENCES

Some perspective on the action of these factors can be obtained by comparing the measures across tasks.　Comparing RT (Figure 10) one sees the
strong developmental change with the MR usually matching the MA group in
performance.　Making the response more complex increased RT as did requiring a cognitive process.　Task demands increased RT and increased the
difference between the non-retarded groups' performance.　The retarded, on
the other hand, become more similar to their MA matched peers.

REACTION TIME

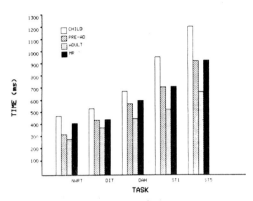

Figure 10
Comparison of RT across tasks for the four groups.
Arranged in putative order of task demands.

Figure 11 presents the CT data across tasks. Increasing task demands,
response complexity and cognitive load increased CT for all groups. The MR
matched their MA matched peers except for the non-warned RT task. For the
MT segment, however, the picture is different (Figure 12). The response
complexity instruction increased MT for all groups but affected the adults
relatively little. The adults' MT was affected equally by the complex DAH
and the memory search requirement. The MT of the retarded was most
affected by the complexity manipulation (DIT/DAH). Cognitive load did not
increase the MT of any group.

CENTRAL TIME

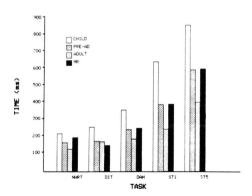

Figure 11
Comparison of central time across tasks for the four groups.

In summary, the MR slowness was primarily in CT due to the processes of response selection and response initiation. There was also a contribution to slowness from muscle recruitment. Decision time added a further small proportion to their RT.

MOTOR EXECUTION TIME

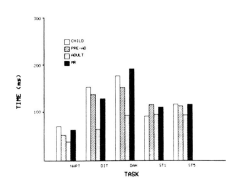

Figure 12
Comparison across tasks of motor execution time for the four groups.

RESPONSE SEQUENCE

There are other data from these tasks that implicate response initiation: the measures of travel time, pause duration and return time. While these are independent of initial RT, there is a high correlation between travel and return time and a moderate one between travel and pause. While the MR had clear differences in central time and in motor time in executing the initial RT response the subsequent parts of the response sequence discriminated the MR even more strongly. Travel time to the appropriate target button was significantly different between groups for both the response complexity and the memory search task (Figure 13). The MR were slower than all non-retarded groups and there was a developmental decrease of travel time in the non-retarded. The MR were proportionately more slow in travel time than on either the CT or MT measures.

TRAVEL TIME

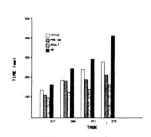

Figure 13
Comparison across tasks of travel time between RT button
and target button for the four groups.

The MR were almost twice as slow as the adults while the children were
about 50% slower than the adults. The more complex response (DAH) had
significantly longer travel times than the simpler response (DIT) across
groups. <u>Pause time</u> on the button showed the groups to be essentially
equivalent for the DAH task. This demonstrated that the interpretation of
the task was the same across age and MR. On the other hand, why were the
DIT and the memory task pause times over 100% longer in the MR. This
could be due to response initiation. Given enough time on the target
button in the DAH response the MR can generate the initiation of the
response back to the home key. Thus, the large effect of pause time in
the DIT and memory search tasks is due to the time to generate response
initiation when the pause on the target button must be executed quickly.
<u>Return times</u> reflect the same group differences as do travel since they
were highly correlated.

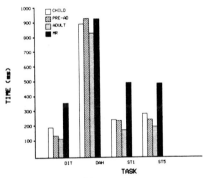

Figure 14
Comparison across tasks of pause time on target button
for the four groups.

The MR were slower than all other groups. DAHS again had longer return
times than the DITS, but all times were faster than for travel times.

RETURN TIME

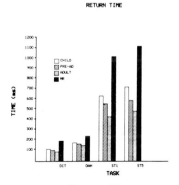

Figure 15
Comparison across tasks of return time from target button back
to RT button for the four groups.

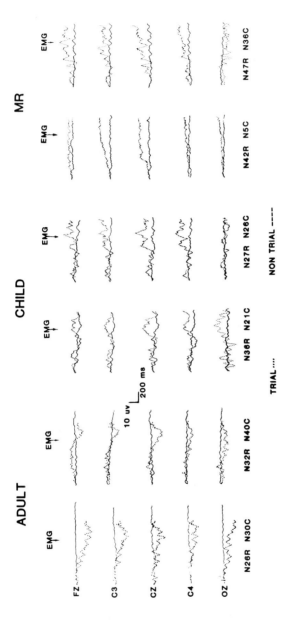

Figure 16

Averaged waveforms of movement-related potentials preceding a voluntary
non-cued button press for adults, children, and MR subjects.
Each column is one subject's data at each brain region. Waveforms were
time-locked to onset of muscle activity (EMG) in the responding
dominant thumb. Solid lines are averaged control trials taken
from the spontaneous EEG between button presses. N equals number of
trials in each average. Positivity of waveforms is upwards.

Cognitive load increased all three measures over the comparable response DIT task. This was most dramatic for return time in which all groups increased substantially from the DIT/DAH task even while memory load itself had little effect. The times in the DIT/DAH task reflect the motor processes during return. The additional time in the memory search task must be due to continued cognitive processing after having made the target response.

NEUROELECTRIC MANIFESTATIONS

What may be some of the neuroelectric processes that underlie slow response initiation and motor performance? There are two pieces of evidence that are of interest: movement related potentials and neural organization. First of all, it is clear the simple measures of evoked potential latencies, at least of the sensory related components that reflect the initial stages of processing, are not contributing to slowness since they were equivalent for the MR, and the non-retarded (for N1 and P1). Similarly, event-related potential (ERP) amplitudes are often similar (Karrer, Warren & Ruth, 1978). This supports the lack of an input of attentional problem associated with slowness. Evidence from the present studies (e.g., the memory search task, Karrer & McDonough, 1980) and previous studies (Karrer & Ivins, 1976) indicates that the neural underpinnings of preparation and expectancy, as indicated by the size of the contingent negative variation (CNV) that occurs between the warning and response signal, are also not different in the MR than in their normal age mates.

MOVEMENT-RELATED POTENTIALS

Of specific concern for motor control are the movement-related potentials (MRP) that precede every voluntary movement. The earliest component of the MRP that precedes movement is the "Readiness potential" that reflects the intentional aspect of organizing the initiation of the movement. This may begin one to two seconds prior to discrete movements. A considerable number of the young adult MR (50%) have movement-related potentials (MRP) that are of opposite polarity than their equal aged normal peers. These positive-going MRPs, are quite similar in waveshape and polarity to those of young children, aged normals (over 65 years) and Parkinsonian patients (Deecke, 1980; Deecke et al., 1977; Karrer, Warren, & Ruth, 1978; Warren & Karrer, 1984a; Warren & Karrer, 1984b). Examples of the different wave-shapes during development can be seen in Figure 16. Normal adults have a

negative-going waveform preceding the onset of muscle activity that
reflects the organization of readiness to respond. There is a developmental change in the waveform with the young and the MR characterized by
positive components preceding movement. We have been trying to determine
the function of this positivity to the behavior of the child and the MR.
Briefly, the size of the positivity appears to index the subjects' effort
at inhibiting what he is not supposed to move -- the control of motor
overflow or associated movement. If one analyzes the waveform as a
function of motor control an orderly relationship is found. Greater
positivity in the waveform occurs in those individuals that have much
associated movement that is successfully controlled on the target trial.
This can be seen in Figure 17 for non-retarded young children. Therefore,

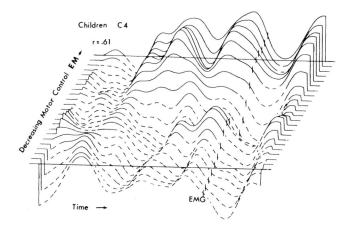

Figure 17
Relation between motor control and movement-related potential polarity
and waveshape at right motor region (C4) for children (age 6-8 yrs.).
All were right-handed. Positivity in the waveform is upwards.

response slowness may in part be due to the use by the MR and young child
of their resources to control non-target associated movements rather than
in executing the target movements. There is also the possibility that the
positivity reflects a different neural arrangement in the MR (see Karrer,
Warren, & Ruth, 1978).

NEURAL ORGANIZATION

Across all of these neuroelectric studies, however, another type of clue
appears that may be the most important, not only for motor behavior slowness, but also for other performance impairments of the mild and moderate
MR. This clue is the topography of the various neuroelectric measures in
the MR compared to the non-retarded. Galbraith first reported some of
this evidence over ten years ago. He found a decrease in amplitude of
visual evoked potentials from posterior to central regions of the brain in
the MR compared to normals (Galbraith et al., 1976). We have found
repeatedly that there are differences in topography even when latencies

and amplitudes may not differ (Karrer & Ivins, 1976). The evidence for
differences in topography has been recently reviewed (Karrer, Nelson &
Galbraith, 1979; Karrer & Warren, 1979).

One way of studying the organization of neural activity that is reflected
in topographical differences is to use EEG coherence measures. EEG coherence basically reflects the relationship of one region of the brain to
another. Galbraith and colleagues (1976) also reported EEG coherence
differences between retarded and nonretarded. Normals had more shared
activity between brain regions. We have found similar results using a
somewhat different measure. In an attempt to develop procedures for
studying neural patterns on the head in the brief time of an event related
potential, we have used correlations of our measures between electrodes
over different brain regions (Gevins, 1983; Gevins et al., 1981). We have
found a developmental pattern into which the MR do not easily fit (Karrer
& Johnson, in press). For example, Figure 18 shows the correlations
between brain regions as a function of development and MR for the non-
warned RT task. There is increasing correlation or linkage between brain

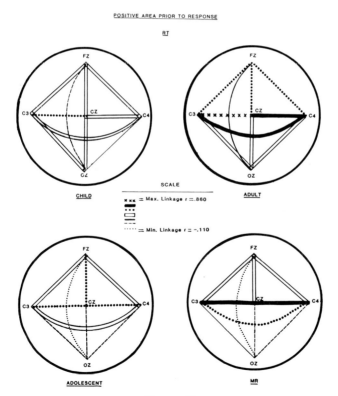

Figure 18
Correlations between brain regions for the four groups
performing a non-warned RT task.

regions with development. Thus, there seems to be an increasing integration of neural activity between cortical regions with age. In overall
strength of linkage (mean Z score), the MR are equivalent to their MA
matched peers but their pattern is clearly different from MA or CA matched
peers. The linkage relates both to IQ and to RT speed in ways that invoke
a localization of function type of concept, i.e., the faster the RT or
higher the IQ, the less the linkage in <u>specific</u> brain regions. At first,
this appears contradictory to the greater overall linkage that occurs with
development. However, differentiation of neural regions may be the
process that makes this result meaningful. It may be that at any developmental level of integration of the brain, the fewer neural regions one
needs to utilize in order to perform a task, the more efficient and
effective the behavior (e.g., IQ or RT). The main point, however, is the
MR pattern of linkage. They do not resemble their CA matched nor their MA
matched peers, nor younger children in the overall linkage between
regions. In fact, by comparing specific brain regions between the MR and
the other groups, it is found that there are regions in the retarded that
match different regions in all three of the non-retarded groups. For
example, in Figure 18, it can be seen that the anterior regions match the
child, the posterior regions resemble the preadolescents, while central
regions either lie between the preadolescents and adults or resemble the
adults. There is clearly something extraordinary about the neuroelectric
organization of the MR. We have done this type of analysis for most of
the tasks in the RT project with similar results. There are two speculations that come to mind to explain this apparently different neural
organization in the MR: there is improper timing in the neural development of the MR such that an aberrant functional hookup between regions
resulted. Or, these moderate to mild MR have acquired strategies for
doing these tasks that are different than the nonretarded and this is
reflected in the regional relationships of neural activity. These
different strategies require the activation of neural systems and
relationships that are inefficient and ineffective leading to the impaired
performance. A further analysis of brain patterns during task performance
is essential to place these exciting speculations upon some empirical
ground.

CONCLUSION

These studies support the role of motor processes in response slowness of
the mild to moderate retarded. These motor processes are response selection, response initiation, as well as muscle execution. When performing a
motor sequence, <u>travel time</u> (movement time of Jensen, 1982) becomes a most
important contributor to slowness. It is not clear whether <u>travel time</u>
and <u>return time</u> contain the process of initiating the direction to the
successive movements or involves the interference of cognitive processing
during transit. Travel time contributes progressively more to total speed
with each movement required (e.g., return time). It is of some importance
that the process of registration of the stimulus, given a testing procedure that assures at least minimal attention, and the process of searching
through memory contribute little or nothing to response slowness in the
MR. If the task calls for a decision on the information in the stimuli,
there is a small increase in processing time. The intention to perform a
motor act, as reflected in the "Readiness potential", is as evident as in
the normal but often reflects the control of unwanted acts rather than the
control of target acts (like the young normal child).

In summary:

1. The process of response initiation, of beginning a motor act, is the major contributor to slowness in simple motor tasks.

2. The neural manifestation of response initiation and motor readiness has a different morphology in the retarded and in younger nonretarded. This morphology may be related to the control of movement and/or neural structures.

3. Motor execution time, the process of activating and recruiting appropriate peripheral muscles adds a small but significant amount to slowness in simple tasks.

4. Response selection adds further slowness in tasks in which two motor responses are possible.

5. Cognitive activity compounds these effects by adding slowness in decision times during recognizing or categorizing stimuli.

6. There are differences in the patterning of neural activity across the brain regions in the retarded that could be associated with differences in structures or in strategies of task performance. The data suggests that neural organization may be an essential part of their impairments.

There are many sources to the slowness of the MR that can be minimized of maximized by the task demands. The present studies have emphasized motor processes. Of greatest importance, perhaps, is the evidence for a different neural organization underlying the performance effects that may pervade various task characteristics.

REFERENCES

Baumeister, A. A., & Kellas, G. (1968). Reaction time and mental retardation. In N. R. Ellis (Ed.), International review of research in mental retardation (Vol 3). NY: Academic.

Berkson, G. (1960). An analysis of reaction time in normal and mentally deficient young men. II. Variation of complexity in reaction time tasks. Journal of Mental Deficiency Research, 4, 59-67.

Clausen, J. (1966). Ability structure and subgroups in mental retardation. Washington, D.C.: Spartan Books.

Deecke, L. (1980). Influence of age on the human cerebral potentials associate with voluntary movements. In D. G. Stein (Ed.), The psychobiology of aging: Problems and perspectives. Amsterdam: Elsevier.

Deecke, L., Englitz, H. G., Kornhuber, H. H., & Schmitt, G. (1977). Cerebral potentials preceding voluntary movement in patients with bilateral or unilateral parkinsonakinesia. In J. E. Desmedt (Ed.), Attention, voluntary contraction, and event-related cerebral potentials. Basel: Karger.

Galbraith, G. C., Gliddon, J. B., & Busk, J. (1976). Electrophysiological studies of mental retardation. In R. Karrer (Ed.), Developmental psychophysiology of mental retardation. Springfield, IL: C. C. Thomas.

Gevins, A. (1983). Brain potential (BP) evidence for lateralization of higher cognitive functions. In J. P. Hellige (Ed.), Cerebral hemisphere assymmetry. NY: Praeger.

Gevins, A., Doyle, J. C., Cutillo, B. A., Schaffer, R. E., Tannehill, R. S., Ghannan, J. H., Gilcrease, V. A., & Yeager, C. L. (1981). Electrical potentials in human brain during cognition: New method reveals dynamic patterns of correlation. Science, 213, 918-922.

Jensen, A. R., & Munro, E. (1979). Reaction time, movement time, intelligence. Intelligence, 3, 121-126.

Karrer, R., & Ivins, J. (1976). Steady potentials accompanying perception and response in mentally retarded and normal children. In R. Karrer (Ed.), Developmental psychophysiology of mental retardation. Springfield, IL: C. C. Thomas.

Karrer, R., & Johnson, C. (in press). Are correlations between leads of slow preparatory ERP components an index of neural organization? In W. C. McCallum, R. Zappoli, & F. Denoth (Eds.), Advances in brain research, Suppl., EEG clin. neurophysiology.

Karrer, R., Nelson, M., & Galbraith, G. C. (1979). Psychophysiology of mental retardation. In N. R. Ellis (Ed.), Handbook of research in mental retardation (2nd Edition). Hillsdale, NJ: L. Erlbaum.

Karrer, R., & Warren, C. (1979). Functional organization of the brain in the mentally retarded: Evidence from event-related potentials. In J. Obiols, C. Ballus, E. Gonzalez Monclus, & J. Pujol (Eds.), Biological psychiatry today, NY: Elsevier/North Holland.

Karrer, R., & Warren, C., & Ruth, R. (1978). Steady potential activity of the brain preceding non-cued and cued movement: Effects of development and mental retardation. In D. Otto (Ed.), Multidisciplinary perspectives on event-related brain potentials. Washington, D.C.: U.S. Government Printing Office, EPA.

Karrer, R., & Warren, C., Daruna, J., & Cone, R. (1981). Temporal segments of response speed during development and in the mentally retarded. Psychophysiology, 18, 178, Abstract.

Klapp, S. T., Wyatt, E. P., & MacLingo, W. (1974). Response programming in simple and choice reactions. Journal of Motor Behavior, 6, 263-271.

Warren, C., & Karrer, R. (1984a). Movement-related potentials in chil-
    dren: A replication of waveforms and their relationships to age,
    performance and cognitive development. In R. Karrer, J. Cohen, & P.
    Tueting (Eds.), Brain and information: Event-related potentials
    (Vol. 425, pp. 489-495). NY: N.Y. Academy of Sciences.

Warren, C., & Karrer, R. (1984b). Movement-related potentials during
    development: A replication and extension of relationships to age,
    motor control, mental status, and IQ. International Journal of
    Neuroscience, 24, 81-96.

FOOTNOTE

1.   These results were first reported in partial form at the AAMD
      meetings, Chicago, 1976 (Karrer, R., Warren, C., & Ruth, R. An
      analysis of response initiation of the retarded) and at the Society
      for Psychophysiological Research meetings, Vancouver, B.C., 1980
      (Karrer, Warren, Daruna & Cone, 1981).

Motor Skill Acquisition of the Mentally Handicapped:
Issues in Research and Training
M.G. Wade (editor)
Elsevier Science Publishers B.V. (North-Holland), 1986

MENTAL DEVELOPMENT, RESPONSE SPEED, AND NEURAL ACTIVITY

Jorge H. Daruna

Department of Psychiatry and Neurology
Tulane University School of Medicine
1415 Tulane Avenue
New Orleans, LA 70112

The notion that intelligent individuals are mentally more agile has been supported by recent behavioral studies. These studies have demonstrated that measures of reaction time derived from a variety of simple tasks are sensitive to cognitive development, correlate with general intelligence, and discriminate between normal and mentally retarded individuals (see Jensen, 1982, for comprehensive review). It follows from such findings that mental development and general intelligence must reflect to a significant degree the basic neural properties which determine the brain's information processing speed.

The present chapter is concerned with delineating neural properties which might underlie the brain's information processing speed by reviewing the evidence linking intelligence (as defined by various psychometric tests) to measures of the brain's electrical activity. The review is restricted to studies conducted within the last twenty years (see Liberson, 1966; Vogel and Broverman, 1964, for reviews of older studies) in which similar measures of neural activity have been examined by independent investigators.* The findings for each individual measure of neural activity are reported and an attempt is made to integrate them into a coherent picture. Inferences are then made regarding the underlying neural properties reflected in the findings as well as their significance for speed of information processing and mental retardation. The chapter concludes with a suggestion for further research.

STUDIES OF BRAIN ACTIVITY AND INTELLIGENCE

There are more than twenty-five relevant papers which have examined either stimulus evoked brain activity (i.e., event related potentials) (See Tables 1-4) or the power spectrum of the spontaneous electroencephalogram (EEG) (See Table 5).

It is evident in Tables 1 through 5 that the studies have examined diverse samples, relied on different measures of intelligence, employed a variety of tasks or stimulus conditions, and differed with respect to recording

---

*The focus on measures examined by more than one independent investigator excludes from consideration several studies which have analyzed the relationship between intelligence and prestimulus neural activity (e.g., Karrer & Ivins, 1976; Karrer, Warren, & Ruth, 1978; Warren & Karrer, 1984) or have quantified EEG activity by visual methods (Giannitrapani, 1969).

technique. The studies are also characterized by various technical flaws, the most severe being the failure to ensure that artifactual activity (i.e., due to eye-blinks, muscle tension, or head movements) did not contaminate the measures of neural activity. As a result of the diverse nature of the studies it is not possible to infer neural properties from findings which are reliable by the criterion of independent replication across methodologically homogeneous studies. Thus, the strategy adopted in this review is to attempt to account for divergent results by considering the methodological and sampling differences across studies, and then, to draw inferences regarding underlying neural properties from the overall pattern of findings.

Table 1

ERP Studies of Younger Subjects (Mean Age < 16 Yrs.)
Using a Monopolar Derivation for Recording

Reference	Sample Character- istics	IQ Tests[@] & Recording Technique #	Stimuli and Task	Significant Findings
Perry et al. (1976)	Normal (N=98) IQ Range: 94-144 Mean=119.5 SD=9.6 Age-Range: 5-6 yrs. Mean=5.7 yrs. Sex-49% males Race-100% Caucasion	WPPSI BW=1-50Hz C-A	S was required to visually fixate for 30 sec upon the center of a 6^0 circle. S was stimulated with flashes (2.35 log ft.-L) at two rates (6/sec, 15 msec duration or 2/sec, 50 msec duration) and with a "sunburst" pattern (2.2 log ft-L 50 msec) at 2/sec. Stimuli were presented within blocks. No response was required.	1) Latency of largest nega- tive peak (in response to 2/sec flashes) directly re- lated to IQ. 2) Maximum amplitude (overall) in- versely re- lated to IQ.
Rhodes et al. (1969)	Bright (N=20) IQ Range: 120-140 Mean=130 Dull (N=20) IQ Range: 70-90 Mean=79 Age-Range: 10-11 yrs. Sex-50% males	WISC BW=0.8-50Hz O-A C-A	S was required to push a button after the 4th and 6th flashes (1 flash per 2 sec) in each sequence of 10. Flashes were	1) Waveform Contour length (100- 250) directly related to IQ 2) Amplitude of P100-N140, N140-P180,

Table 1--Continued

Reference	Sample Characteristics	IQ Tests[@] & Recording Technique #	Stimuli and Task	Significant Findings
			reflected from a white half-dome at 3 different intensities (.65, 1.15, and $2.05 \times 10^{+2}$ lumens /cm^2).	and P180-N230 directly related to IQ. 3) Latency of N230 at O1 & O2 inversely related to IQ.
Osaka & Osaka (1980)	Normal (N=8) IQ Range: 110-130 Mean=118 Retarded (N=8) IQ Range: 54-76 Mean=66 Age-Range: 12-13 yrs. Race-100% Oriental	Suzuki-Binet TC=.3 sec. O-A	S was required to fixate on center of white screen (900cd /m^2) and passively view flashes of 1msec duration presented at 1/ sec. No response directly required.	1) Latency of N70 inversely related to IQ 2) Amplitude of P100-N120 & N120-P170 directly related to IQ. 3) Total power & power above 10 Hz directly related to IQ.
Hendrickson (1982)	Normal (N=219) IQ Mean=107.7 SD=13.9 Age mean=15.6 yrs. SD=1.13 yrs. Sex-55% males	WAIS BW=?-OO C-M	S passively listened to tones (1000 Hz, 85 db, 30 msec) presented via earphones at pseudo randomly ordered intervals between 1 and 8 sec. No response was required.	1) Waveform contour length (0-256 msec) directly related to IQ.
Dustman et al. (1976)	Normal-High SES Not Poor (N=57) IQ-Range: 70-131 Mean= 109.8 SD=11.6 Normal-Low SES (N=114) IQ-Range: 62-133	WISC CFIT O-A C-A	See Rhodes et al. (1969)	High SES 1) Amplitude of N150 & P200 at O2 inversely related to IQ. 2) Latency of P200 at C3

Table 1--Continued

Reference	Sample Character-istics	IQ Tests[@] & Recording Technique [#]	Stimuli and Task	Significant Findings
	Mean: 87.8 SD=13.5 Age-Range: 4-15 yrs. Mean=9.8 yrs. SD=3.1 yrs.			and N250 at C3 & C4 directly re-lated to IQ. Low SES 3) Amplitude of N90 at O1 inversely re-lated to IQ.
Bigum et al. (1970)	Normal (N=24) Down's Syndrome (N=24) Age-Range: 6-16.6 yrs. Sex-38% males	? BW:0.8-250Hz O-A C-A	S passively (?) viewed flashes (10 usec,1.15x 10^2 phots) pre-sented at a rate of 1 every 2-3 sec. S was also presented with electric shocks (0.1msec) 2.5 times thres-hold intensity delivered to the index finger in order to evoke somatosensory responses. Flash and shock ses-sions were ran-domly ordered within each experimental ses-sion. No response was required.	Visual Modality 1) Amplitude of N60-P80 at O1 & O2 directly related to IQ 2) Latencies of P140, N175, P235 & N290 at O1 & O2 were inverse-ly related to IQ. 3) Amplitude of N190-P260 at C3 & C4 was inversely re-lated to IQ. 4) Latencies of N60 & N190 at C3 & C4 were directly re-lated to IQ.
Callaway (1975)	Normal (N=119) Age-Range: 6-15 yrs. Sex-51% males	VMI WISC BW:DC-50Hz C-A C-C	S passively viewed flashes (intensity=8) reflected from a white half-dome. S then passively lis-	Auditory Modality 1) Amplitude of N100-P200 directly re-lated to IQ. 2) Latency of P80 & P200

Table 1--Continued

Reference	Sample Character- istics	IQ Tests[@] & Recording Technique [#]	Stimuli and Task	Significant Findings
			tened to tones (1000 Hz, 70 db, 500 msec). In- terval between stimuli varied between 1.5 and 3 sec. No response was required.	directly re- lated to IQ.
Thatcher et al. (1982)	Normal (N=191) Age-Range: 5-16 yrs. Sex - 54% males Race - c.a.87% Caucasian	WPPSI WISC-R BW:5-30Hz O-A P-A C-A	S passively viewed flashes rear projected on screen sub- tending 12 deg. of visual angle. S passively listened to clicks presented either at 1/sec or at random interstimulus intervals between 1 and 3 sec. No response was required.	1) None

[@] Armed Forces Qualifications Test (AFQT), Bender-Gestalt (B-G), Culture Fair Intelligence Test (CFIT), Columbia Mental Maturity Test (CMMT), Cattell and Peabody Tests (CPT), General Classification Test (GCT), Large-Thorndike Test (L-T), Measures of Fluid and Crystallized Intelligence (MFCI), Otis Quick Scoring Test (OQST), Primary Mental Abilities Test (PMAT), Peabody Picture Vocabulary Test (PPVT), Raven Advanced Progressive Matrices (RAPM), Raven Standard Progressive Matrices (RSPM) Stanford-Binet Intelligence Test (S-B), SRA Achievement Series (SRA), Visual-Motor Integration Test (VMI), Wechsler Adult Intelligence Scale (WAIS), Wechsler Intelligence Scale for Children (WISC)-Revised (WISC-R), and Wechsler Preschool and Primary Scale of Intelligence (WPPSI).

[#] Amplifier band width (BW) and/or Time Constant (TC)

Electrode location-Central (C), Earlobe (A), Frontal (F), Mastoid (M), Occipital (O), Parietal (P), and Temporal (T).

Table 2

ERP Studies of Older Subjects (Mean Age > 16 Yrs.)
Using a Monopolar Derivation for Recording

Reference	Sample Character- istics	IQ Tests[@] & Recording Technique #	Stimuli and Task	Significant Findings
Callaway (1975)	Navy Recruits "mostly normal" (Ns=46-145) for different samples Age-Range:16-21 yrs. Sex-100% male Race-c.a. 64-78% Caucasion	AFQT GCT TC=0.3 BW=0.1-50Hz C-A	Task demands changed for different sam- ples. 1) Pas- sively listen to tone (60db, 500msec) pairs followed by passive viewing of flash pairs. Interstimulus interval 1.5 sec. within a pair and 7 sec. between pairs. 2) S presented with tones (1 KHz, 65db, 50msec) and flashes (50msec) and asked to either passively view them or press button to occasion- ally dim flashes. 3) S pressed button to self-present tone, passively viewed 2 flashes and repeated the process again.	Visual Modality 1) None Auditory Modality 2) Latency of P60 & P180 direct- ly related to IQ.
Dustman and Callner (1979)	Normal (N=66) IQ-Mean=115.5 SD=8.2 Down's Syndrome (N=66) IQ-Mean=31.6 SD=4.5 Age-Range: 5-62 yrs. Sex-50% male	S-B OQST WISC WAIS O-A C-A F-A	S was passively stimulated in three modali- ties within a session. Stimu- li were flashes (10msec, 12 lux), clicks (.25msec,80db) and shocks to to the right index finger.	Visual and Audi- tory Modalities 1) Contour length (80-220 msec) was inversely related to IQ. 2) Change in con- tour length with stimulus repetition was directly re- lated to IQ.

Table 2--Continued

Reference	Sample Character-istics	IQ Tests[@] & Recording Technique [#]	Stimuli and Task	Significant Findings
			Interstimulus interval varied between 2 to 4 secs. No response was required.	
Shagass et al. (1981)	Normal (N=20) Raven's IQ Mean=61 SD=27 Psychiatric Patients (N=80) Raven's IQ Mean=53 SD=30 Age-Range: 16-67 yrs. Sex-54% male	RSPM TC=.45 sec O-A T-A C-A F-A	S was passively stimulated in three modali-ties within a session. Stimuli were a checkerboard pattern (8 msec, 1.2ftL), clicks (.1msec, 50db) & elec-tric shocks to the median nerve (wrist). Adja-cent stimuli were never in the same modal-ity. Inter-stimulus interval ranged between 1.5 and 2 sec. No response was required.	Visual Modality 1) Amplitudes (75-450 msec) directly re- lated to IQ in normals. 2) Latency of P200 directly related to IQ in normals. Auditory Modality 1) Contour length (18- 460 msec) inversely re- lated to IQ in patients. 2) Amplitude (40-450 msec) directly re- lated to IQ in normals. 3) Amplitude (0-100 msec) inversely re- lated to IQ in patients. 4) Amplitude (100-450msec) directly re- lated to IQ in patients.
Blink-horn and Hend-rickson (1982)	Normal (N=33) Superior IQ Range Age-Range: 18-36 Sex - 50% male	RAPM BW=?-00 C-M	Passive listen-ing to tones (1000 Hz, 85db, 30msec) with eyes closed.	1) Contour length (0-256 msec) direct- ly related to IQ.

Table 2--Continued

Reference	Sample Character- istics	IQ Tests[@] & Recording Technique #	Stimuli and Task	Significant Findings
			Random inter- stimulus inter- val between 1 and 8 sec. No response was required.	
Strau- manis et al. (1973)	Normal (N=20) IQ-Above Average Range Retarded (N=32) IQ-Range: 14-44 Mean=30 Age-Range: 17-33 yrs. Mean=21.7 Sex-44% male	RSPM S-B CPT TC=.24 sec C-M	Passive listen- ing to clicks (.1msec, 60db) presented every 2 sec. No response was required.	1) Amplitude of P50 was in- versely re- lated to IQ.
Schafer (1982)	Normal (N=74) IQ Range: 98-135 Mean=118 Retarded (N=52) IQ Range: 18-68 Mean=37 Age-Range: 15-57 Mean=28.6 yrs. Sex-48% male	WAIS S-B Leiter BW=3-30Hz C-A	S passively listened to clicks (60db) 1 per 2 sec. S self initiated clicks by button press at irregular intervals. S passively listened to clicks controlled by tape recording of self-initiated clicks.	1) Amplitude change across conditions directly re- lated to IQ.

@# See Table 1

Table 3

ERP Studies of Younger Subjects (Mean Age < 16 Yrs.)
Using a Dipolar Derivation for Recording

Reference	Sample Character- istics	IQ Tests[@] & Recording Technique #	Stimuli and Task	Significant Findings
Engle and Hender- son (1973)	Normal (N=119) IQ-Mean=95.5 SD=14.6 Age-Range: 7-8 yrs. Sex-55% male Race-64% Caucasian	WISC B-G O-F O-C	S passively viewed a flash (intensity=8) triggered at the discretion of a technician who continuously observed S. No response was required.	1) None
Flinn et al. (1977)	Normal (N=64) IQ-Dist. below 80 (N=6) 80-129 (N=50) above 130 (N=8) Median=110 Age-Range: 12-13 yrs. Sex-0% male	L-T SRA WISC BW=0.3-50Hz P-F	S passively viewed a flash (2-4x10^5 lumens) presented every 1.6 sec. No response was required.	1) Power at lower fre- quencies ($<$ 12Hz) inversely re- lated to IQ. 2) Power at higher fre- quencies ($>$ 30Hz) directly re- lated to IQ.
Gucker (1973)	Normal (N=17) IQ-Range: 92-137 Age-Range: 8-13 yrs.	WISC PPVT P-F	S passively received with eyes closed a flash (inten- sity = 16) triggered by an EEG zero crossing detector. No response was required.	1) Latency to third base- line crossing was inversely related to IQ
Ertl (1973) Ertl and Schafer (1969)	Normal (N=573) IQ-Mean=105.2 SD=13.1 Age-Range: 7-15 yrs.	WISC PMAT OQST BW=3-50Hz	S passively viewed flashes presented with an interstimulus interval which	1) Latency to baseline crossing be- tween 30 and 200 msec was

Table 3--Continued

Reference	Sample Character-istics	IQ Tests[@] & Recording Technique [#]	Stimuli and Task	Significant Findings
	Mean=10.8 SD=2.2	P-F	ranged from .8 to 1.8 sec. No response was required.	inversely related to IQ. 2) Power at higher frequencies (18-29Hz) in the range of 48 to 192 msec was directly related to IQ
Davis (1971)	Normal≈(N 1000) Age-Range: 5-14 yrs. Uneven Dist. Preschoolers 1st & 7th Graders Race-50% Caucasian	WPPSI WISC PMAT P-F	S passively viewed flashes. No response was required.	1) None.

[@][#] See Table 1

Table 4

ERP Studies of Older Subjects (Mean Age > 16 Yrs.)
Using a Dipolar Derivation for Recording

Reference	Sample Character-istics	IQ Tests[@] & Recording Technique [#]	Stimuli and Task	Significant Findings
Callaway (1975)	See Table 2	BW=5-50Hz P-C P-F	See Table 2	1) Latency of P185 was inversely related to IQ in Black recruits. 2) Latency to first baseline crossing

Table 4--Continued

Reference	Sample Character- istics	IQ Tests[@] & Recording Technique [#]	Stimuli and Task	Significant Findings
				was inversely related to IQ in Caucasian recruits.
Chalke and Ertl (1965)	Graduate Students (N=33) IQ-Superior Range Arm Cadets (N=11) IQ-low average Range Retarded (N=4) IQ-Range: 50-65 Age-Range: 17-41 yrs. Mean=28 yrs.	? P-F	S passively viewed flashes presented at random intervals. No response was required.	1) Latencies to the 3rd, 4th and 5th base- line-crossing were inverse- ly related to IQ.
Weinberg (1969)	Normal (N=42) IQ-Range: 77-146 Age-Range: 18-39 yrs.	WAIS TC=0.3 sec 0-0	S passively viewed flashes (20msec, 10^5 lumens) presented at an average interval of 2 sec. No response was required.	1) Total power and power in the 12-14Hz band were directly re- lated to IQ.
Shucard and Horn (1972; 1973)	Normal (N=108) Age-Range: 16-68 yrs. Sex-56% males	MFCI BW:3-200Hz P-F	1) S was required to press button to each flash (in- tensity=1,10 usec) which occurred at random intervals between 1-4 sec. 2) S was required to silently count flashes. 3) S was required to passively view flashes.	1) Latencies of peaks between 50 and 400 msec were in- versely re- lated to IQ. 2) Amplitude (over all peaks) change as a function of task demands was directly re- lated to IQ.

Table 4--Continued

Reference	Sample Character- istics	IQ Tests[@] & Recording Technique [#]	Stimuli and Task	Significant Findings
Galbraith et al. (1970)	Normal (N=16) Retarded (N=24) IQ-Range: 26-66 Mean=46.7 Age-Range: 7-32 yrs. Mean=17.8 yrs.	? BW=0.6-18Hz 0-0 0-P	S was required to fixate on center and was presented with a circular light display which contained a black line triangle. The stimulus was presented for 100 msec at a rate of 1 every .8 sec and randomly to the left, right, or both visual fields. No response was required.	1) Latencies of P60 at anter- ior-left and P280 at posterior midline were inversely re- lated to IQ. 2) Amplitude (overall) was directly re- lated to IQ. 3) Contour length (125- 450msec) ra- tio (Lateral right/poster- ior-midline) in response to stimuli in left visual- field was directly re- lated to IQ in retarded subjects.
Rust (1975)	Twins (N=84) Prisoners (N=149) "Miscellaneous" (N=63) Age-Range: 17-44 yrs. Mean= 27.2 yrs. Sex-80% male	RSPM TC=0.3 sec C-T	S passively listened to tones (1000Hz, 1sec) with eyes closed. For the initial group intensity was 95db and interstimulus interval was 33sec. For a second group additional conditions were added at 55db and 75db, with a ran- dom interstimulus interval between 4 and 9 sec. No response was required.	1) None

@# See Table 1

Table 5

Recent EEG Studies Using Fourier Analysis

Reference	Sample Character- istics	IQ Tests[@] & Recording Technique #	Stimuli and Task	Significant Findings
Ahn et al. (1980)	U.S. Normals (N=360) IQs 90 Barbedos Normals (N=91) IQs 85 Learning Disabled (N=143) IQ-Range: 65-84 Age-Range: 5-16 yrs.	PPVT WISC-R O-P C-C T-T T-F	Passive state eyes closed.	1) Power in the slow frequen- cy bands (delta and theta) was inversely re- lated to IQ.
Katada et al. (1981)	Normal (N=58) Retarded (N=63) IQ-Mean=61.3 SD=7.6 Age-Range: 3-18 yrs.	? O-A P-A C-A T-A F-A	Passive state eyes closed.	1) Dominant al. alpha compon- ents (i.e., frequency with maximum power) was inversely re- lated to IQ.
Corning et al. (1982)	Clinic Referred Children (N=92) Age-Range: 9-14 yrs. Sex-88% males	WISC-R BW:.3-70Hz O-A P-A T-A C-A F-A	Passive state eyes closed.	1) Power in the delta and theta bands was inversely related to IQ 2) Intercorrela- tions between EEG epochs recorded from all homolo- gous sites, except frontal and temporal, were inverse- ly related to IQ.
Gasser et al. (1983)	Normal (N=31) Mildly Retarded	WISC CMMT	Passive state eyes closed.	1) Power in the theta band was inversely

Table 5--Continued

Reference	Sample Character- istics	IQ Tests[@] & Recording Technique #	Stimuli and Task	Significant Findings
	(N=25) IQ-Range: 50-70 Age-Range: 10-13 yrs.	BW:.16-70Hz O-A C-A P-A F-A		related to IQ
Thatcher et al. (1983)	Random Sample (N=191) IQ-Range: 44-150 Mean=107 SD=17.4 Age-Range: 5-16 yrs.	WPPSI WISC-R BW:0.5-30Hz O-A C-A P-A T-A F-A	Passive state eyes closed.	1) EEG coherence (a measure of similarity between signals at different scalp loca- tions) was inversely related to IQ for all fre- quency bands.

@# See Table 1

EEG AND EVENT-RELATED-POTENTIALS

The EEG is a record in time of the amplified voltage differences between two electrodes. The voltage differences are generated by the ionic currents which accompany synaptic modulation of neurons in the cortex (Elul, 1972). The actual records of such activity depends on the location of the electrodes as well as other aspects of the recording technique (Lindsley & Wicke, 1974). For instance, the effect of reference electrode location is illustrated in Figure 1 where it is evident that EEG amplitude depends on whether a given electrode is referred to a nearby scalp site (bipolar derivation) or to a more distant "inactive" site such as the ear lobe (monopolar derivation).

Quantification of the EEG has become more precise by the application of Fourier Analysis. This technique essentially decomposes the EEG into a series of pure sine waves of different amplitudes (Glaser & Ruchkin, 1976). The obtained distribution of squared amplitudes as a function of sine wave frequency is known as the EEG's power spectrum. It provides a compact picture of the EEG and highlights subtle aspects of the activity such as the exact frequency at which maximum power occurs (See Figure 1).

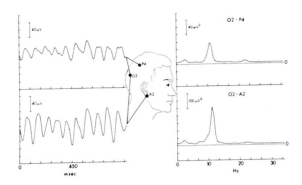

Figure 1
Spontaneous EEG recorded from the occiput (O2) referred to a
parietal scalp site (P4) (biopolar derivation) or to the earlobe (A2)
(monopolar derivation) and the corresponding power spectra.
Note the prominent effect of recording derivation on amplitude
as well as the more subtle effect on peak frequency.

Event-related-potentials (ERPs) represent the brain's responses to particular stimuli. In order to obtain FRPs, discrete stimuli (e.g., tones) must
be repeatedly presented to the subject. The EEG epochs immediately following each stimulus presentation are then averaged across presentations in
order to extract the stimulus evoked activity, which in the single EEG
epochs is somewhat obscured by the spontaneous EEG activity (See Figure 2).
The averaging procedure works because the spontaneous activity tends to be
out-of-phase across presentations and is thus cancelled by the averaging,
whereas the stimulus evoked activity remains in-phase and is therefore
enhanced by the averaging (John, Ruchkin & Vidal, 1978).

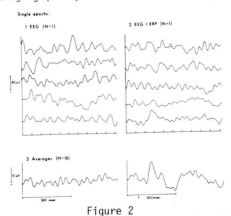

Figure 2
(1) Single traces of spontaneous EEG activity and (2) EEG plus tone (T)
evoked activity (ERP) recorded from frontal scalp (F4) referred to
earlobe (A2). (3) Average activity. Note the similarity across
single traces and the effect of averaging, which serves to attenuate
the spontaneous activity and extract the stimulus evoked activity.

Among the most frequently derived ERP measures are the amplitude of specific components or peaks and their latency (i.e., time from stimulus onset to the occurrence of the peak or components). Other measures which have also been studied are: the "time to baseline crossing", which is a latency measure obtained from single trial ERPs; the length of the contour along the ERP waveform between two points in time; and the power spectrum of the ERP (See Figure 3).

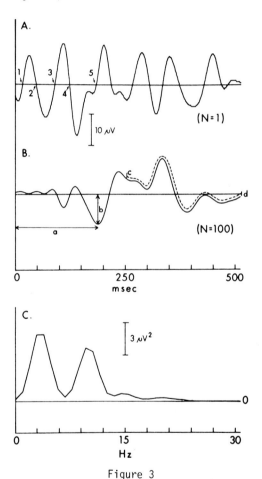

Figure 3
A.   Single EEG trace recorded between parietal (P4) and frontal (F4)
scalp sites in response to a light flash. Successive baseline
crossings are indicated by the numbers 1 to 5.
B.   Average of one hundred single EEG traces recorded between P4 and the
earlobe (A2) illustrating measures of: (a) latency and
(b) amplitude (baseline-to-peak) of the second positive (P2)
peak or component, and (c-d) contour length (distance along
the waveform) between 250 and 500 msec.
C.   Power spectrum of visual evoked potential in B.

RELATION OF EEG AND ERP MEASURES TO INTELLIGENCE

Latency. The relationship between latency and intelligence seems dependent on recording technique (i.e., monopolar vs. bipolar). On the whole the monopolar studies yield a more contradictory picture. Some studies have found the relation between latency and intelligence to be inverse (i.e., the shorter the latency, the higher the intelligence) (Osaka and Osaka, 1980; Rhodes, Dustman, & Beck, 1969); others have found it to be direct (Callaway, 1975; Dustman, Scheckenberg, & Beck, 1976; Perry, McCoy, Cunningham, Falgout, & Street, 1976; and Shagass, Roemer, Straumanis, & Josiassen, 1981); and still others have found the relationship to be component specific (Bigum, Dustman, & Beck, 1970) or simply absent (Callaway, 1975; Karrer, this volume; Schafer, 1982; Straumanis, Shagass, & Overton, 1973; Thatcher, McAlaster, Horst, & Lester, 1982).

An attempt to reconcile these differences on the basis of consistent methodological differences across studies reveals that the studies which have observed an inverse relationship are also the only ones which have examined children between 10 and 13 years and have compared extreme groups (i.e., high vs. low intelligence). However, the remaining studies cannot be consistently discriminated on methodological grounds and so the discrepant findings may reflect sampling biases or methodological factors not determinable from the published reports.

The bipolar studies have been somewhat less contradictory. Most of these studies have found latency to be inversely related to intelligence (Callaway, 1975; Chalke & Ertl, 1965; Ertl & Shafer, 1969; Galbraith, Glidden, & Busk, 1970; Gucker, 1973; Schucard & Horn, 1972), whereas none of the studies has reported a significant direct relationship. However, several studies have failed to find any consistent relationship (Callaway, 1975; Davis, 1971; Engle & Henderson, 1973; Rust, 1975).

An analysis of methodological differences between the two groups of studies reveals that three of the four studies which found no relationship were characterized by a confounding between intelligence and race, something which did not appear to be a problem for any of the studies reporting an inverse relationship. The fourth study (Rust, 1975) in the null group was also markedly deviant both in methodology and sample characteristics from those reporting a significant relationship (See Table 4).

Overall it appears that the bipolar technique is most consistent in showing an inverse relationship between latency and intelligence across methodologically heterogeneous studies, provided that intelligence is not grossly confounded with other subject characteristics. This probably reflects the fact that the bipolar technique is more sensitive than the monopolar technique to differences in the phase of neural activity across cortical regions. It suggests that intelligence is associated with the degree to which higher frequency activity is present and out-of-phase across cortical areas.

Amplitude. Amplitude has been found to be directly related to intelligence by some of the studies (Callaway, 1975; Galbraith et al., 1970; Osaka & Osaka, 1980; Rhodes et al., 1969; Shagass et al., 1981), others have found the relationship to be inverse (Dustman, et al., 1976; Perry et al., 1976; Straumanis et al., 1973), still others have found it to be component specific (Bigum et al., 1970; Shagass et al., 1981) or simply absent (Rust,

1975; Schucard & Horn, 1973; Thatcher et al., 1982).

At first glance these results appear contradictory. However, examination
of sample characteristics and methodological factors reveal that the
discrepancies may reflect differences between studies in the age group and
intelligence range of the subjects studied, as well as differences in
recording technique. Age is a particularly crucial variable because
amplitude is non-monotonically related to age (e.g., Callaway & Halliday,
1973), exhibiting relative maxima during early childhood, middle childhood
(ca. 9 years) and early adolescense (ca. 14 years). Given this underlying
relation between ERP amplitude and age and the assumption that mental
development should parallel neural maturation, one would expect the direction of the intelligence-amplitude relation to be dependent on age. For
instance, an inverse relation would be expected in early childhood, a
direct relationship in early adolescence and inconsistent results should be
observed in studies combining both children and adolescents, since within
different age ranges the direction of the amplitude-intelligence relation
should change. These expectations actually fit nicely what has been
observed in studies of subjects under 16 years of age (Bigum et al., 1970;
Callaway, 1975; Dustman et al., 1976; Osaka & Osaka, 1980; Perry et al.,
1976 Rhodes et al., 1969; Thatcher et al., 1982).

During adulthood amplitudes tend to stabilize and one would expect little
relationship to intelligence, unless extreme groups are being compared
(e.g., normal vs. retarded) or attentional factors, which are known to
affect amplitude (Callaway, 1975), are systematically related to intelligence. In the case of extreme groups, one would expect the mentally
retarded to have a larger amplitude, as is typical of younger individuals.
This was found by Straumanis et al. (1973). However, the latter employed a
bipolar derivation, which would be expected to attenuate highly synchronized activity, and so despite apparent differences these studies are
actually in agreement, by showing that neural activity is more synchronized
in the mentally retarded. The role of attentional factors may explain the
direct relation found by Shagass et al. (1981) in a sample of adult
psychiatric patients, since impairments in attention are characteristic of
psychiatric patients and can be expected to affect both their performance
on intelligence tests and their ERP amplitudes.

In general these studies indicate that the intelligence-amplitude relation
probably reflects a combination of changes due to maturation and attentional factors, particularly since it appears that more intelligent
individuals are better able to modulate the arousal processes underlying
attention and thus ERP amplitude (See Modulation of Amplitude and Contour
Length).

Contour Length. Waveform contour length has been found to be directly
related to intelligence (Blinkhorn & Hendrickson, 1982; Galbraith et al.,
1970; Hendrickson, 1982; Rhodes, et al., 1969), inversely related to
intelligence (Dustman & Callner, 1979; Shagass et al., 1981), or not
related to intelligence (Bigum et al., 1970; Shagass et al., 1981).

It seems evident here as was true for amplitude that the presence and
direction of any relationship is partially dependent on the age range as
well as the intelligence range of the samples under study. This is hardly
surprising since the contour length is dependent not only on frequency but
also on amplitude and is thus non-monotonically related to age (Dustman &

Beck, 1966).

Studies comparing extreme groups find a direct relationship between contour length and intelligence in young adolescents (Rhodes et al., 1969), an inverse relationship in a predominately adult sample (Dustman & Callner, 1979) and no relationship in a mixed sample of children and adolescents (Bigum et al., 1970). This is exactly the picture obtained with amplitude measures and suggests that these findings are primarily due to amplitude differences.

For the remaining studies the role of frequency content as well as that of attentional factors appear to be more significant. This is suggested by the finding of a direct relationship in a sample of adolescents (Hendrickson, 1982), an age group in which one would expect an inverse relationship based on age related changes in amplitude. Similarly, the findings of a direct relationship in a sample of mentally retarded subjects (Galbraith et al., 1970) and in one of gifted adults (Blinkhorn & Hendrickson, 1982) suggests a frequency content and/or attentional effect. However, the failure to find any relationship in a sample of normal adults and in inverse relation in a sample of psychiatric patients of average intelligence (Shagass et al., 1981) indicates that the relationship in adults may depend on the intelligence range examined and/or other subject characteristics.

Modulation of Amplitude and Contour Length. The extent to which amplitude changes as a function of instructions to attend or ignore the stimuli, or as a function of uncertainty regarding the exact time of stimulus delivery, has been found to be directly related to intelligence (Schafer, 1982; Schucard & Horn, 1973). Similarly, the degree to which contour length changes as a function of stimulus repetition has been found to correlate with intelligence (Dustman & Callner, 1979). These studies have shown that greater change is associated with higher intelligence. They demonstrate that the ability to modulate neural responsiveness is a correlate of mental development and intelligence.

Power Spectra. The recent studies which have examined the spontaneous EEG consistently demonstrate that less intelligent individuals have significantly more power at lower frequencies (Ahn, Prichep, John, Baird, Trepetin, & Kaye, 1980; Corning, Steff, & Chaprin, 1983; Gasser, Von Lucadou-Muller, Verleger, & Backer, 1983), tend to have a lower dominant frequency (Katada, Ozaki, Suzuki, & Suhara, 1981), and show more similarity (higher coherence) in the activity at different scalp sites (Corning et al., 1983; Thatcher, McAlester, Lester, Horst, & Cantor, 1983).

The ERP studies are generally consistent with this picture by showing that lower intelligence is associated with more power at lower frequencies (Flinn, Kirsch, & Flinn, 1977) or less power at higher frequencies (Ertl, 1973; Osaka & Osaka, 1980; Weinberg, 1969), as well as more similarity between ERPs recorded from different scalp locations (Karrer, this volume; Thatcher et al., 1983).

These are among the most consistent findings and suggest that greater independence across neural generators within cortical regions as well as a more rapid cycling by individuals generators parallels mental development.

Summary and Implications. There appear to be specific associations between

measures of neural activity and intelligence. The latency findings suggest
that intelligence is associated with the extent to which event related
activity contains higher frequency components that are relatively out-of-
phase across cortical regions. The amplitude findings seem to reflect
maturational changes, in particular the declining interdependence among
generators and the increasing ability to control the degree of synchrony
among generators. The latter is also supported by the findings that
individuals of higher intelligence show greater amplitude modulation.
Finally, the contour length, power spectra, and coherence findings further
support an association between intelligence and both the speed at which
individual generators cycle and the extent of their independence.

On the whole the results are generally consistent with the interpretation
that mental development, and therefore speed of information processing at
the behavioral level, is paralleled by those structural or functional
changes which lead neural generators (most probably ensambles of cortical
columns) to oscillate more rapidly, to achieve greater independence and to
be more responsive to modulation. As a result of these properties cortical
regions would be expected to display both greater stability and greater
plasticity in their information processing capability. The greater
stability results from more rapid and independent cycling among generators,
which ensures that a cortical region's state of readiness will be less
variable over time. The greater plasticity results from the precision with
which phase relations can be modulated across regions in search for optimal
pathways (more efficient strategies?) along which to channel activity.
These speculations, in turn, suggest that aberrations in the organization
of cortical columns must underly mental retardation. Some aberrations have
already been observed in the profoundly retarded (e.g., Purpura, 1975) and
it seems likely from the evidence reviewed here, that other aberrations,
perhaps or a more subtle nature, will eventually be found to be associated
with less severe forms of mental retardation.

Conclusion. This review has delineated properties of neural activity which
are associated with intelligence. Such properties, in turn, suggest
possible mechanisms whereby the brain is able to stabilize and decrease
information processing time and thus the timing of overt movements.
However, despite the fact that one can conceptually link neural activity
and motor speed, it does not appear that they are redundant measures when
it comes to predicting intelligences (e.g., Jensen, Schafer, & Crinella,
1981). Therefore, a more complete characterization of information processing in the mentally handicapped could be obtained by studying neural
activity in conjunction with motor indices of information processing. By
this approach it may be possible to detect patterns of neural activity
which precede instances of optimal performance in mentally handicapped
individuals. Such knowledge could then be used to enhance their performance by either presenting information contingent on key patterns of neural
activity or by attempting to train the individual to sustain optimal
patterns of neural activity.

REFERENCES

Ahn, H., Prichep, L., John, E. R., Baird, H., Trepetin, M., & Kaye, H.
    (1980). Developmental equations reflect brain dysfunctions. Science,
    210, 1259-1262.

Bigum, H. B., Dustman, R. E., & Beck, E. C. (1970). Visual and somato-sensory evoked responses from mongoloid and normal children. Electroencephalography and Clinical Neurophysiology, 28, 576-585.

Blinkhorn, S. F., & Hendrickson, D. E. (1982). Averaged evoked responses & psychometric intelligence. Nature, 295, 596-597.

Callaway, E. (1975). Brain electrical potentials & individual psychological differences. New York: Grune & Stratton.

Callaway, E., & Halliday, R. A. (1973). Evoked potential variability: Effects of age, amplitude and methods of measurement. Electroencephalography and Clinical Neurophysiology, 34, 125-133.

Chalke, F. C. R., & Ertle, J. P. (1965). Evoked potentials & intelligence. Life Sciences, 4, 1319-1322.

Corning, W. C., Steff, R. A., & Chaprin, I. C. (1982). EEG slow frequency & WISC-R correlates. Journal of Abnormal Child Psychology, 10, 511-530.

Davis, F. B. (1971). The measurement of mental capability through evoked-potential recordings. Educational Records Research Bulletin. No. 1. Greenwish, Conn.

Dustman, R. E., & Beck, E. C. (1966). Visually evoked potentials: Amplitude changes with age. Science, 151, 1013-1015.

Dustman, R. E., & Callner, D. A. (1979). Cortical evoked responses and response decrement in nonretarded and Down's syndrome individuals. American Journal of Mental Deficiency, 83, 391-397.

Dustman, R. E., Schenkenberg, T., & Beck, E. C. (1976). The development of the evoked response as a diagnostic & evaluative procedure. In R. Karrer, (Ed.), Developmental psychophysiology of mental retardation: Concepts & studies. Springfield, IL: Charles C. Thomas.

Elul, R. (1972). The genesis of the EEG. International Review of Neurobiology, 15, 228-272.

Engel, R., & Henderson, N. D. (1973). Visual evoked responses IQ at school age. Developmental Medicine & Child Neurology, 15, 136-145.

Ertl, J. P., & Schafer, E. W. P. (1969). Brain response correlates of psychometric intelligence. Nature, 223, 421-422.

Ertl, John P. (1973). IQ evoked responses & fourier analysis. Nature, 241, 209-210.

Flinn, J. M., Kirsch, A. D., & Flinn, E. A. (1977). Correlations between intelligence & the frequency content of the visual evoked potential. Physiological Psychology, 5, 11-15.

Galbraith, G. C., Glidden, J. B., & Busk, J. (1970). Visual evoked responses in mentally retarded & non-retarded subject. American Journal of Mental Deficiency, 75, 341-348.

Gasser, T., Von Lucadou-Muller, O., Verleger, R., & Bacher, P. (1983). Correlating EEG & IQ: A new look at an old problem using computerized EEG parameters. Electroencephalography & Clinical Neurophysiology, 55, 493-504.

Giannitrapani, D. (1969). EEG average frequency and intelligence. Electroencephalography and Clinical Neurophysiology, 27, 480-486.

Glaser, E. M., & Ruchkin, D. S. (1976). Principles of Neurobiological Signal Analysis. New York: Academic Press.

Gucker, Donald K. (1973). Correlating visual evoked potentials with psychometric intelligence: Variations in technique. Perceptual & Motor Skills, 37, 189-190.

Hendrickson, D. E. (1982). The biological basis of intelligence. Part II: Measurement. In H. J. Eysenck (Ed.), A model for intelligence. New York: Springer-Verlag.

Jensen, A. R. (1982). Reaction time and psychometric g. In H. J. Eysenck (Ed.), A model for intelligence. New York: Springer-Verlag.

Jensen, A. R., Schafer, E. W. P., & Crinella, F. M. (1981). Reaction time, evoked brain potentials and psychometric g in the severely retarded. Intelligence, 5, 179-197.

John, E. R., Ruchkin, D. S., & Vidal, J. J. (1978). Measurement of event-related potentials. In E. Callaway, P. Tueting, & S. H. Koslow (Eds.), Event-related brain potentials in man. New York: Academic Press.

Karrer, R., & Ivins, J. (1976). Steady potentials accompanying perception and response in mentally retarded and normal children. In R. Karrer (Ed.), Developmental psychophysiology of mental retardation. Springfield, IL: Charles C. Thomas.

Karrer, R., Warren, C., & Ruth, T. (1978). Slow potentials of the brain preceding cued and noncued movement: Effects of development and mental retardation. In D. Otto (Ed.) Multidisciplinary perspectives on event related brain potentials. Washington, D. C., Government Printing Offices.

Katada, A., Ozaki, H., Suzuki, H., & Suhara, K. (1981). Developmental characteristics of normal and mentally retarded children's EEGs. Electroencephalography and Clinical Neurophysiology, 52, 192-201.

Liberson, W. T. (1966). EEG & intelligence. Proceedings of the American Psychopathological Association, 56, 514-543.

Lindsley, D. B., & Wicke, J. D. (1974). The electroencephalogram: Autonomous electrical activity in man and animals. In R. F. Thompson & M. M. Patterson (Eds.), Bioelectric recording techniques. Part B. New York: Academic Press.

Osaka, M., & Osaka, N. (1980). Human intelligence & power spectral analysis of visual evoked potentials. Perceptual & Motor Skills, 50, 192-194.

Perry, N W., Jr., McCoy, J. G., Cunningham, W. R., Falgout, J. C., & Street, W. J. (1976). Multivariate visual evoked response correlates of intelligence. Psychophysiology, 13, 323-329.

Purpura, D. P. (1975). Dendritic differentiation in human cerebral cortex: Normal and aberrant developmental patterns. In G. W. Kruetzberg, (Ed.), Advances in neurology, 12, New York: Raven Press.

Rhodes, L. E., Dustman, R. E., & Beck, E. C. (1969). The visual evoked responses: A comparison of bright & dull children. Electroencephalography & Clinical Neurophysiology, 27, 364-372.

Rust, J. (1975). Cortical evoked potential, personality, & intelligence. Journal of Comparative Physiological Psychology, 89, 1220-1226.

Schafer, W. P. (1982). Neural Adaptability: A biological determinant of behavioral intelligence. International Journal of Neuroscience, 17, 183-191.

Shagass, C., Roemer, R. A., Straumanis, J. J., & Josiassen, R. C. (1981). Intelligence as a factor in evoked potential studies. I. Comparison of low and high IQ subjects. Biological Psychiatry, 16, 1007-1030.

Shucard, D. W., & Horn, J. L. (1972). Evoked cortical potentials & measurement of human abilities. Journal of Comparative Physiological Psychology, 8, 59-68.

Schucard, D. W., & Horn, J. L. (1973). Evoked potential amplitude change related to intelligence & arousal. Psychophysiology, 10, 445-452.

Straumanis, J. J., Shagass, C., & Overton, D. A. (1973). Auditory evoked responses in young adults with Down's Syndrome and idiopathic mental retardation. Biological Psychiatry, 6, 75-79.

Thatcher, R. W., McAlaster, R., Horst, R. L., & Lester, M. L. (1982). Evoked potential correlates of cognitive functioning in children. In A. Rothenberger (Ed.), Event-related potentials in children, Amsterdam: Elsevier Biomedical Press.

Thatcher, R. W., McAlaster, R., Lester, M. L., Horst, R. L., & Cantor, D. S. (1983). Hemispheric EEG asymmetrics related to cognitive functioning in children. In E. Perecman (Ed.), Cognitive processing in the right hemisphere. New York: Academic Press.

Vogel, W., & Broverman, D. M. (1964). Relationship between EEG & test intelligence: A critical review. Psychological Bulletin, 62, 132-144.

Warren, C., Karrer, R. (1984). Movement-related potentials during development: A replication and extension of relationships to age, motor control, mental status and IQ. International Journal of Neuroscience, 24, 21-26.

Weinberg, H. (1969). Correlation of frequency spectra & averaged evoked
    potentials with verbal intelligence. <u>Nature</u>, <u>224</u>, 813-815.

Motor Skill Acquisition of the Mentally Handicapped:
Issues in Research and Training
M.G. Wade (editor)
© *Elsevier Science Publishers B.V. (North-Holland), 1986*

EVOKED POTENTIALS, RESPONSE TIMING, AND MOTOR BEHAVIOR: A RESPONSE

Gary C. Galbraith, Ph.D.

MRRC-UCLA Research Group
Lanterman State Hospital
P.O. Box 100-R
Pomona, California   91769

OVERVIEW

Coordinated and skilled movements depend upon spatial-temporal patterns of
interaction not only between different neuromuscular control centers, but
between sensory and motor centers as well. Thus, the study of motor
behavior requires the use of experimental and/or statistical techniques
which are sensitive to interaction patterns among diverse brain regions.
The chapters by Daruna and Karrer (this volume) illustrate the application
of a variety of such techniques; in the present chapter this theme is
further developed.

Normal sensorimotor performance thus depends upon integrative and adaptive
capacities of the involved sensory and motor systems. Displacing the
optical array during sensorimotor training provides a means of studying
adaptive processes that are hypothesized to be the same neural processes
as those involved in normal visual-motor performance. In the present
chapter several experiments are described which point to the value of
studying adaptation to optical displacement in mentally retarded individuals.

The present chapter concludes with a consideration of synaptic temporal
variability. Although the data presented are based upon recordings of the
short-latency auditory evoked response (ABR), it is assumed that these
neural events are representative of other brain systems, including those
involved in sensorimotor integration. The results suggest that increased
synaptic instability may account for impaired motor control in mentally
retarded individuals.

CENTRAL TOPOGRAPHIC ORGANIZATION

The chapter by Karrer concluded with an interesting discussion of the
pattern of 'linkages' among five recording sites on the scalp (C3, C4, Fz,
Cz, and Oz). Linkage, in this case, was operationally defined as the
intercorrelation between the negative potential areas occurring prior to a
self-initiated motor response, and prior to a reaction time response,
recorded at each electrode site.

In general, Karrer's results showed increasing linkage (higher correlations) as a function of age, at least in the more anterior electrode
derivations. However, electrode combinations involving the posterior
region of the head (Oz-C3 and Oz-C4) showed little or no change with age.

Moreover, these posterior linkages consistently yielded the lowest overall correlation coefficients. These findings are qualitatively similar to the results of Busk and Galbraith (1975), in which a measure derived from the EEG linear coherence function was lowest among posterior electrode derivations during performance of eye-hand coordination tasks. Anatomical studies indicate that there are no direct fiber projections from visual cortex to motor cortex (Myers, 1967; Pandya & Kuypers, 1969). This may account for the generally lower linkage levels between Oz and the C3 or C4 electrodes, as well as the failure of these posterior electrode combinations to show any consistent age-related trends.

Daruna's chapter summarized data which showed that intelligence is related to various measures of brain activity which may be used to assess interactions among neural generators. Particularly interesting in this regard is the paper he cited by Thatcher, McAlaster, Lester, Horst, and Cantor (1983), which reported a robust inverse relationship between IQ and baseline EEG coherence in the theta $\overline{(3.5\ to}\ 7.0\ Hz)$ frequency band. Thatcher et al. (1983) also studied coherence in academic groups ranging from gifted to very low achievers. Coherence in the delta (0.5 to 3.5 Hz) band was inversely related to academic performance. Karrer also presented data which showed that more intelligent (or faster responding) subjects had lower levels of inter-electrode linkage.

Although Busk and Galbraith (1975) did not study intelligence per se, they did show that a measure of weighted-average EEG coherence significantly decreased following learning of a visual-motor skill. Perhaps those same patterns of neural organization that characterize motor learning also underlie the broader dimension of intellectual functioning. That is, higher intelligence may be characterized by increased neural efficiency, which could find expression in greater regional specialization, or independent of function. This could account for the fact that higher IQ, and/or better motor performance, are significantly associated with lower coherence or linkage patterns.

As noted, Karrer reported generally increasing correlations between brain regions with development in nonretarded subjects. Among mentally retarded individuals, however, there was a greater variety of linkage patterns. Thus, some electrode combinations were more similar to the adolescent or adult (age-matched) controls, while other electrode combinations yielded the lower linkage patterns characteristics of younger children. These results led Karrer to suggest a possible developmental asynchrony between different brain regions in mentally retarded individuals. Such developmental asynchrony would seriously impact studies of EEG linkage in mentally retarded individuals, since quite different results could be obtained depending upon placement of the electrodes.

The hypothesis that mentally retarded individuals differ in their pattern of central topographic organization is not new. Working within a theoretical framework of Gestalt psychology, and based upon the performance of mentally retarded individuals in a perceptual task, Spitz (1963) suggested four interesting postulates. Only Postulate IV concerns us here: "In retardates, there is less spread of electrochemical activity from stimulated cells into the surrounding cortical field" (Spitz, 1963, p. 30).

Based upon this postulated reduction in 'spread of electrochemical activity', it follows that one would expect lower linkage between brain

areas in persons with reduced intelligence. Generally speaking, this is
what Karrer reported. Yet, Thatcher et al. (1983) report that coherence
increases as intellectual functioning decreases. Note, however, that their
results are most pronounced in the lower EEG frequency ranges, i.e., delta
(0.5 to 3.5 Hz) and theta (3.5 to 7 Hz). In considering this fact, along
with the implications of bipolar versus monopolar evoked potential recording techniques, Daruna made the important suggestion "... that intelligence is associated with the degree to which higher frequency activity is
more out-of-phase relative to lower frequency activity across cortical
areas." Thus, electrophysiological support for Postulate IV might best be
obtained by an analysis of higher EEG frequencies, and during conditions
of sensory stimulation (using bipolar recording techniques).

In our laboratory we have found support for Postulate IV. Thus,
Galbraith, Gliddon, and Busk (1976) reported lower EEG coherence for
mentally retarded subjects. These results may differ from those of
Thatcher et al. (1983) in part because the EEG was recorded primarily
during conditions of photic driving (up to 16 flashes/sec), and the
weighted-average measure of coherence included higher EEG frequencies
(encompassing harmonics of the stimulus frequency).

Galbraith, Gliddon, and Busk (1970) also reported visual evoked potential
data that supported Postulate IV. Bipolar visual evoked responses (VERs)
were recorded from relatively close (5-8 cm) electrode placements over the
posterior aspect of the head. (This particular study is one of those
included in Daruna's category of 'bipolar studies', which have more
consistently yielded significant correlations with IQ than studies using
monopolar recording derivations.)

The results are shown in Figure 1, which displays the topographic distribution of the largest positive VER amplitude presented separately for
retarded and nonretarded groups. The results are expressed as a percentage of the amplitude recorded over the primary receiving cortex, which
is thus normalized to 100 percent. Although such normalization auto-
matically forces the comparison VER to a value of 100 percent for each
group, it is important to note that the absolute amplitudes for this
particular electrode derivation were quite similar in the two groups.

Control   Mentally retarded

Figure 1
Topographic distribution of bipolar visual evoked response (VER)
amplitudes in control (nonretarded) and mentally retarded subjects.
The results are expressed as a percentage of the amplitude recorded
from one electrode placed above the inion, and a second electrode
5 cm distant along the midline.
(Used by permission, Galbraith, Gliddon, & Busk, 1970.)

The mentally retarded group evidences a marked decline in the local spread of VER amplitudes into nearby associative cortical fields as predicted by Postulate IV (Spitz, 1963).

Additional evidence that is consistent with a postulated reduction in the spread of electrochemical effects in the cortex of mentally retarded individuals comes from the anatomical studies of Huttenlocher (1974). The technique in this case relied upon a quantitative analysis of the dendritic branching of pyramidal neurons in layers of the neocortex. Basal dendrite arborizations were quantified by counting the intersections of dendritic branches with concentric circles drawn at multiples of 25 micra around the center of the cell body. Figure 2 shows that profoundly retarded children under the age of five years show far less dendritic arborization than a six-month old control.

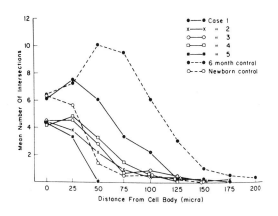

Figure 2
Graphic presentation of basal dendritic spread in pyramidal neurons of cortical layer 3. The points indicate the mean number of intersections of basal dendrites with concentric circles drawn at multiples of 25 micro from the perikaryon. "Zero" distance indicates the primary dendritic branches. (Used by permission, Huttenlocher, 1974, Fig. 5.)

Elul, Hanley, and Simmons (1975) analyzed the probability distribution of EEG amplitude in a group of Down syndrome children and age-matched normal controls. The trend in the normal group was towards a first-order Gaussian distribution, while the Down syndrome children had a strongly non-Gaussian distribution. These authors conclude that the non-Gaussian behavior of the EEG in Down syndrome may be the result of impoverished synaptic contacts on cortical neurons.

Thus, results from a broad range of perceptual, electrophysiological, and anatomical studies indicate that patterns of central topography are different in mentally retarded individuals. Abnormal patterns of central nervous system connections would clearly impact the neural organization required to mediate coordinated and skilled sensorimotor behavior.

VISUAL-MOTOR ADAPTIVE BEHAVIOR IN MENTALLY RETARDED INDIVIDUALS

I would not like to discuss an experimental paradigm that offers promise in the study of motor performance in mentally retarded individuals, viz., sensorimotor adaptation induced by viewing through a displacing prism.

Displacing the optical array during sensorimotor training initially results in reaching errors. However, these errors are reduced or eliminated with further visual-motor experience, i.e., there is adaptation depends upon the same neural processes as those involved in the establishment and maintenance of normal visual-motor performance (Cohen, 1967; Freedman, 1968; Hamilton & Bossom, 1964; Held, 1961; Taub, 1968).

Scheel and Galbraith (1977) recorded the EEG from institutionalized, mentally retarded individuals, while performing during a prismatic adaptation task (reaching with a pointer while viewing through a 20-diopter, 11.3^{0}, base right prism). The results showed significant negative correlations between pointing scores and alpha intensity in the 8.6 to 10.3 cycle/second band. Thus, higher alpha intensity was associated with poorer prismatic adaptation. However, this was true only for premotor (Fz) and motor areas (c3 and C4), and not for the occipital (Oz) area. Alpha-like activity recorded over motor regions, the so-called sensorimotor ("mu") rhythm, has been reported during the voluntary suppression of movement (Sterman & Wyrwicka, 1967). Although all subjects performed the pointing task, perhaps the presence of sensorimotor alpha indicates a suppression in the effectiveness of self-produced movements, which are known to be essential for visual-motor adaptation.

These results indicate that patterns of organization in the EEG may provide useful information concerning functional adaptive motor states in mentally retarded individuals. Also, it appears that optical rearrangement is a useful technique in the study of motor behavior among mentally retarded individuals. It would be interesting to know the relationship of mu to the positive-going Bereitschaft potentials that Karrer found in his mentally retarded subjects.

As used in the field of mental retardation and developmental disabilities, the term 'adaption' typically refers to the adjustment to natural and social environmental demands (Heber, 1959; Nihira, 1973). Indeed, the current American Association on Mental Deficiency (AAMD) definition of mental retardation includes, in addition to psychometric test results, evidence of a deficit in adaptive behavior (Grossman, 1973). Specific attributes of adaptive skills can be assessed by such instruments as the AAMD Adaptive Behavior Scale (ABS) (Nihira, Foster, Shellhass, and Leland, 1969; 1974), which measures three general factorial dimensions: I--Personal Self-Sufficiency, II--Community Self-Sufficiency, and III--Personal-Social Responsibility.

Scheel and Galbraith (1980) were interested in the possible relationship between adaptation as measured by the ABS, and experimentally induced adaptation to optical rearrangement. They studied whole-body sensorimotor adaptation by requiring mentally retarded subjects to make numerous visual-motor adjustments while wearing 20-diopter prisms, including navigating an obstacle course similar to that used in movement education (Winneck, 1979). Whole-body sensorimotor adaptation was used in order to maximize the strength of prismatic effect.

Since the prism displaces optical images to the right, subjects initially reach incorrectly to the right of what is seen. Adaptation, then, consists of recalibrating one's reach to the left of the apparent viewed position. Figure 3 shows the distribution of pointing responses in 35 subjects immediately following prismatic exposure, while viewing through a 0-diopter (clear glass) lens. In this case, subjects who had adapted would now reach to the left of the viewed target. The results show a wide distribution of scores, which can generally be categorized into adaptors and non-adaptors.

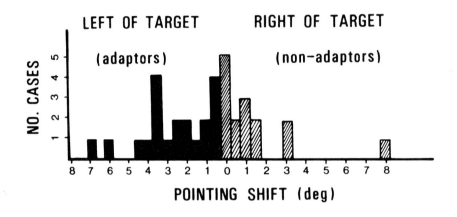

Figure 3
Frequency distribution of off-target pointing shift due to prism aftereffect. Expected pointing shift is to the left of target (Adaptors). A zero shift or shift to the right of target represents an atypical response to prism adaptation (Nonadaptors). Pointing shift measured in degrees (deg.). (Used by permission, Scheel & Galbraith, 1980.)

It was found, overall, that adaptors had significantly higher ABS scores (F = 10.16, 1/33 df, p < .01). Individual t tests showed that adaptors had significantly higher scores for Factors I and II, but not for Factor III (see Table 1). Interestingly, the behavioral items in Factor I include walking and running, body balance, and a variety of other skills that clearly depend upon sensorimotor integration. Factor II also includes items that would seem to depend upon sensorimotor integration, such as sense of direction, writing, and job complexity. Factor III, on the other hand, includes items that are more appropriate to an individual's motivation and socialization.

Thus, there appears to be a meaningful relationship between adaptive behavior as measured in the laboratory, and adaptive behavior appropriate to real-life situations. Once again, adaptation to optical rearrangement appears to be a viable and useful tool for assessing sensorimotor integrative abilities in mentally retarded individuals.

Table 1

Mean Adaptive Behavior Scale Factor Scores.[a]

Factor[b]	Adaptors	Nonadaptors
Factor I	72.0	65.1
Factor II	90.0	67.7
Factor III	41.4	37.9

[a]From Scheel & Galbraith, 1980

[b]Factor I = Personal Self-Sufficiency; Factor II = Community Self-Sufficiency; Factor III = Personal-Social Responsibility.

RESPONSE TIMING AND SOME TEMPORAL PARAMETERS OF NEURAL FUNCTIONING

Several papers in the present volume (see chapters by Vernon; Zelaznik; and Karrer) have reported data on reaction time (RT) performance in mentally retarded individuals. The data consistently show that such individuals respond with slower RTs than nonretarded controls, and that the relative slowing increases as the information conveyed by the stimulus display increases. Karrer showed that this increased latency cannot be attributed to afferent (input) processes, but is due mainly to increases in central processing time, with a small contribution from efferent (output) processes.

A number of studies have consistently shown that the strongest (negative) correlation of any of the RT parameters with psychometric g is intra-individual variability of RT (e.g., Carlson & Jensen, 1982; Jensen, 1980; Jensen & Munro, 1979). Increased RT variability has been attributed to the increased processing demands of greater information uncertainty (Jensen & Munro, 1979; Vernon, 1981).

Using a standardized and simple stimulus configuration, such as only eight possible light displays in a choice reaction time paradigm, why should there be a range of inter-individual processing demands? Although overly simplistic, there is heuristic value in a model of neural functioning that postulates reduced 'efficiency' or 'reliability' in coding and processing information. Since the effects of unreliable processing can compound at successive stages of the system, the final output would be more variable, both in terms of accuracy and speed of response.

Hendrickson (1982) presents just such a model, in which the representation of information in the central nervous system is assumed to be coded as a chain of logically related neuronal pulse trains. The substrates of veridical perception or cognition thus depend upon the correct recognition of pulse trains at successive stages of processing. The characteristic probability of correct recognition for an individual, R, is assumed to

operate independently at each synaptic junction. Thus, for a chain of N
successive events, the final probability of correct recognition is R^N.
Because N can be large, especially when complex central processing is
involved, even slight inter-individual differences in R-values can lead to
sizable quantitative differences in final outcome. For example, higher
R-values would permit much longer time periods of error-free reverberation
of information, which in turn could greatly enhance memory processes.
Presumably, high-IQ people have high levels of R. The concept of 'recognition failure' is summarized as follows:

> We believe that all individuals can be characterized by the
> extent to which recognition failures occur or do not occur.
> This characterization can be expressed as a single parameter, a
> probability of recognition occurring when it should occur.

> The actual parameter as it might apply at a single synapse need
> not apply to other synapses, but what seems to be likely is that
> the distribution of individual synaptic probabilities will have
> a characteristics mean value for the individual as a whole.

> The greater or lesser characteristic probability of correct
> pulse train recognition at the synapse for given individuals we
> believe to be the biological basis of intelligence (Hendrickson,
> 1982, p. 184).

Since the Hendrickson model is based upon temporal chains of neuronal
discharges (spatial parameters are not considered), the model is most
affected by the magnitude of temporal error in the intervals between
successive pulses. The greater the temporal variability, the greater the
probability of a recognition failure.

For the past several years, the present author has been studying trial-to-
trial temporal variability of the auditory brain-stem evoked response
(ABR). Components of the ABR are known to originate in successive synaptic stages of the auditory projection pathway, and are thought to depend
upon 'synaptically secure' neurons which discharge with brief and stable
firing latencies (Buchwald, 1983). Hence, ABR waveform morphology is
reliable, and component latencies can be measured with sub-millisecond
precision.

It has been our working hypothesis that synaptic security is compromised,
or reduced, in mentally retarded individuals (this hypothesis is similar
to that proposed by Hendrickson, 1982). Reduced synaptic security would
result in less stable firing latencies, which in turn should be reflected
in greater trial-to-trial variability of neuronal responses. We have
studied the ABR, rather than long-latency evoked potentials, because of
(a) the anatomical (synaptic) specificity of successive ABR components,
and (b) the possibility of measuring quite subtle temporal events (in the
range of microseconds).

Although cognitive and intellective deficits are typically attributed to
disturbances in higher cortical functioning, it is possible that disturbances may be introduced (and subsequently compounded) at the earliest
levels of synaptic processing. Moreover, we have assumed that synaptic
processes measured in the brain-stem auditory pathway are representative
samples of processes that may occur elsewhere in the CNS -- especially in

genetically determined forms of mental retardation, such as in Down's syndrome (DS).

Several studies have shown that short-latency ABR amplitudes in DS individuals are smaller than amplitudes recorded from nonretarded controls (Galbraith, 1984; Galbraith, Aine, Squires, & Buchwald, 1983; Squires, Aine, Buchwald, Norman, & Galbraith, 1980; Squires, Galbraith, & Aine, 1979). Reduced ABR amplitudes could be due to greater temporal variability (increased time 'jitter') of the neural events underlying the computer-averaged ABR.

In order to quantify the degree of temporal variability we have performed a latency compensation analysis (LCA) of single-trial ABR recordings. Details of the LCA methodology have been presented elsewhere (Galbraith, 1984). To summarize, however, each individual trial sample is cross-correlated with the ABR waveform obtained by averaging across all trials. Separate correlation coefficients are computed as each individual sample is lagged in 40 microsecond increments through a range of ± 360 micro-seconds. This procedure is carried out for a minimum of 1000 trials that constitute the total ABR wave form. It is thus possible to characterize each trial sample by (a) the largest correlation coefficient among the set, and (b) the particular lag value at which the largest coefficient occurs.

By knowing the distribution of lag values, a modified ABR waveform can be computed by temporally realigning all individual trails. Thus, instead of aligning on the stimulus, each trial is temporally shifted so as to align on the particular lag associated with the largest correlation. As seen in Figure 4, this invariably results in significantly enhanced ABR component amplitudes.

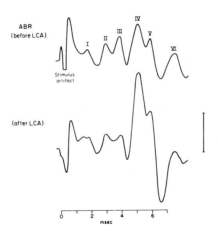

Figure 4
Amplitude of auditory brain stem evoked response (ABR) before (top) and after (bottom) latency compensation analysis (LCA). Successive waves following stimulus are indicated by numerals I to VI. Time calibration is in milliseconds; amplitude calibration is 0.5 uV.

Our primary interest, however, concerns whether or not DS individuals are characterized by greater temporal variability in the neuronal events reflected in the ABR. This has been assessed in two pilot studies by comparing the standard deviation of lag values, computed in a variety of experimental conditions, obtained from DS and age-matched, nonretarded individuals.

In one study, trial-to-trial ABR variability in the DS group (N=5) was greater in 10 of 12 stimulus conditions. Although the actual mean differences were small, the result is statistically significant using a binomial test ($p < 0.019$, one-tailed). In the second study, we compared university undergraduates and DS (N=9) individuals. A repeated measures analysis of variance showed significantly greater variability for the DS group (F = 8.894, 1, 16 df, $p < 0.01$).

These findings support the hypothesis that central dysfunction in DS individuals may be characterized by disturbances in the temporal stability of neural events. These results are thus in agreement with the Hendrickson (1982) model, which postulates that increased recognition failure (lower intelligence) is due primarily to a disruption in the temporal stability of chains of neuronal discharges.

Of course, results obtained from ABR recordings address only the initial stages of coding in the auditory sensory pathway. However, it seems reasonable to assume that the sampled coding patterns are representative of other neural systems, including the motor system. Thus, increased synaptic variability could significantly disrupt motor control processes. Such effects could account for at least some of the increased RT variability observed in mentally retarded individuals.

CONCLUSIONS

Even the simplest of motor skills requires a high degree of interaction and feedback between sensory and motor subsystems. Moreover, the patterns of interaction are dynamic. Drawing upon the work of Paillard (1960), Busk and Galbraith (1975) state that...

> In the early stages of acquiring complex skilled movements many motions are unnecessary and involve other parts of the body. As learning progresses, more and more motor control is relegated to feedback circuits such as the cerebellar-cerebral system which relies upon proprioceptive information from the appropriate muscles. Movements become increasingly refined until they reach a level of integration which is characterized by minimal effort and specialized responses from the specific muscle groups necessary for the task. Such increased efficiency in motor output would seem to imply a similar efficiency in the neural systems mediating this behavior. (Thus)...visual motor learning can be equated with reduced task complexity and hence lower coupling (between different brain regions) (p. 420).

Interestingly, this is the same argument that Karrer uses to explain reduced linkage and the positive waveform topography found in mentally retarded individuals. Specifically, the size of positivity appeared to reflect the effort at inhibiting associated movements that were inappropriate to the target movement.

Such neural interactions assume functional anatomical interconnections among involved brain regions. Yet, evidence from several sources indicates that mentally retarded individuals are characterized by diminished patterns of functional connectivity. In addition, there is evidence that the temporal coding of sensory (and presumably, motor) pathways is more variable in the retarded. These factors would combine to disrupt sensorimotor behavior.

Yet, individual differences can be assessed by a variety of useful techniques, ranging from whole-body adaption to displacement of the optical array, to the assessment of electrophysiological variability and linkage patterns. By this means, it should be possible not only to better understand the mechanisms involved, but to identify those candidates who will benefit most from habilitative sensory-motor training.

REFERENCES

Buchwald, J. (1983). Generators. In E. J. Moore (Ed.), Bases of auditory brain-stem evoked responses) (pp. 157-195). New York: Grune and Stratton.

Busk, J., & Galbraith, G. C. (1975). EEG correlates of visual-motor practice in man. Electroencephalography and Clinical Neurophysiology, 38, 415-422.

Carlson, J. S., & Jensen, C. M. (1982). Reaction time, movement time, and intelligence: A replication and extension. Intelligence, 6, 265-274.

Cohen, M. M. (1967). Continuous versus terminal feedback in prism aftereffects. Perceptual and Motor Skills, 24, 1295-1302.

Elul, R., Hanley, J., & Simmons, J. Q., III. (1975). Non-Gaussian behavior of the EEG in Down's syndrome suggests decreased neuronal connections. Acta Neurologica Scandinavica, 51, 21-28.

Freedman, S. J. (1968). On the mechanisms of perceptual compensation. In S. J. Freedman (Ed.), The neuropsychology of spatially oriented behavior (pp. 231-240). Homewood, IL: Dorsey Press.

Galbraith, G. C. (1984). Latency compensation analysis of the auditory brain-stem evoked response. Electroencephalography and Clinical Neurophysiology, 58, 333-342.

Galbraith, G., Aine, C., Squires, M., & Buchwald, J. (1983). Binaural interaction in auditory brainstem responses of retarded and non-retarded individuals. American Journal on Mental Deficiency, 87, 551-557.

Paillard, J. (1960). The patterning of skilled movements. In J. Fields, H. W. Magoun, & V. E. Hall (Eds.), Handbook of physiology-neurophysiology, (Vol. 3, pp. 1679-1708). American Physiology Society, Washington, D.C.

Pandya, D. N., & Kuypers, H. G. J. M. (1969). Cortico-cortical connections in the rhesus monkey, Brain Research, 13, 13-36.

Scheel, V., & Galbraith, G. C. (1977). Electroencephalographic correlates of prism adaptation in mentally retarded individuals. American Journal of Mental Deficiency, 82, 292-298.

Scheel, V., & Galbraith, G. C. (1980). Adaptation to visual-motor rearrangement of mentally retarded individuals: Relationship to Adaptive Behavior Scale scores. American Journal of Mental Deficiency, 84, 627-632.

Spitz, H. H. (1963). Field theory in mental deficiency. In N. R. Ellis (Ed.), Handbook of mental deficiency (pp. 11-40). New York: McGraw-Hill.

Squires, N., Aine, C., Buchwald, J., Norman, R., & Galbraith, G. (1980). Auditory brainstem response abnormalities in severely and profoundly retarded adults. Electroencephalography and Clinical Neurophysiology, 50, 172-185.

Squires, N., Galbraith, G., & Aine, C. (1979). Event-related potential assessment of sensory and cognitive deficits in the mentally retarded. In E. Callaway & D. Lehmann (Eds.), Event related potentials in man: Application and problems (pp. 397-413). New York: Plenum.

Sterman, M. B., & Wyrwicka, W. (1967). EEG correlates of sleep: Evidence for separate forebrain substrates. Brain Research, 6, 143-163.

Taub, E. (1968). Prism compensation as a learning phenomenon: A phylogenetic perspective. In S. J. Freedman (Ed.), The neuropsychology of spatially oriented behavior. Homewood, IL: Dorsey Press.

Thatcher, R. W., McAlaster, R., Lester, M. L., Horst, R. L., & Cantor, D. S. (1983). Hemispheric EEG asymmetries related to cognitive functioning in children. In E. Perecman (Ed.), Cognitive processing in the right hemisphere. New York: Academic Press.

Vernon, P. A. (1981). Reaction time and intelligence in the mentally retarded. Intelligence, 5, 345-355.

Winneck, J. P. (1979). Early movement experiences and development habilitation and remediation. Philadelphia: Saunders.

Section IV
Training and Motor Skills

Motor Skill Acquisition of the Mentally Handicapped:
Issues in Research and Training
M.G. Wade (editor)
© *Elsevier Science Publishers B.V. (North-Holland), 1986*

PROCESS AND CONTEXT IN ENSURING COMPETENT MOTOR BEHAVIOR
BY MENTALLY RETARDED PEOPLE

Dr. James Hogg

Hester Adrian Research Centre
The University Manchester M13 9PL
England

SUMMARY

Competent motor behavior is required in virtually all self-help,
vocational and many leisure activities. The lack of competence manifest
in many retarded people's motor behavior, therefore, severely impairs
their ability to adapt and to lead an optimally normal life. The motor
component of competent adaptive behavior while being critical to success
is only one vehicle of its realization. At the outset, therefore, we
adopt a somewhat wide perspective on this issue by viewing motor
competence as the effective realization of goal directed actions. Several
'layers' of motor and cognitive activity can therefore be identified as
necessary prerequisites for such realization, from the ongoing monitoring
of movement, to the organization of components of movement, to the
structure of action sequences, and the realization of actions as social
acts.

The attempt to relate specific developmental and experimental research to
intervention practice is illustrated from the author's own developmental
studies. While the feasibility of establishing such links is acknowledged, it is suggested that the most realistic approach to synthesizing
motor research and intervention is by informing, in a broadly based way,
programming activities on the basis of existing research on motor and
related processes. The methodological adequacy of comparative studies
(nonretarded persons vs. persons with mental retardation) and the quantity
of information derivable from them is too limited and limiting to approach
the overall problems of goal-directed actions and problems in their
realization. While an experimental psychology of mental retardation may
be a legitimate pursuit in its own right, the value of experimentation
with a view to influencing intervention might be more in the study of
mentally retarded people in their own right and the extent to which
component processes can be modified by carefully controlled conditions.

It is suggested that recent developments in applied behavior analysis,
notably General Case Programming, provide a well-grounded body of procedures in which to consider the application of theories and experimental
findings on motor competence.

* * * * *

The diversity of neurological, physical, and psychological deficits that
influences competent motor behavior in those classified as profoundly,
severely, moderately and mildly retarded precludes any hope that by

drawing on any single source of neurological or psychological information
we can, at one fell swoop, alleviate their difficulties. Within all these
groups, however, motor problems are to be found. At the profound end of
the range the almost inevitable presence of neurological damage or
abnormality will manifest itself in conditions such as cerebral palsy,
while in the severe to moderate range less obvious neurological abnormalities, most clearly evident in those with Down syndrome, are hypothesized
to have specific effects on motor competence. In these groups and in the
mild retardation category, difficulties probably related to specific
cognitive impairments will also play their part in reducing motor
competence.

For the purposes of this paper, my concern is with motor incompetence as
it is possibly determined by psychological factors rather than with
difficulties arising from obvious gross physical impairment. There is,
however, a grey area between these influences. Many severe and moderately
retarded individuals will exhibit neurological abnormalities which might
be expected to affect motor behavior. Much play is made, for example,
with the small cerebellum relative to their overall brain size of Down
syndrome people and this in turn is used to 'explain' poor motor learning
and programming of movements. However, it is possible to start at the
level of psychological analysis with such individuals, without recourse to
somewhat suspect neurologizing.

I have used in my title and in the opening paragraphs of this paper the
term 'motor competence'. Connotatively I use this term to convey something less sophisticated than 'motor skill' with its suggestion of special
expertise but to indicate behavior more advanced than mere movement which
can be aimless or even involuntary. If I were asked to be more specific I
would refine this characterization by reference to recent developments in
theories of goal-directed action as introduced by Harre' (1982) and von
Cranach (1982). Here action is distinguished from mere movement and von
Cranach (1982) defines a goal-directed action (GDA) as referring to "...
an actor's goal-directed, planned intended and conscious behavior, which
is socially directed (or motor controlled)" (p. 36).

von Cranach adds to this definition two further distinctions. He distinguished 'an act' from an action by emphasizing that a goal-directed action
is considered an act when it occurs in a specific social setting directed
to a specific goal that can be socially identified as appropriate to that
setting. Finally, he emphasizes that any goal-directed action is it
itself a complex behavioral system. Thus, I am using the term motor
competence to describe goal-directed actions (as defined) which frequently
will have the status in von Cranach's terminology of 'an act'. For the
majority of people such actions do not require special skill but are
nevertheless well beyond the demands of 'mere movement' in their execution. For any of us lacking a particular behavior demanding motor
competence, then, its acquisition may indeed be seen as skill acquisition,
however transitory the period is for which we would regard the behavior as
skilled. Note, however, that such a view of competence goes beyond the
ability to produce a series of goal-directed actions and embraces the
social appropriateness of the action when it is viewed as an act.

I will come back to GDA theory later in this paper. Not only do I want to
examine the relevance of this view for the study and development of motor
competence in retarded children and adults, but I want to relate it to

some of the important developments that have taken place in our approach
to the education and training of retarded people. Some of you may already
be going through a mental 'translation' in which you see von Cranach's
'act' in terms of a behavior generalized to a wider social setting than
that in which it was trained, while relating social settings (von Cranach
refers to a specific social setting as 'situatedness') to the various
ecologies in which the behavior is deemed appropriate.

The apparent shortcomings in motor competence in many severely, moderately, and mildly retarded people do not typically concern us because they
have been shown to have short reaction times, difficulties in utilizing
proprioceptive feedback, or problems in programming repetitive movements
in experimental tasks. They concern us because a wide range of basic
adaptive actions, both practical and social, are dependent for their
realization on motor control both bodily and particularly with respect to
the use of hands. With regard to the latter, Piaget (1953) commented that
"... With the mouth, the eye, and the ear, the hand is one of the most
essential instruments of which the intelligence, once it has been
established, will make use" (p. 88). These actions embrace most self-help
activities, washing, dressing, etc., household chores, and so on. In the
vocational and leisure spheres motor competence is essential in producing
work and participating in sports and other activities. Yet, it is the
attempt to relate these two distinct areas, the experimental-research
characterizing motor performance and the wider difficulties encountered by
the retarded person, that has preoccupied researchers and professional
teachers and trainers for some time (see Connolly, 1975). This attempted
synthesis is not, of course, limited to the area of motor behavior, but
covers other psychological domains. To this general point, however, must
be added the admission that for many research workers the attempt to
develop an 'experimental psychology of mental retardation' has been an end
in itself with no explicit concern for relevance to intervention.
Similarly, those concerned with applied behavioral analysis have shown
lack of interest in available experimental or developmental findings,
proceedings as they have through pragmatic shaping of their own procedures
in the light of program successes and failures. In this paper, however, I
want to continue to explore the relation between developmental and experimental research on the one hand and education and training of motor
competence on the other. In due course, I will return to GDA theory and
place some of my observations within this framework. Since my intention
is essentially illustrative I will not try in any way to be comprehensive
in my coverage. I will draw upon some of my own work since it was the
outcome of these studies that gave impetus to the position adopted in this
paper.

The impetus to develop research on motor skills in young children stemmed
from a consideration of the curriculum for young mentally handicapped and
nonhandicapped children involved in an experimental preschool project. A
major gap in available information appeared in the area of fine motor
skill. Laboratory studies had little relevance to the concerns of preschool education, while the proliferation of fine motor skill checklists
struck me as diffuse in their content and somewhat aimless in their outcome.

A tradition of research did exist, however, which emphasized the structure
and function of prehensile or manipulative behavior. This could be found
in Piaget's (1953) account of early prehensile development and White's

(1971) innovatory studies on visually directed reaching and, in somewhat
older children, the work of Bruner (1970) and Connolly (1973). The
suggestion of these last two authors was essentially a model of skill
acquisition in young children that has been referred to as "a modular
model of skill". They offered a computer model of skill acquisition in
which a specific behavior was seen to be made up of sub-behaviors
organized in a sequential fashion. The overall determinant of any given
sequence was a hypothesized program, the individual behavioral components
of the sequence being underlain by sub-routines. The program itself could
be organized hierarchically, specifying a general outcome and then assem-
bling different sub-routines in its realization. From this standpoint
motor competence involved the development of refined sub-routines underlying, for example, different manual grips, that could be assembled with
increasing efficiency to meet any specific goal. These would be 'run-off'
in an increasingly invariant fashion, while the need to attend less and
less to feedback would, in the terminology of motor control theory, free
the attention to process information from other sources -- a shift from a
closed loop system to open loop. Here, indeed, was a pertinent theory.
Not only had it been developed to apply to motor skill during the exact
period in which I was interested, about one to five years of age, but it
also mapped on to the procedures of applied behavior analysis. The
overall control program was directly analogous to the behavioral program
geared to teach a specific skill. The subroutines underlying the subcomponents paralleled the components of the skill revealed through task
analysis. Even the refinement of sub-components into an invariant form
and sequence paralleled the specification of criterial performance in most
programs.

There was, however, little empirical support for this position. Indeed,
in many respects, its operationalization was extremely problematical.
However, here was an opportunity to start to look at the development of
fine motor skill in young children, and to guide and refine our behavioral
programming in the light of these findings. We undertook both a longitudinal study stretching over eight months from approximate 12-20 months
and a cross sectional study (extending up to about 36 months) with groups
of nonretarded preschool children (Moss and Hogg, 1982). Briefly, however, the upshot of our observations of sequences of nursery curriculum-
type activities (joining rods, inserting and removing them from holes and
so) was that invariance of performance during both acquisition of competence and during its refinement was the exception and not the rule. The
more competent in executing a task the child was, the more he or she
produced a variety of different and often novel action sequences. The
older a preschool child was, the more variable he or she became in organizing and realizing sequences of movements. In so far as Connolly and
Bruner's hypothesis went, variability rather than invariance characterized
motor performance in our tasks.

This result needs to be placed in a framework that goes beyond an immediate concern with the modular model of skill acquisition. We can first
consider the result with respect to GDA theory into which we can introduce
a more specific developmental dimension of cognition. von Cranach has
produced the following diagram to illustrate the relation between
cognition, behavior and social meaning.

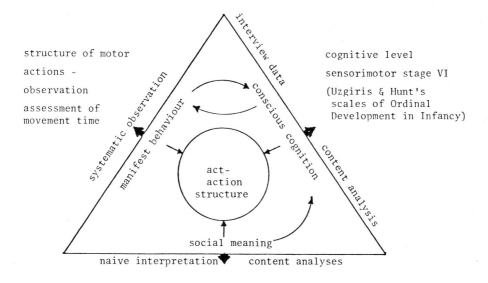

structure of motor
actions -
observation
assessment of
movement time

cognitive level
sensorimotor stage VI
(Uzgiris & Hunt's
scales of Ordinal
Development in Infancy)

social meaning,e.g. free play vs. self help

Figure 1
Expanded from von Cranach's "conceptual triangle"
in relation to the study of skilled action in young children

In our own study, we have explicitly considered manifest behavior through
observation and measurement of movement times. Implicitly, we have taken
one dimension of social meaning that we could characterize as 'play' with
the experimental materials. Where should we take this study in the light
of von Cranach's triangle of concepts? First, it would be of value to
explicitly assess cognitive change. It is not necessary to insist on
conscious cognition, and indeed, the verbal reports on which GDA theorists
draw would here be inappropriate with such young children -- as they would
with many retarded individuals. However, this period from 12-20 months
coincides well with the movement into Piaget's sensorimotor Stage VI --
invention of new means to achieve ends, and we might complete this side of
the triangle through assessment of the development of such cognition using
the relevant scale from Uzgiris and Hunt's Ordinal Scales of Development
(Uzgiris and Hunt, 1975), or through the development of cognitive structures as proposed by Greenfield (1978).

The dimension of social meaning also requires comment. In studies of the
organization of work activities in industry it is well established that
the degrees of freedom in the execution of a given plan vary. Rothe
(1978), (cited by Hacker, 1982, p. 87) proposed a scale as follows:

(i)   jobs without any degree of freedom for individual decision
       making and goal setting;

(ii)   jobs with degrees of freedom, which allow goals concerning
       the speed of action;

(iii) jobs with goals concerning the sequence of operations;

(iv)   jobs with goals concerning means and procedures;

(v)   jobs with goals concerning the characteristics of the
       result.

Into our own approach to this question then, we might introduce a variation in the degrees of freedom operating in the young child's social
milieu. A self-help task is likely to be more constrained with respect to
its realization than our own manipulative task. Dalgleish (1977), working
on Connolly's modular model did indeed find progressive refinement of
spoon-use in line with his predictions. What is required on the base of
the triangle then, is variation in the social meaning of tasks in order
that we gain a true picture of the structure of motor actions and their
development.

With respect to training retarded individuals in motor competence, two
important points emerge from this second look at our own study. First, we
are concerned to encourage action sequences that reflect appropriate
planning of component steps to a given goal. The cognitive operations
required are first going to be generalized across a range of curriculum or
vocational domains. Ideally, we are teaching to plan in a strategic
fashion. For young or profoundly retarded individuals, the cognitive
changes reflected in Piaget's Sensorimotor Stage VI are crucial, and
indeed, Kahn (1977) has shown that means-end behavior can be taught to
profoundly retarded individuals, though much remains to be done in this
direction. At a more advanced level we would be striving to encourage in
some measure the qualities attributed to effective industrial workers by
Hacker (1982, p. 93):

(i)   the most effective workers developed a more sophisticated
       network of goals and sub-goals;

(ii)   they use more effective signals, that inform about future
       states of the technological process;

(iii) they know better the probability of important events, e.g,
       faults, thus using more effective strategies of fault
       finding;

(iv)   they predict the future course of processes more accurately;

(v)   they predict a wider range of possible steps of a program
       including their consequences and alternatives.

Second, and parallel to these high level, strategic, developments, we are
going to be concerned too with many routinized tasks of important adaptive
significance. Reason (1984) has considered the behavioral and cognitive
nature of such tasks and I believe his analysis has implications for

understanding and encouraging the adaptive behavior of retarded people. He has recently summarized a long-standing view in psychology that the development of highly routinized actions in everyday life permit the gradual withdrawal of conscious attention to a given task. This view, which we have already noted has been applied to the development of motor competence in young children by Connolly and by Bruner, also reflects the computer analogy those authors invoke. Reason writes:

> In the modern idiom, one might say that repeated performance of a task permits the central processor to delegate control to largely automatic subroutines, the sequencing and timing of which are governed by superordinate executive programs, or plans (p. 519).

Many of the actions that we take for granted in our everyday life and which form the focus for intervention with mentally retarded people come within the category described by Reason-tasks such as dressing, washing, making tea or coffee and so on. Reason's analysis of these tasks is of special interest in this context:

(a) because of the light it throws on failures in motor competence in such situations,

(b) because of the model this analysis generates, and

(c) because it presents use with a clear illustration of how GDA can be analyzed.

Reason's studies were primarily based on analyses of diaries of failures in action sequences in everyday life, failures such as putting the coffee pot without having put water in and so on. He showed that it was indeed the most routinized actions that were subject to such errors and that similarity of location, movement and objects with the intended action were the clearest determinants of the error. Reason distinguished between action and non-action slips, the former concerned with control or atten- tional failure, the latter with failures of encoding, storage or retrieval. For Reason, the intention is to use error classification based on conceptual rather than behavioral analysis, though in passing he does produce a behavioral taxonomy particularly relevant in analyzing failures of action whether in our own behavior or those we have thought:

1. Repetition: Some actions in the intended sequence are repeated unnecessarily.

2. Wrong object(s): The intended actions were made, but in relation to the wrong object(s).

3. Intrusion: Unintended actions (other than those associated with repetitions or wrong object(s) become incorporated into the sequence at some point.

4. Ommission: Intended actions (other than those arising from repetitions, wrong objects, or intrusions) were left out of the sequence (p. 531).

It is beyond the scope of this paper to show how Reason relates what he

calls a "heuristic model of action" to a cognitive or <u>conceptual</u> classification of errors in action in which sometimes distinct <u>behavioral</u> categories of error are shown to result from common failures in the cognitive
action-components of model which embraces both intention and action-
systems as well as memory, need and feedback systems.

As with our discussion of limited subcomponents of action above, we would
suggest that analysis of action errors and perhaps some consideration of
the cognitive failures resulting in errors would be of value to teachers,
therapists and trainers in considering programming failures during
acquisition and generalization. With retarded people, action errors are
as likely to be as predictable and therefore comprehensible as with
non-retarded individuals and application of Reason's analysis provides a
systematic approach to these errors. Errors of this type are clearly
distinguishable from failures in the execution of a movement derived from
more fundamental incompetencies in the realization of a movement in
itself.

In emphasizing action in everyday life, Reason also takes us back to the
concerns of GDA theory with its location of behavior in the defined social
context in which it is intended and realized. The enhancement of motor
competence must, in this view, go beyond a narrow emphasis on motor
control or even motor planning. The starting point for its consideration
is a social one though as I have argued, the whole gamut of physiological
and psychological information available to us can be used to understand
and inform successful and unsuccessful intervention. It might be objected
that I have so far ignored the potential contribution of studies of motor
behavior <u>per se</u> in pursuit of this wider cognitive framework. Clearly
information on motor processes is of great relevance to the realization of
action plans and with differing degrees of thoroughness proponents of
laboratory research have urged the significance of their findings for
education and training. At their weakest, the authors of an experimental
paper may add to their Discussion, almost by way of an afterthought: "The
results have clear implications for remediating motor deficits in this
population." The hollowness of this claim has been readily exposed when
as reviewer I have requested elaboration of this point in a revised paper.
At the other extreme, however, we find the rigorously argued case for the
relevance of information on basic processes to training of the kind
provided by Wade, Hoover, and Newell (1983).

The argument developed by Wade and his colleagues, evolves in the
following way: Motor incompetence in mentally retarded people impairs
their ability to participate in a more fully normalized life, especially
with reference to vocational activities and leisure pursuits such as
sport. An essential requirement of the motor component of these
activities is the ability to process information on which to organize
(psychologically and ultimately neuromuscularly) appropriate motor
behaviors.

A long tradition of research, which we can conveniently note the start of
with Berkson's (1960 a, b, c) studies, has demonstrated poorer performance
by retarded people in information processing than matched control
subjects. This tradition of work suggests that these relative shortcomings occur not only at the response organization end of the process, as
suggested in the work of Wade and co-workers, but also in the initial
analysis of the stimulus configuration which has to be responded to, as

indicated by Nettlebeck and his co-workers, e.g., Nettlebeck and Brewer (1976).

When these laboratory findings are related to performance in the wider ecology, then incompetencies in work or leisure settings are hypothesized to result from failures in information processing. In addition, any attempt to remediate these shortcomings by teachers and trainers can be enhanced by informing the analysis of the training task by a knowledge of these experimentally demonstrated motor inadequacies. In the light of the argument, Wade et al. (1983) propose "a human factors approach to training", a marriage between a fuller understanding of operator capacity and task analysis. In this the task analyzer utilizes known differences between retarded and non-retarded people to modify training analyses or to circumvent particular constraints by appropriately designing the task.

While Wade's analysis of the link between experimental research and training is far more rigorous than my own modest effort to relate the developing structure of motor behavior to preschool curriculum activities, they bear some comparison. First, we have both opted for theory and experimental method relevant to specific curriculum domains for limited populations of retarded people. In looking for "a marriage" we have perhaps necessarily excluded wide areas of motor research highly relevant to motor activities. It can be argued, for example, that postural control has a profound bearing on fine motor skill (see Woolacott and Shumway-Cook, this volume) but such information does not readily lend itself to assimilation when we single-mindedly adopt our initial theoretical stance. Other areas of experimental research are also ignored in attempting to facilities the marriage. What, for example, is the role of proprioceptive and visual feedback, use and integration of which has also been suggested to affect the motor performance of mentally retarded people (Anwar, 1983)? How does a programmed, component movement in a sequence of actions become refined, a topic dealt with by Schmidt (1975) in his motor schema theory?

It would be easy to go on, but it is not my intention to appear to be intellectually throwing up my hands in horror at the possibility of bringing together this vast amount of information and synthesizing it in the context of mental retardation. What I would suggest, and propose to argue, is that we need to stand back from our immediate attempt to relate specific models of motor behavior to intervention practices and define a context in which this information can be placed, I am thinking here not only of the overall context that we might consider to be the motor domain, but the place of motor behavior in the full life of the mentally retarded person as a social being, a concern that I share with Wade. Let me then, suggest why if we are going to attempt a marriage of the sort proposed, it should be a very modern marriage, i.e., retaining the main relationship while being open to others.

For the purposes of this discussion, I will raise a number of questions concerning the relation between experimental and developmental research into motor competence with mentally retarded people and the effective implementation of training programs involving a major motor component.

First, drawing on von Cranach, I have suggested that motor competence entails goal-directed action and is dependent upon a complex behavioral system. Within the essentially reductionist tradition of research on

motor functioning with which we are all familiar, it is clear that no
single model of such functioning can explain or inform the totality of
requirements for competent behavior. Thus, any competent action requires
not only the important phase of information transmission and response
organization, but also the development of generalized programs and their
refinement as described by Schmidt (1975), and their organization into
complex sequences of behavior executed in appropriate conditions.
Analytically it is necessary to map the operations involved in motor
performance onto any given task for the educator or trainer to be able to
use this specific information. This, of itself may be a difficult operation, but not inherently impossible. Second, however, to utilize the
relevant information from theories of motor performance do we actually
need to have demonstrated that on average a group of mentally retarded
people do perform more poorly than suitable matched controls (given that
the inherent problems of matching groups of experimental subjects of
differing levels of development remain essentially unresolved)? I would
suggest that such comparative studies are of limited value in terms of
yielding information relevant to teaching and training. The fundamental
information is available independent of such comparisons and can be
related to and translated into the training setting given sufficient
knowledge of the theoretical field and fine enough analysis of the
training task. Where experimental paradigms are of value is in demonstrating the conditions under which relevant specific processes can be
modified and generalized to non-programmed situations or tasks. Wade et
al. (1983) describe the selective modification of discrete components of
motor skill in a laboratory task indication that apparently highly
restricted and fundamental components can be improved in mentally retarded
people--a demonstration not dependent on comparative studies. Indeed,
Baumeister (1967) has argued that the proper study of retarded people is
retarded people themselves.

In passing, it is worth noting that such improvement has been related to a
distinction between modifiable control processes and unalterable
structural processes developed initially by Atkinson and Schiffrin (1968)
in memory theory, an important consideration for those concerned with
intervention. Here the control process is akin to computer softwear and
'reprogramming' can lead to greater efficiency or success. Structural
processes are comparable to hardwear and are essentially unmodifiable.
With respect to training motor or other forms of cognitive process it is
questionable whether this distinction can be maintained either theoretically or pragmatically. It appears to propose a dichotomy that cannot
readily be established. Wade et al. (1983) suggests that:

> If no training technology exists which would allow the teaching
> of a certain task component, this component should be called
> functionally structured, and the stimulus, transfer, or response
> requirement could be reduced (p. 187).

However, the interest of the laboratory training experiment might well be
taken to point to what is likely to be modifiable in the less constrained
setting of a training program. If under carefully controlled conditions a
component of motor performance is unmodifiable, perhaps we would be less
optimistic in changing it outside the laboratory. It would appear to be
this rather than any validity in the control-structure distinction that is
of value.

We now have available a wide repertoire of teaching and training techniques that have undergone systematic evaluation over the past few
decades. The use of task analysis to teach competent action with its
implications for stimulus presentation and sequencing of reinforcement and
feedback has amply demonstrated that historically our expectations of
retarded people have been too limited (e.g., Gold, 1973). The fundamental
suggestion of this paper is that a fuller understanding of the processes
implicated in motor competence in the wider experimental and developmental
literature can inform this intervention activity directly. Whether direct
comparative studies are needed as a prerequisite to this activity is, we
have suggested, questionable, though it is unlikely that adequate replication of the totality of mainstream motor competence work will ever prove
feasible. What is now needed is a detail specification for teachers and
others of the core of available information on motor processes and how
this can be employed in initial development and monitoring of their
programs at the level that has begun to be worked out for language and
communication intervention. Thus, a motor competence curriculum will cut
across a large section of the traditional curriculum, and will utilize
this wider information resource selectively in different areas.

Let me offer one brief example: The development of components of action
has been a major concern of those teaching the least able of the mentally
retarded population, though with increasing task complexity this issue can
become a focus for any population, or indeed any of us who have tried to
learn a new skill.

Though task analysis a given sub-behavior is defined and subsequently
taught. Schmidt's (1975) motor schema theory is of special relevance
here. He is concerned with the conditions under which a relatively
restricted behavior hypothesized as being underlain by a motor program
develops and is flexibly applied. Schmidt accounts for this flexibility
by postulating the development of recall and recognition schema that
evolve through feedback from a variety of stimulus inputs occurring
before, during and after a movement had been executed. There are a number
of implications for training of this account which has proved considerably
more successful in predicting skill acquisition in children than adults
(Shapiro & Schmidt, 1982). One of the most robust is that schema formation develops most effectively in conditions under which variable practice
permits a variety of different inputs at the various stages of the action.
Where such inputs remain relatively more consistent during constant
training schema formation is less effective. The test of schema formation
is by introduction of novel values of the task, e.g., in a throwing task
to different intermediate distances and also beyond the range of training
distances.

It is interesting to consider the implications of this model for intervention. First, it suggests that even in the early phases of training, where
the task analysis and the trainee's performance dictate teaching of
limited movements, effective generalization can be built in at the
component stage. Thus, Stokes and Baer's (1977) training by multiple
exemplars developed within the pragmatic tradition of applied behavior
analysis finds a theoretical analogue in Schmidt's theory. However, can
this theory take us beyond existing practices in the applied analysis of
motor behavior? After all, the behavior analyst might well argue that the
development of teaching sufficient exemplars was not actually dependent on
schema theory. In line with the earlier observations on experimental

information, I believe that schema theory can take us beyond a simple
parallel based on variable versus constant training. As a theory, it
emphasizes the place of biofeedback in the development of a flexible,
applicable motor schema. It therefore suggests that in training under
variable conditions (or training with multiple exemplars) emphasis is
placed upon ensuring feedback at different points in the action. In
addition to systematic reinforcement of the action emphasis should
therefore be place on attending responses to a variety of sources of
information available in the task, e. g., initial limb positions, point of
visual fixation, topography of the movement during its execution (perhaps
through emphasis on attention to proprioceptive feedback -- "feel your arm
move") and outcome -- the last not being signalled simply through success
(reinforcement) or failure (non-reinforcement) but by direct feedback on
terminal stimulus conditions. It does not surprise me that when we begin
to talk in these terms the appearance and content of a training session
begins to look more like what we would see the good teacher or therapists
engaged in when actually working with a retarded person, though refined by
direct reference to schema theory. Similarly, failure to analyze
adequately the initial stimulus conditions again producing an inadequate
schema can be considered in relation to work on information processing and
the consequences of limited channel capacity.

If we now move from the specific to the general we return to the parallel
between GDA's view of the social character of actions and acts in relation
to the more familiar view of motor competence as the appropriate emission
of target behaviors in appropriate ecologies. The movement towards an
ecological perspective on behavior both within developmental psychology
and applied behavior analysis has been apparent over recent years.
Adjustment to this changing view by applied behavior analysts has
typically taken the form of considerations of generalization is that of
General Case Programming (Becker & Englemann, 1978) with its emphasis at
the outset on community and living-environment-referenced outcomes to
training. Colvin and Horner (1983) have demonstrated that application of
GCP to motor competence in an illustrative study of screwdriver-use.
Generalization of motor competence in this or other targeted tasks is
achieved in which:

(a) the instructional universe is defined;

(b) the range of relevant stimulus and response variation within
     this instructional universe is defined;

(c) examples from the instructional universe for training and
     probe testing are selected;

(d) training examples are sequenced;

(e) training examples are taught;

(f) testing with non-trained probe examples is undertaken.

The effectiveness of this procedure which bears some relation to Schmidt's
variable training procedure is demonstrated in this and other studies. It
is clear, however, that to limit such an approach to stimulus and response
class considerations is to neglect the other possible sources that
contribute to motor competence that we have described, as well as ignoring

incorrect performances (errors) that might arise from the mechanisms
proposed by Reason (1984). Nevertheless, General Case Programming offers
the most thoroughly worked out behavioral approach to teaching motor
competence, and the one with which information from the wider literature
on motor performance could most usefully be integrated. Like GDA theory
General Case Programming permits a consideration of the wider social
setting which carries us from 'mere movement' into the realm of 'action'
and 'acts'.

REFERENCES

Anwar, F. (1983). Vision and kinesthesis in motor movements. In J. Hogg
& P. J. Mittler (Eds.), Aspects of competence in mentally handicapped
people: Advances in mental handicap research (Vol. 2). Chichester:
Wiley.

Atkinson, R. C., & Shiffrin, R. M. (1968). Human memory: A proposed
system and its control processes. In K. W. Spence & J. T. Spence
(Eds.), The psychology of learning and motivation: Advances in
research and theory (Vol. 2). London: Academic Press.

Baer, D. M., Rowbury, T. G., & Goetz, E. M. (1976). Behavioral traps in
the preschool: A proposal for research. In A. D. Pick (Ed.),
Minnesota symposia on child psychology (Vol. 2). Minneapolis:
University of Minnesota Press.

Baumeister, A. A. (1967). Problems in comparative studies of mental
retardates and normals. American Journal of Mental Deficiency, 71,
864-875.

Becker, W. C., & Engelmann, S. (1978). Systems for basic instruction:
Theory and applications. In A. Catania & T. Brigham (Eds.), Handbook
of applied behavior analysis: Social and instructional processes.
New York: Irvington.

Berkson, G. (1960a). An analysis of reaction time in normal and mentally
deficient young men. I. Duration threshold experiment. Journal of
Mental Deficiency Research, 4, 51-58.

Berkson, G. (1960b). An analysis of reaction time in normal and
mentally deficient young men. II. Variation of complexity in
reaction time tasks. Journal of Mental Deficiency Research, 4,
59-67.

Berkson, G. (1960c). An analysis of reaction time in normal and
mentally deficient young men. III. Variation of stimulus and of
response complexity. Journal of Mental Deficiency Research, 4,
69-77.

Bruner, J. S. (1970). The growth and structure of skill. In K. Connolly
(Ed.), Mechanisms of motor skill development. London: Academic
Press.

Colvin, G. T., & Horner, R. H. (1983). Experimental analysis of
    generalization: An evaluation of a general case program for teaching
    motor skills to severely handicapped learners. In J. Hogg & P. J.
    Mittler (Eds.), Aspects of competence in mentally handicapped people:
    advances in mental handicap research. Chichester: Wiley.

Connolly, K. (1973). Factors influencing the learning of manual skills
    by young children. In R. A. Hinde & J. Stevenson-Hinde (Eds.),
    Constraints on learning. London: Academic Press.

Connolly, K. (1975). Behavior modification and motor control. In C. C.
    Kiernan & F. P. Woodford (Eds.), Behavior modification with the
    severely retarded. Amsterdam: Associated Scientific Publishers.

Dalgleish, M. (1977). The development of tool using skills in infancy.
    Unpublished doctoral dissertation, University of Sheffield.

Gold, M. W. (1973). Research on the vocational habilitation of the
    retarded: The present, the future. In N. R. Ellis (Ed.),
    International review of research in mental retardation. London:
    Academic Press.

Greenfield, P. M. (1978). Structural parallels between language and
    action in development. In A. Lock (Ed.), Action, gesture and symbol:
    The emergence of language. London: Academic Press.

Hacker, W. (1982). Objective and subjective organization of work
    activities. In M. von Cranach & R. Harre' (Eds.), The analysis of
    action. Cambridge: Cambridge University Press.

Harre', R. (1982). Theoretical preliminaries to the study of action. In
    M. von Cranach & R. Harre' (Eds.), The analysis of action.
    Cambridge: Cambridge University Press.

Hogg, J. (1981). Learning, using and generalizing manipulative skills in
    a preschool classroom by non-handicapped and Down's syndrome
    children. Educational Psychology, 1, 319-340.

Kahn, J. V. (1977). On training generalized thinking. San Francisco,
    CA: Paper presented at American Psychological Association. (ERIC
    Document No. ED 165 348).

Moss, S. C., & Hogg, J. (1983). The development and integration of fine
    motor sequences in 12 to 18-month old children: A test of the
    modular theory of motor skill development. Genetic Psychology, 107,
    145-187.

Nettlebeck, T., & Brewer, N. (1976). Effects of stimulus-response
    variables on the choice reaction time of mildly retarded adults.
    American Journal of Mental Deficiency, 81, 85-92.

Piaget, J. (1953). The origin of intelligence in the child. London:
    Routledge and Kegan Paul.

Reason, J. (1984). Lapses of attention in everyday life. In R. Parasuraman & D. R. Davis (Eds.), Varieties of attention. London: Academic Press.

Rothe, S. (1978). Arbeitsinhalt and Moglichkeiten zur selbstandigen Zielsetzung. Dresden: Informationen der Technischen Universitat Dresden, No. 22-17-78.

Schmidt, R. A. (1975). A schema theory of discrete motor skill learning. Psychological Review, 82, 225-260.

Shapiro, D. C., & Schmidt, R. A. (1982). The schema theory: Recent evidence and developmental implications. In J. A. S. Kelso & J. E. Clark (Eds.), The development of movement control and coordination. Chichester: Wiley.

Stokes, T. J., & Baer, D. M. (1977). An implicit technology of generalization. Journal of Applied Behavior Analysis, 10, 349-367.

Uzgiris, I., & Hunt, J. M. (1975). Assessment in infancy: Ordinal scales of psychological development. Urbana, Illinois: University of Illinois Press.

Von Cranach, M. (1982). The psychological study of goal-directed action: Basic issues. In M. von Cranach and R. Harre' (Eds.), The analysis of action. Cambridge: Cambridge University Press.

Wade, M. G., Hoover, J. H., & Newell, K. M. (1983). Training and trainability in motor skills performance of mentally retarded persons. In J. Hogg & P. J. Mittler (Eds.), Aspects of competence in mentally handicapped people: Advances in mental handicap research (Vol. 2). Chichester: Wiley.

White, B. L. (1971). Human infants: Experience and psychological development. Englewood Cliffs, NJ: Prentice-Hall.

Motor Skill Acquisition of the Mentally Handicapped:
Issues in Research and Training
M.G. Wade (editor)
  Elsevier Science Publishers B.V. (North-Holland), 1986

GENERALIZATION AND MOTOR CONTROL: IMPLICATIONS FOR INSTRUCTION
WITH LEARNERS WHO EXHIBIT SEVERE DISABILITIES

Robert H. Horner

University of Oregon

The activity which is the subject of this report was supported
in whole or in part by the U.S. Department of Education,
Contract 300-82-0362. However, the opinions expressed herein do
not necessarily reflect the position or policy of the U.S.
Department of Education, and no official endorsement by the
Department should be inferred.

Within the field of Applied Behavior Analysis there is a growing interest
in building a technology that results in performance of newly acquired
skills across nontrained, appropriate situations and materials (Baer,
1981; Drabman, Hammer & Rosenbaum, 1979; Horner, Bellamy, & Colvin, 1985;
Stokes & Baer, 1977). To date, this technology has emphasized problems
and solutions that address the role of stimulus generalization (and the
lack thereof) in applied settings (Sanders & James, 1983). As the
implications of this technology have been extended to learners who exhibit
severe disabilities, it has become clear that functional generalization
requires attention to motor control variables as well as traditional
stimulus control variables (Campbell, 1983; Bunker & Moon, 1983). This
chapter describes the importance of response variables (i.e., motor
control) in building generalized skills. Recent research addressing the
role of response variables in building generalized skills is reviewed, and
suggestions are offered for research that will be of direct utility in
developing a functional technology of generalization.

DEFINING THE PROBLEM: RESPONSE VARIATION AND GENERALIZED RESPONDING

From an applied perspective, responses have been learned to a functional
level of generalization when three criteria are met: (a) the response is
performed across the full range of "appropriate" stimulus situations, (b)
the response is _not_ performed in inappropriate stimulus situations, and
(c) the response endures over time. Most responses (skills) taught to
people with and without handicaps involve relatively simple responses.
The skill becomes complicated, or difficult due to the complex stimulus
discriminations involved. Reading, for example, requires verbal responses
that most people find easy to emit. The complexities of reading arise
from discriminating when to emit those responses, not how. Similarly,
when people with severe retardation are taught to cross streets, the
difficulty of the task typically lies in learning the generalized discriminations that index when to cross, not in learning the motor skill of
walking from one side of a street to the other. Because the generaliza-

tion of most skills lies in teaching complex discriminations, the role of response variables has been overshadowed. Recently, however, the importance of response variation in the generalization of adaptive behaviors has become more evident. When the skill under analysis includes motor topographies that vary with new, "appropriate" stimulus situations, instructional procedures must ensure that the learner knows both how and when to respond when presented with these novel situations. This requirement holds particular relevance for people with severe disabilities who are learning skills that must be performed in natural environments.

The ability to perform community-based skills across all appropriate situations in an environment often means performing the skills with different variations of a response in different situations. The use of hand tools such as screwdrivers and wrenches involves performing a basic class of response topographies (Bellamy, Wilson, Adler, & Clarke, 1980). Each job, however, will require use of the tool at a different angle, different intensity or different rotation. A competent individual is defined by his or her ability to both perform the tool-use response with the range of necessary topographies, and to select the correct topography for a particular job. This involves much more than recognizing that a stimulus situation is an instance of a "job that requires using a screwdriver." The learner must also select the correct instance from he response class "screwdriver use" that is uniquely suited to the demands of that job.

This problem is also apparent in nonvocational skills. A person learning to use laundromats, manipulate faucets, or turn on lights must deal with the same issues. Light switches, for example, may be activated by a variety of responses (i.e., flipping, pushing, twisting). Achieving the functional effect of the light coming on is dependent upon selecting the response topography that fits the particular situation. A learner with severe retardation who is taught only to flip standard wall switches may very likely "generalize" this skill to flipping the switches on nontrained table lamps that require a "twist" response. This inappropriate variation of the trained response would occur because of the limited variation of the motor skill the learner had acquired, not because of insufficient stimulus generalization. If a technology of generalization is to meet the needs of learners with severe disabilities, it must be useful not only for teaching the learner the range of stimulus situations where a skill should be performed, but also for teaching how to select the response variation that is functional for a particular novel situation.

Operant psychologists have addressed this issue under the title "response generalization" or the teaching of "response classes" (Garcia, Baer, & Firestone, 1971; Millenson & Leslie, 1979; Peterson, 1968; Skinner, 1938; Solnick & Baer, 1984). A response class has been defined as a cluster of behaviors that produce a common effect, and are susceptible as a group to modification via manipulation of consequences. Recently, Johnston and Pennypacker (1980) have argued that defining a response class also involves specifying that a set of responses are controlled by a definable class of stimuli. This approach is consistent with Becker and Engelmann's definition of "operations" (Becker, Engelmann, & Thomas, 1975), and fits well with the applied approach of designing instruction so that after some members of a response class are taught, all members of the class will be more likely to occur in appropriate stimulus situations.

Becker, Engelmann, and Thomas (1975) offer one conceptual analysis of how to teach responding to novel situations where an untaught variation of a skill is required. They propose a strategy labeled "general case instruction" that requires selection of teaching examples that sample the range of both stimulus and response variation the learner will encounter after instruction. In recent years this approach has been applied successfully with response classes such as mechanical parts assembly (Bellamy, Oliver, & Oliver, 1977), generalized use of vending machines (Sprague & Horner, 1984), generalized telephone use (Horner, Williams, & Steveley, 1984), generalized soap dispenser use (Pancsofar & Bates, in press), and generalized tool use (Colvin & Horner, 1983; Horner & McDonald, 1982; Walls, Seinicki, & Crist, 1981). The primary emphasis in these studies has been the performance of a newly acquired skill under nontrained stimulus conditions. In each case, however, learners were required to emit nontrained variations of a trained response. Their ability to perform successfully lends credence to the Becker-Engelmann model of analysis. Of particular note across the studies, however, has been the consistent pattern of generalization errors that have been reported. It is possible that a careful analysis of the error patterns that learners perform after instruction may suggest adaptive directions for building a technology of generalization that teaches responses classes (Horner, Bellamy, & Colvin, in press).

GENERALIZATION ERROR PATTERNS

The errors that learners make during instruction are typically a function of their not knowing a task. As a result, we have come to equate errors with ignorance. Horner, Bellamy, and Colvin (in press) suggest that this assumption is invalid with generalization errors (i.e., errors that occur after the learner has successfully completed training and is exposed to novel situations). Generalization errors may provide a valuable window through which the deficiencies of instruction can be seen.

One pattern of generalization errors has been identified by Engelmann and Carnine (1982), and Horner et al. (in press) as particularly relevant for the development of response classes. This pattern is characterized by learners who, after acquiring one topography for performing a response, apply that same topography to new situations; even when a different variation of the target response is needed to produce the desired effect. This error pattern has been labeled "response distortion" (Colvin & Horner, 1983; Engelmann & Carnine, 1982; Rose & Horner, 1982). The result of this error pattern is that the learner faced with a novel situation performs a response variation that is of the appropriate class, but is not an effective method of achieving the functional effect. The structure of the response distortion error pattern is diagrammed in Figure 1.

R.H. Horner

Response (R)

	R_1	R_2	R_3	R_4	R_5	R_6
T_1	X	X	X	X	X	X
T_2	X	X	X	X	X	
T_3	X	X	X	X		
T_4	X	X	X			
T_5	X	X				
T_6	X					

Task (T)

Figure 1
The relationship between topographical variations of a response (R)
and their utility with stimulus variations of task (T).
Xs denote situations where the particular topography
would produce the effect needed for the task (T).

Any response (e.g., rotating a screwdriver) can be performed with a range of variations. The responses R1, R2, etc., in Figure 1 refer to variations of the target response R (e.g., use of a screwdriver). Similarly, the tasks T1, T2, etc., are variations of the task T (e.g., tighten a screw). The Xs within Figure 1 indicate those tasks where a particular response variation will produce the desired effect. Spaces in Figure 1 that do not contain an X identify situations where performance of that response topography will not result in the desired effect. The particular format shown in Figure 1 is constructed to fit the examples of screwdriver use where R1 is a precise use of the tool and R6 is a response variation with considerable slop. With task variation T1 (e.g, a large Philips screw and screwdriver) any of the response variations will be effective. With task variation T6, however, (e.g., a small slotted screw and small standard screwdriver) only the most precise response variation will result in the screw being tightened. The error pattern of response distortion would occur when the objective was to teach the learner to respond successfully across the full range of task variations T1-T6, but as a function of the way instruction occurred the learner acquired response variation R4 as his dominant strategy for using a screwdriver. The learner would have acquired a skill that was functional across some new task variations but not across the range needed for competent performance in the natural environment.

Although no experimentally controlled studies have examined response distortion directly, several recent reports have included error data consistent with the response distortion logic. Horner and McDonald (1982) taught four high school students with IQs below 50 to crimp/cut biaxle capacitors. The task involved taking small circuit board components (see Figure 2), and placing each of the wire leads into the jaws of a plier-like tool that, when closed, would both cut the lead to a desired length and place a small bend (crimp) near the head of the component. Horner and McDonald compared two instructional approaches to determine the best method of teaching a skill that would generalize across the full range of components a worker in normal industry would be expected of the task. After the students had mastered the skill of crimp/cutting with one type of biaxle capacitor they were given a probe trial with 20, nontrained capacitors. These 20 nontrained capacitors had been systematically selected to sample the range of different capacitors encounted in industry. The results indicate that the four students generalized the basic response they had learned to all 20 new capacitors, but that the particular topography they used was only effective in an average of 3.68 of the 20 nontrained examples. With exceptional consistency, the students cut new capacitor leads too low, unevenly, or with unacceptable angles in the crimp. While the authors did not measure the topographies of the responses used when errors were made, the types of errors suggest that instruction with one capacitor had resulted in acquisition of a response distortion. For example, smaller capacitors required that the plier-tool be given an extra nudge to move it up close to the ceramic head of the capacitor before the tool was closed. This ensured that the placement of the crimp (bend) in the lead was in the correct position. This nudging was not required of the mid-size, training capacitor. If the students were making errors with small capacitors because they were failing to nudge the tool into place there should have been a correlation between generalization errors where the crimp was too low on the lead and the size of the capacitor. In fact there was a -.76 correlation between capacitor size and the probability of errors due to leads being cut too low. While

these data do not provide experimental verification of response distortion, they are consistent with the pattern of errors predicted from the
response distortion analysis.

Figure 2
Examples of the biaxel capacitors used by Horner and McDonald (1982).
The capacitor on the right has been crimped/cut.

Sprague and Horner (1984) provide another potential demonstration of
response distortion in their report on generalized vending machine use by
students with severe retardation.   The gist of their study is that
instruction using multiple teaching examples, where those examples sample
the range of situations the student is expected to encounter after
instruction, is more effective for teaching generalized skills than
instruction using a single teaching example or multiple examples that do
not sample the range of situations to be encountered.   Six students with
moderate or severe retardation were trained to use vending machines either
by training with a single machine, training with multiple, similar
machines, or training with multiple machines that systematically sampled
the superiority of training with multiple machines that sample the
relevant stimulus and response variation.   As previously unreported result
from this study was the pattern of errors that students made in their
efforts to activate nontrained vending machines.   Vending machines are
activated by a variety of responses: pressing a button, pulling a lever,
sliding a plastic door, etc.   When students had been trained with either
(a) a vending machine that required that they press a panel with the item
logo on it, or (b) several machines that involved pushing a button or
panel, they were very likely (72%) to push on the plastic door of a
machine that required activation by sliding the door sideways.   Only after
students experienced training with the range of different response topographies required of all types of machines did they slide the door on those
few nontrained machines that required activation by sliding a door.   It is
possible that the students discriminated that the door was related to
activating the machine, but because their prior training had only taught

one response variation (push) they used that "distorted" variation with the novel vending machine.

Colvin and Horner (1983) also report results that are consistent with the response distortion analysis. In their study eight students with moderate or severe retardation were taught generalized screwdriver use. A graduated easy-to-hard sequence was used to teach the multiple motor skills involved in placing a screw in a hole, positioning a screwdriver, and tightening the screw. The first five "lessons" in the program to teach screwdriver use involved work on the flat plane of a table. Only after reaching competence with different screwdriver types and sizes on the 0 degree plane did a student move to lesson six where the working surface shifted to a 60 degree tilt. Figure 3 provides results on the average number of trials to criterion for all lessons in the package. Lesson six required nearly twice the number of trials 0 and other lesson to reach criterion. This was true even though the students had already been successful using the same screwdriver in the previous lesson. Discussions with the trainers, and direct observation by the authors suggests that during training with lessons 1-5 on a 0 degree plane (flat on the table), the students had learned a response variation that involved considerable downward force during the screw tightening sequence. When this downward force was applied on a 60 degree plane, the screwdriver head invariably slipped out of the screw. The impressions of the trainers was that Lesson 6 was "difficult" because students were unlearning a response variation (distortion) that had become well practiced in the previous lessons. Once again, these data lack the experimental control that would allow documentation of a functional relationship between the generalization error pattern and the training sequence. They are, however, very consistent with the errors that would be predicted from the response distortion analysis.

To date, research addressing generalization has focused too exclusively on the performance of correct responses. Seldom have research reports defined the type of generalization errors that learner perform (c.f. Stella & Etzell, 1983, for an excellent exception). Before the issues surrounding response distortion can be adequately tested, more fine grained measurement of motor performance during generalization tests is needed.

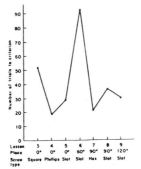

Figure 3
The average number of trials to criterion by lesson for subjects
in Colvin and Horner's study (1983) on generalized screwdriver use.

TOWARD A TECHNOLOGY OF INSTRUCTION THAT AVOIDS RESPONSE DISTORTION

Education for learners experiencing severe mental disabilities will be
useful only to the extent that acquired skills are performed across the
range of situations the students experience in their day-to-day routines.
Brown and his associates (Brown, Neitupski, & Hamre-Neitupski, 1976) have
expressed this sentiment by challenging teachers to use the "criterion of
ultimate functioning" as their standard for terminating instruction. This
criterion demands that a learner be able to perform a skill with the
precision, fluency, rate and level of generalization needed to make the
skill a functional part of the student's lifestyle. Although not overtly
discussed by Brown, et al. (1976), this criterion must also include that
students perform the range of response variations needed for complex motor
skills to be performed in nontrained situations. One training approach
that responds to the type of generalization technology we need, comes from
the direct instruction strategy of "general case instruction" (Becker &
Engelmann, 1978; Engelmann & Carnine, 1982).

General case instruction refers to those behaviors performed by a teacher
or trainer that increase the probability that skills learned in one
training situation will be successfully performed with different
materials, in different settings and with different people. "The general
case has been taught when, after instruction on some tasks in a particular
class, any task in that class can be performed correctly" (Becker &
Engelmann, 1978, p. 325). Originally developed to teach math, reading,
and language skills (Becker, Engelmann, & Thomas, 1975) the general case
approach has recently been adapted for use with severely disabled learners
(Horner, McDonnell, & Bellamy, in press; Horner, Sprague & Wilcox, 1982).
The general case approach builds on the foundation of our existing arsonal
of instructional techniques (prompting, reinforcing, correcting, fading)
by adding guidelines for selecting and sequencing teaching examples.
These guidelines arise from the following six steps for using the general
case approach.

1. Define the "instructional universe" of stimulus situations
    where the learner will be expected to perform the skill
    after instruction.

2. Examine the "instructional universe", and define the extent
    to which the relevant stimuli and responses vary from
    situation to situation.

3. Select a small set of teaching examples that systematically
    sample the range of relevant stimulus and response
    variation.

4. Sequence the teaching examples to avoid response distortion.

5. Teach

6. Test the level of generalization to which the skill is
    learned by exposing the learner to nontrained situations
    where the newly acquired skill is both appropriate and
    inappropriate.

Define the universe of instruction. The first step in performing a general case analysis is to define the full range of stimulus situations where the response will be required. This set of situations may vary depending on the behavior under analysis, the existing competencies of the learner and the characteristics of the settings where performance is desired. A critical assumption of the general case approach, however, is that generalized responding is not an amorphous phenomenon, but a result of skill instruction that has a clear target. Without defining the class of situations where the target skill will be desired, the teacher does not have the foundation from which to design a functional general case program.

The instructional universe should be designed to fit the unique needs of the learner and the demands of the task. For generalized vending machine use the instructional universe might be "all vending machines in town." Similarly, the instructional universe for generalized dressing with one learner might be "all clothing items in all home, school and community settings." With another learner who experiences more severe disabilities the instructional universe for dressing might be "all pullover shirts." The instructional universe denotes value judgments on the part of the programmer. It is important that these judgments are overt and specified before instruction begins if a functional, generalized skill is to be learned.

Define the range of relevant stimulus and response variation. Once the instructional universe is specified, the teacher should logically examine the examples in the instructional universe and determine the range of variation the learner will be expected to perform across. Much of the research to date has focused on how to define relevant stimuli, and sample the range of relevant stimulus variation (Becker & Engelmann, 1978; Engelmann & Carnine, 1982; Horner, McDonnell, & Bellamy, in press; Sprague & Horner, 1984). Of greater significance for the present chapter is the equally important step of defining the range of response variations the learner will need to perform in different situations. An example of this variation might be dialing a telephone via (1) standard push button, (2) princess push button, (3) pay phone push button, (4) standard rotor, and (5) princess rotor. Each of these dialing responses is unique, and a learner who is expected to use telephones across a full range of community settings should have the ability to dial each type of telephone. Similarly the motor skills required for eating food may required defining the varying response topographies demanded of fork use versus spoon use across differing types of food. General case instruction requires careful examination of the range of response variations the learner will be expected to perform. As a function of this analysis the teacher should select a set of teaching examples that present the learner with the full range of response variations she/he will be expected to perform. Using these examples during instruction should teach the learner both the range of response topographies that produce the desired effect, and the stimulus conditions that should be associated with each response variation.

Sequence the teaching examples. The general case guidelines for sequencing teaching examples focus on ensuring that the rate of acquisition is as fast as possible. When teaching a complex motor skill, it is recommended that the teaching examples be sequenced so that (a) multiple examples are presented in a single session; and (b) a mix of difficult and easy examples are presented as early as possible. This will avoid the response distortion problem described by Colvin and Horner (1983) where learners acquire a response topography in the early stages of training that must be unlearned as more difficult examples are presented. In general it is suggested that teachers begin instruction with a mix of examples (i.e., 60% easy, 20% moderate difficulty, 20% criterion difficulty). The learner may need extra physical or prosthetic assistance with the more difficult examples, but the difficult examples will serve to prevent the development of dysfunctional response variations that might be learned with a typical easy-to-hard sequencing strategy.

Teach. There is no substitute for quality instruction. The general case approach is a strategy for allowing good teachers to build generalized skills. It is not an approach that will overcome instruction that involves poor prompting, ineffective reinforcement, slow pacing, and poorly timed correction. The exciting aspect of general case instruction is that it is a technology that can translate good teaching skills into functional lifestyle skills for learners.

Tests. The final step in the general case approach is to test the learner. Testing may occur prior to and during acquisition, but is critical to the general case approach when the learner actually reaches the instructional criterion. The student who has been trained to shop in stores should be tested in several nontrained stores. The student who has been trained in generalized tool use, should be asked to perform a series of nontrained tasks that sample the range of the skill s/he just learned. The testing process not only guarantees that the target skill has been learned to a generalized criterion, but provides critical information on how training should be modified if the student is not successful in the nontrained situations.

FUTURE RESEARCH DIRECTIONS

The full breadth of the challenge to design an applied technology of generalization is just becoming understood. As we strive for solutions at least three issues will be important for researchers: (a) Selection of dependent variables, (b) Documentation of the problem of response distortion, and (c) Experimental analysis of solutions to the problem of response distortion.

Selection of Dependent Variables. One of the possible reasons why our technology of teaching generalized skills has not kept pace with other advances in instruction is because few researchers have emphasized responding across the full range of natural conditions as an important dependent variable. All too often researchers have been content to assess the "generalizability" of a newly acquired skill by presenting one or two randomly selected, nontrained situations. Demonstrations of this type do not allow assessment of whether the learner can perform the new skill across the full range of natural situations s/he will encounter in the natural environment. The first issue in need of research attention is a shift to using dependent variables that adequately sample the stimulus and response variations a learner will encounter in nontrained situations. A second concern related to the selection of dependent variables is inclusion of measures that report generalization errors as well as generalization successes. These measures will attend to the type of error made (i.e., topography, latency, duration, perseverance) in addition to error frequency, and will provide a direct method of building instructional procedures that avoid and remediate generalization errors.

A third dependent variable of interest in future research needs to be the efficiency of instruction. We are now convinced that learners with severe handicaps can acquire a myriad of functional skills, but a key to success- ful education will be the efficiency with which our technology of instruc- tion can teach behaviors that result in lifestyle changes. The ability to teach generalized skills will be a major issue in instructional effi- ciency. Procedures that focus on generalized behaviors, and that avoid teaching irrelevant behaviors that must be unlearned later in a sequence will have dramatic impact on the quality of life experienced by learners with severe handicaps.

Documentation of Response Distortion. To date most curriculum development and research efforts have focused on the problems of stimulus generaliza- tion. Especially for learners with several handicaps, however, the issues surrounding response variables (i.e., generalized motor control) are of equal concern. Research is needed that examines the relationship between current instructional procedures and the development of response distor- tion. Although several examples of distorted responding were presented in this chapter, no experimentally controlled analysis exists that ties these response errors to particular instructional procedures. The theory that underlies response distortion is as yet untested.

Analysis of Solutions to Response Distortion. Should the error pattern of response distortion be found to follow the structure defined in this chapter, a critical focus of future research efforts will be to examine instructional procedures to avoid its development. Three starting point in this process are suggested by the general case approach. The first involves attending to the range of response variation the learner will be expected to use, and selecting teaching examples that systematically sample this variation. The second attends to the sequencing of teaching examples, and encourages the inclusion of examples of differing difficulty as early as possible in the scope and sequence of a program. Analysis of this scope and sequence change would lie in the efficiency with which a generalized response was acquired. An easy-to-hard sequence, for example, would be expected to teach the same level of generalization as a general case sequence if the same teaching examples were used. The difference would lie in the time (and trials) saved in the general case sequence because students would not learn inappropriate response topographies in the early stages of the lesson plan that would need to be unlearned in latter stages.

A final area of research analysis may lie with the criterion used by teachers to terminate instruction. White (1984) has argued that the "fluency" with which a response is learned affects the degree to which it will generalize and maintain. This hypothesis is consistent with the general case emphasis on bringing the response under sufficient control that multiple variations are likely. As teachers become more interested in the response variations their students perform there will be renewed interest in the logic behind our criteria for determining when a skill has been learned to an adequate level of competence.

SUMMARY

The recent recognition that the education of learners with severe handicaps must be "functional" has led to a renewed interest in the generalizability of acquired skills. With few exceptions, however, our applied
analyses of generalized skills have focused on stimulus variables. The
development of generalized motor control has not been defined as an issue.
With learners who are acquiring skills with difficult motor components,
however, the ability of the learner to use the skill with the range of
topographical variations demanded by his/her environment may be the key to
making that skill a functional part of the learner's lifestyle. The
present chapter builds one case for the role that motor control may play
in the development of an applied technology of generalization. This case
revolves around analysis of the generalization error pattern labeled
"response distortion."

One promising approach to the problem of response distortion is available
from Becker and Engelmann's model of general case instruction. The
general case approach includes response variables as well as stimulus
variables in building instructional programs, and offers specific recom-
mendations for both avoiding the development of response distortion as
well as remediating this error pattern should it occur. To date, the
general case approach has been used successfully to teach a number of
generalized skills that include complex motor responses. In most cases,
however, the focus of the studies has been on stimulus variables.
Insufficient data have been collected to evaluate the specific recommenda-
tions related to response distortion.

In addition to defining the role of response variation in an applied
technology of generalization, and describing one instructional approach
for building generalized responding, the present chapter suggests several
avenues for future research. It is the firm belief of the author that
applied researchers will benefit from attending both to the methodological
and instructional implications of the general case approach.

REFERENCES

Baer, D. M. (1981). How to plan for generalization. Lawrence, H & H
    Enterprises, Inc.

Becker, W. C., & Engelmann, S. E. (1978). Systems for basic instruction:
    Theory and applications. In A. Catania & T. Brigham (Eds.), Handbook
    of applied behavior analysis: Social and instructional processes.
    New York: Irvington Publishers.

Becker, W., Engelmann, S., & Thomas, D. (1975). Teaching 2: Cognitive
    learning and instruction (pp. 57-92). Chicago: Science Research
    Associate.

Bellamy, G. T., Oliver, P., & Oliver, D. (1977). "Operations" in
    vocational training for the severely retarded. In C. Cleland, J.
    Schwartz, & L. Talkington (Eds.), Research with the profoundly
    retarded Vol. 3. Austin, TX: The Western Research Conference.

Bellamy, T., Wilson, D. J., Adler, E., & Clarke, J. Y. (1980). A strategy for programming vocational skills for severely handicapped youth. Exceptional Education Quarterly, 1, 85-97.

Brown, L., Nietupski, J., & Hamre-Nietupski, S. (1976). The criterion of ultimate functioning. In M. Thomas (Ed.), Hey, don't forget about me! (pp. 2-15). Reston, VA: CEC Information Center.

Bunker, L. K., & Moon, S. (1983). Motor skills. In M. E. Snell (Ed.), Systematic instruction of the moderately and severely handicapped (2nd ed.). Columbus, OH: Charles E. Merrill.

Colvin, G. T., & Horner, R. H. (1983). Experimental analysis of generalization: An evaluation of a general case program for teaching motor skills to severely handicapped learners. In D. Hogg & P. Mittler (Eds.), Advances in mental handicap research: Volume 2. Aspects of competence in mentally handicapped people (pp. 309-345). Chichester, England: John Wiley & Sons Limited.

Drabman, R. S., Hammer, D., & Rosenbaum, M. S. (1979). Assessing generalization in behavior modification with children: The generalization map. Behavioral Assessment, 1, 203-219.

Engelmann, S., & Carnine, D. (1982). Theory of instruction: Principles and applications. New York: Irvington Publishers.

Garcia, E., Baer, D. M., & Firestone, I. (1971). The development of generalized imitation within topographically determined boundaries. Journal of Applied Behavior Analysis 4, 101-112.

Horner, R. H., Bellamy, G. T., & Colvin, G. T. (in press). Responding in the presence of nontrained stimuli: Implications of generalization error patterns. Journal of the Association for Persons with Severe Handicaps.

Horner, R. H., McDonnell, R. S. (1982). A comparison of single instance and general case instruction in teaching a generalized vocational skill. Journal of the Association for the Severely Handicapped, 7, 7-20.

Horner, R. H., McDonnell, J. J., & Bellamy, G. T. (in press). Teaching generalized behaviors: General case instruction in stimulation and community settings. In R. H. Horner, L. H. Meyer, & H. D. Fredericks (Eds.), Education of learners with severe handicaps: Exemplary service strategies.

Horner, R. H., Sprague, J., & Wilcox, B. (1982). Constructing general case programs for community activities. In B. Wilcox & T. Bellamy (Eds.), Design of high school for severely handicapped students (pp. 61-98). Baltimore: Paul H. Brookes.

Horner, R. H., Williams, J. A., & Steveley, J. D. (1984). Acquisition of generalized telephone use by students with severe mental retardation. manuscript submitted for publication.

Johnston, J. M., & Pennypacker, H. S. (1980). Strategies and tactics of human behavioral research. NJ: Lawrence Erlbaum Associates, Publishers.

Millenson, J. R., & Leslie, J. C. (1979). Principles of behavioral analysis (2nd ed.). New York: MacMillan.

Pancsofar, E. L., & Bates, P. (in press). The impact of the acquisition of successive training exemplars on generalization by students with severe handicaps. Journal of the Association for the Severely Handicapped.

Peterson, R. F. (1968). Some experiments on the organization of a class of imitative behaviors. Journal of Applied Behavior Analysis, 1, 225-235.

Rose, H., & Horner, R. (1982). Avoiding response distortion with severely handicapped students. Direct instruction news, 2(1).

Sanders, M. R., & James, J. E. (1983). The modification of parent behavior: A review of generalization and maintenance. Behavior Modification, 7(1), 3-28.

Skinner, B. F. (1938). The behavior of organisms. New York: Appleton.

Solnick, J. V., & Baer, D. M. (1984). Using multiple exemplars for teaching number-numeral correspondence: Some structural aspects. Analysis and Intervention in Developmental Disabilities, 4, 47-63.

Sprague, J. R., & Horner, R. H. (1984). The effects of single instance, multiple instance and general case training on generalized vending machine use by moderately and severely handicapped students. Journal of Applied Behavior Analysis, 17, 273-278.

Stella, M. E., & Etzel, B. (1983). Effects of criterion-level probing on demonstrating newly acquired discriminative behavior. Journal of the Experimental Analysis of Behavior, 39, 479-498.

Stokes, T. F., & Baer, D. M. (1977). An implicit technology of generalization. Journal of Applied Behavior Analysis, 10, 349-367.

Walls, R. T., Sienicki, A., & Crist, K. (1981). Operations training in vocational skills. American Journal of Mental Deficiency, 85(4), 368-376.

Motor Skill Acquisition of the Mentally Handicapped:
Issues in Research and Training
M.G. Wade (editor)
© *Elsevier Science Publishers B.V. (North-Holland), 1986*

TRAINING FOR TRANSFER: GUIDELINES FOR PROMOTING
FLEXIBLE USE OF TRAINED SKILLS

Ann L. Brown and Joseph C. Campione

University of Illinois

Preparation of this manuscript was supported in part by Grants
HD-05951 and HD-15808 from the National Institute of Child
Health and Human Development and by Fellowship funds from the
Spencer Foundation awarded to the first author during her tenure
at the Center for Advanced Study in the Behavioral Sciences,
Stanford.

Generalization of learning is a critical issue for those who would devise
intervention procedures to help the mentally retarded, or any other group
needing help in mastering an arena of skill. Quite simply, the practical
value of training must be assessed against certain cost/benefit analyses
that include stringent criteria of the significance and durability of the
change, and the range of situations over which it is accomplished. By the
significance of the change, we mean that the effects of training should
result in worthwhile improvement on an important task, important in the
sense that it renders learners better able to cope with the contingencies
of everyday life, including academic milieux. Training should also result
in durable change in that the improvement stands the test of time; if the
effects are fragile and fleeting, they are of no practical significance.
The third criterion refers to the issue of transfer or generality of
learning. The outcomes of training should be relatively general, in the
sense that the new skill(s) can be used over the range of situations where
it would be appropriate. If the effect of instruction is restricted to
the training situation or little beyond, the practical significance is
reduced.

How one effects worthwhile, durable and generalizable learning, and
indeed, whether it is, in principle, possible to engineer such change by
training, is an issue of paramount theoretical importance that has
generated controversy for more than a century (Becker, Englemann, &
Thomas, 1975; Borkowski & Cavanaugh, 1979; Brown, 1974, 1978; Brown &
Campione, 1978, 1981, 1984; Campione & Brown, 1977, 1978; Campione, Brown,
& Ferrara, 1982; Gagne, 1962; Judd, 1980; Katona, 1940; Orata, 1928;
Osgood, 1949; Ruger, 1910; Schultz, 1960; Stokes & Baer, 1977; Thorndike &
Woodworth, 1901). The issue is particularly pressing for the management
and treatment of retarded learners, again a problem recognized early
(Woodworth, 1919), but still a perennial issue in the psychology of
learning and instruction (Brown & Campione, in press).

Regardless of one's theoretical bias, which class of learning theories one
espouses, etc., the central problem remains the same -- how to persuade

learners to use the fruits of past learning in novel domains; how to
induce the flexible use of acquired knowledge (Brown & Campione, 1981).
Therefore, although we are clearly novices in the training of motor
skills, knowing little or nothing about motor skill development, spontaneous or induced, and knowing little or nothing about motor skill development, spontaneous or induced, and knowing little or nothing about the
learning of severely retarded individuals, we believe that the theoretical
and practical problems of those seeking to engineer change are quite
similar. Even though we work with mildly retarded students who are
attempting to come to grips with the demands of basic academic learning,
and the participants at this conference work primarily with more severely
impaired individuals, the similarities in our prescriptions for training
are more notable than the differences. Indeed, it is particularly
striking that findings from such diverse areas, motivated by what some
might regard as conflicting theoretical stances, applied behavior analysis
and cognitive skills training, should result in such generality.

We begin this discussion by providing a thumb-nail sketch of the major
findings concerning the training and transfer of cognitive skills. We
then point out the similarity of these findings to those discussed by
Horner and Hogg for the training of motor responses. Finally, we pick up
an important theme of both the Hogg and Horner papers, i.e., the importance of analyzing errors when diagnosing learnings.

TRAINING COGNITIVE SKILLS: THE PROBLEM OF ACCESS

If we were asked to give a "one-line" diagnosis of the problems that
characterize mildly retarded students' learning of academic subjects, it
would be inflexible access. By access we refer to the ability to operate
fluidly and intelligently with one's own knowledge base, in particular the
ability to use flexibly and appropriately the information and skills one
has acquired. This is a problem for slower learners. Consider, for
example, the results of a typical cognitive training study of the 1970s.
A group of students is trained to rehearse a list of picture names until
they are sure that they can remember them all. After extensive training
they perform the task well, whenever the instructor tells them to. After
a delay the students are brought back to the laboratory and given the
identical problem to solve, but are not told to use laboratory and given
the identical problem to solve, but are not told to use the rehearsal
strategy -- and they don't. Why not? Of course, they could have simply
forgotten the learned skill. But this was not the case because when the
experimenter gave a gentle reminder, "Hey, didn't you learn how to do this
before?", some students started up again. Others needed a more explicit
prompt, "Didn't it help you when you said the names over and over?",
before they resumed strategic activity. But for the majority of the
students, the learned strategy was available, in that it wasn't necessary
for them to relearn it, but it was not spontaneously accessible, in that
students did not use it on their own volition.

That was a real experiment by the way, conducted with mildly retarded
grade schoolers (Brown, Campione, & Barclay, 1979), and it is interesting
to note that the delay in question was extensive (one year). But it is a
typical finding of cognitive skills training studies of the 1960s and
1970s (Borkowski & Cavanaugh, 1979; Brown, 1974, 1978; Brown & Campione,
1978, 1981; Butterfield & Belmont, 1975; Campione & Brown, 1977, 1978,

1984; Flavell, 1970). It was studies such as this that led to a wide-spread diagnosis of the learning of mildly retarded children as being particularly welded to the situation in which it was acquired (Brown, 1974). Although lack of flexibility in academic learning is a problem for all learners, it is particularly so for the slower learner (Campione & Brown, 1984; Campione et al., 1982). The problem of inert knowledge (Whitehead, 1915), knowledge that is rote learned but rarely used, let alone used flexibly, is of special concern when the students have a history of academic delay. Students must be helped to access the know-ledge they have.

Within the cognitive skills literature, it helps to make the distinction between multiple and reflective access (Brown & Campione, 1981; Pylyshyn, 1978). Multiple access to the fruits of past learning is shown by the ability to use knowledge flexibly, i.e., a particular behavior is not delimited to a constrained set of circumstances, it is not welded to a particular situation. At the most flexible level, knowledge is informationally plastic in that is can be systematically varied to fit a wide range of conditions that have little in common at the surface level but share a common structure at the deep level. In other words, learners can use their information appropriately in a wide range of situations taken from the same conceptual family as the training task. Reflective access refers to the ability to talk about, as well as use, the knowledge one has, to discuss it with others, to reflect upon one's own knowledge access involves understanding one's own understanding, which many claim to the be hallmark of higher intelligence.

The general diagnosis is that retarded learners, to a greater extent than others, are troubled by problems of access. This difficulty is character-ized by problems of both multiple access, or the ability to take their own thinking as an object of thought, to talk about, question and refine their own knowledge. It is certainly possible to instruct slower students to use a variety of strategies successfully; indeed, with intensive well-designed training their performance improves dramatically, particularly when the training concentrates on both inculcating the desired strategies and providing detailed instructions concerning self-regulation. But retarded children still experience great difficulty in using their new knowledge, and this diagnostic failure is particularly likely to occur if explicit instruction in self-regulatory mechanisms is not provided (Brown, Bransford, Ferrara, & Campione, 1983; Campione et al., 1982; Paris, Newman, & McVey, 1982).

PROGRAMMING TRANSFER

Faced with this persistent restriction on the outcome of instruction, researchers with a background in applied behavior analysis began intensive work on the problem of training for transfer, or programming generaliza-tion. Stokes and Baer (1977) pointed out that it was unduly optimistic to sit around waiting for transfer to happen; the message was -- if you want transfer, you will have to program it. And General Case Instruction, introduced by Becker, Engelmann, & Thomas (1975), provided a detailed blueprint for how to achieve generalized response learning, an advance summarized in both the Horner and Hogg papers (this volume). From a different intellectual tradition, cognitive skills training, there were contemporaneous blueprints for how to train for transfer where the object

of training was a more complex form of thinking. A list of eight guidelines that has influenced our own work was published in 1978 (Brown &
Campione, 1978), and is remarkably similar to those emerging from the
applied behavior analysis school, even though the two groups of
researchers did not cross reference each other, and were not aware of the
similarity. We share these guidelines with you, first because of the
striking analogy with the steps outlined in the Horner paper and second
because of their practical utility to our research program -- before
following the guidelines, our studies had generally been ineffectual at
inducing generalized learning, after adopting them, out studies have
resulted in durable and generalized improvement.

1. Know your domain. One cannot hope to induce transfer within a domain
unless one understands that domain. At one level this is a call for
detailed task analyses of both the training and transfer domains (Brown,
1978; Campione et al., 1982). But at the very simplest level the message
is -- if the experimenter and any intelligent adult would not regard the
training and transfer tasks as part of the same domain, don't expect the
slow learner to either. Thus, one measure of the suitability of the
transfer domain is that spontaneous users of the strategy on the training
vehicle would also use it on the transfer test. As Horner points out, a
thorough knowledge of the domain would permit one to devise learning and
transfer probes that form a representative sample of the occasions where a
skill could appropriately be applied. Near and far tests of transfer
reveal the extent of flexible use of information (Brown, 1978; Brown &
Campione, 1984). But one must know the domain, and if that domain is at
all complex, as it is with any academic skill, then an initial step is
laborious analysis of the task domain in which one wants to effect change.

2. Know your learner. Just as it is necessary to know the task domain,
it is also necessary to know the learner. As Hogg points out, it is
important to consider the developmental status of the learner who is to be
the subject of training. Not all learners are alike; there is considerable variability among novices faced with a new task, even if on some
criteria the novices are selected from the same group (i.e., mildly
retarded learners). All learners are not equal across tasks even is their
conventional "labels" would suggest otherwise. It is a truism in educational psychology that instruction should he tailored to the competence of
the learner; issues of learner readiness are also long-standing concerns
of the field. Recent advances in cognition and instruction have centered
on just this issue, how to map instruction onto the partial knowledge that
the learner brings, or doesn't bring, to the instructional context. We
now know just how difficult it is for learners to abandon their naive
theories and replace them with more sophisticated knowledge, even when
they are relatively sophisticated learners (college students) exposed to
extensive direct instruction (McCloskey, Caramazza, & Green, 1980;
Schoenfeld, 1980). This issue is only now receiving the attention it
deserves in those whose business it is to instruct the retarded learner.
Even slow learners are not tabula rasa; quite the contrary, immature
thinkers may not have the knowledge we wish they had, but they do have a
wise variety of misconceptions about learning that must be overcome before
progress can be made. Know your learner is then a call for detailed
developmental analysis of the way novices become experts; before one can
guide a novice one must know the steps along the way to success.

3. Train in multiple contexts to finesse the welding problem. If a major

stumbling block is that students tend to use a skill only in settings in which it was trained, then one answer is to train in more than one setting. If the learner is instructed in the use of a strategy or skilled in more than one appropriate setting, this should reduce the tendency for strict situationally-specific learning to occur. The need to such training has been recognized for many years (see Katona, 1940, for a review of the first half of the century), but the exact technology of how many and what settings is still to be determined. For example, one can have too many as well as too few exemplars (Morrisett & Hovland, 1959), and as Horner points out, the exemplars should be representative of appropriate occasions of use.

The importance of self-management. The next few desiderata for effective training have to do with recruiting the learner's cooperation and collab-oration. The aim is to keep learners informed of what we are all trying to do -- to make them coinvestigators of their own learning (Bereiter & Scardamalia, in press). The aim is to make the learner, as fully as is possible, an informed participant in the training process. We want the learner, as well as the psychologist, to understand the significance of the instruction (Brown et al., 1983), of why a particular form of strategy should be applied, of when, where and how to use it. We want the learner to see that the use of a particular strategy works for them. In the final analysis, we would like learners to take charge of their own learning, to become the self-directed learner that has been the goal of training since at least the time of Binet (Binet, 1909; Brown, in press). It is because of these issues of awareness, cooperation, and self-management that those in the business of training cognitive skills have become concerned with problems of metacognition, learners' knowledge and control of their own learning processes (Brown, 1975, 1978; Flavell & Wellman, 1977). In a review of the cognitive skills literature from this perspective, Brown, Campione, and Day (1981) characterized the majority of cognitive skills training studies as being primarily blind, blind in the sense that the student is kept in the dark concerning the nature of the enterprise in which both the learner and the instructor are engaged. Blind studies are contrasted with informed, self-control studies where students are helped to gain control of their own learning efforts and are fully informed of why, when and how to learn in a particular way. Some concrete suggestions of how to orchestrate informed training follow.

4. Given direct feedback concerning the effectiveness of the trained skill. As instructors, we select skills for instruction when we have theoretical or practical reasons for believing that they work. We believe that is the students use them they will get better -- we watch this working and record the progress. Often, however, the learners are by no means aware of the utility of the strategy. If the students do not know they are using a new skill or that it works for them (works in the sense of cognitive economy, i.e., performance gets better without heroic effort), then why should they maintain the skill when the social pressure to use it goes away -- let alone transfer it flexibly and incorporate it into their own skills repertoire? Ergo, include in any training package explicit feedback concerning the effectiveness and cognitive economy of the activity in question.

5. Direct instruction in generalization. Young or slow children in a training study are often unaware that separate phases of the experiment are indeed related. It is not surprising, therefore, that the utility of

a prior solution or strategy to a new variant of the training task does
not occur to them spontaneously. But, if the aim of training is flexible
generalization, then it seems reasonable to include in the training
package direct instruction concerning generalization. For example, one
could tell learners that the trained behavior could help them on a variety
of similar tasks and that the trick is to know which ones. One could then
expose learners to a variety of prototypic tasks (those on which experienced users of the strategy would always attempt to use it), and the
utility of the strategy in such situations could be explained and demonstrated. At that point, inappropriate tasks could be considered, and the
reason why the trained behavior would not be helpful could be pointed out.
Finally, the learners could be presented with a generalization test
containing new prototypic and inappropriate tasks and their intelligent/
unintelligent application of the strategy examined. Ergo, tell learners
about the range of utility of the strategy as directly as possible, given
their extant cognitive status.

6. Direct instruction in self-management. If one wants students to "take
charge of their own learning," the banner cry of the learning to learn
school, then given them practice in doing so, allow them to take more and
more of the responsibility.

7. Expert scaffolding. Expert scaffolding refers to situations where an
expert (a teacher, a peer, a coach, a parent, a master craftsman, etc.)
guides the novice to greater levels of participation. The expert
initially takes on the lion's share of the action. Novices are encouraged
to watch and then to participate in group activity before they are able to
perform unaided, the social context supporting the individual's efforts.
The expert models and explain, relinquishing part of the task to the
novices only at the level each one is capable of negotiating at any one
point in time. Increasingly, as a novice becomes more competent, the
expert increases her demands, requiring participation at a slightly more
challenging level. Expert scaffolding is the instructional philosophy
that lies behind successful instruction by (1) computers in such areas as
physics (Heller & Hungate, 1984) and electronics trouble-shooting (Brown,
Burton, & deKleer, 1982; Sleeman & Brown, 1982); (2) teachers in story
telling (McNamee, 1981), listening and reading comprehension (Brown &
Palincsar, in press), and writing (Applebee & Langer, 1984; Scardamalia,
1984); (3) peers in study strategies and problem solving (Bloom & Broder,
1950; Frase & Schwartz, 1976); and (4) parents in picture book "reading"
(DeLoache, 1984; Ninio & Bruner, 1978), joint counting games (Saxe,
Gearhart, & Guberman, 1984), and problem solving (Wertsch, 1979).

8. Training in situ. The final guideline is to make every attempt to
situate training in as close a fascsimile of the target task as possible.
For example, if the aim is to train reading strategies, it is advisable to
do it in the context of reading. This may seem obvious, but a favorite
form of instruction is to decompose the target task into its subcomponents
and then train each subcomponent in turn, in isolation from the target
task. The responsibility for putting the pieces together is too often
left to the learners' own devices. Just as retarded children have
particular problems with lateral transfer, using knowledge broadly, they
also have a great deal of difficulty with vertical transfer (Gagne, 1965),
recombining learned subcomponents into usable packages. As both Hogg and
Horner point out, careful attention must be paid to the natural environments or contexts in which the skills must eventually be employed.

A SUCCESSFUL COGNITIVE SKILLS TRAINING STUDY

To illustrate the above points with one concrete example, we will describe briefly a recent series of studies, conducted in our laboratory, that did result in satisfactory generalization and transfer. The students were junior high school poor readers with marginal academic competence (IQs in the high 70s to mid 80s, several years delayed on standardized achievement tests). The skills in question were basic to reading comprehension. The instructional procedure was called reciprocal teaching. (For full details of this complex program, see Brown & Palincsar, in press, and Palincsar & Brown, 1984).

Reciprocal teaching is an example of expert scaffolding in the classroom. The basic procedure is simple. A teacher and a group of students take turns leading a dialogue concerning the meaning of a section of text they are jointly attempting to read and understand. The dialogue includes spontaneous discussion and argument and four main comprehension-fostering activities: summarizing, questioning, clarifying, and predicting. The adult teacher assigns a segment of the passage to be read and either indicates that it is her turn to be the teacher or assigns a student to teach it. After all have read the segment silently, the teacher (student or adult) for that segment summarizes the content, asks a question that a teacher or test might reasonably ask, discusses and clarifies any difficulties, and finally makes a prediction about future content. All of these activities are embedded in as natural a dialogue as possible, with the teacher and the students giving feedback to each other. In addition to the daily dialogues, the students took an independent comprehension test daily and recorded their own progress.

Simple as the procedure sounds, it embodies the essence of the eight guidelines for inducing changed outlined above. First, the four comprehension fostering were selected on the basis of detailed task analyses of reading comprehension (know your domain). Specifically, they are strategies that serve an important dual function, that of enhancing comprehension while simultaneously providing an opportunity for the learner to monitor whether understanding is occurring. For example, if one cannot paraphrase the content this is a sure sign that adequate understanding is not being reached, and that remedial action is called for (see Brown, Palincsar & Armbruster, 1984, for a discussion of this point). Second, the training was ideally tailored to the learners (know your learner). The students in these studies were diagnosed as particularly deficient in reading comprehension; their decoding skills were adequate. Third, training was in multiple contexts; the students worked on two new texts each day, one in the dialogue sessions, the other in the test taking mode.

Fourth, turning to the actual teaching procedure, reciprocal teaching is a form of expert scaffolding. In the beginning, the teacher actively modeled the desired comprehension activities, thereby making them overt, explicit, and concrete. This is important because comprehension-fostering and monitoring activities are usually difficult to detect in the expert reader, as they are executed covertly. The reciprocal teaching procedure provided a relatively natural forum for the teacher to engage in the strategies overtly, and hence to provide a model of what it is that expert readers do when they try to understand and remember texts. The modeling also served to demonstrate to the students concrete ways of monitoring their own learning through methods they can readily understand.

Fifth, training was in situ in that the strategies were always modeled in appropriate contexts, not as isolated, decontextualized skills. The four key strategies of summarizing, questioning, clarifying and predicting were embedded in the context of the dialogue between students and teacher that took place during the actual task of reading with a clear goal of deriving meaning from the text. Each separate activity was used in response to a concrete problem of text comprehension. Summarizing was modeled as an activity of self-review. Its purpose was to state to the teacher or the group what had just happened in the text and as a self-test that the content had been understood. If an adequate synopsis could not be reached, this fact was not regarded as a failure to perform a particular skill but as an important source of information that comprehension was not proceeding as it should, and remedial action such as re-reading or clarifying was needed. Questioning was not an isolated activity, but a continuing goal of the whole enterprise -- to what reasonable test could one's new learning be put? Clarifying occurred only if there were confusions, either in the text or in the student's interpretation of the text. Similarly, prediction was attempted if the students or teachers recognized any cues that served to herald forthcoming material. In short, all of the activities were undertaken when appropriate in the context of actually reading with the goal of understanding and remembering.

Sixth, there was continual attention to the metacognitive aspects of the learning situation, i.e., direct instruction was given in generalization. The students were fully informed of the need for strategic intervention, of where and when to be strategic, and of the fact that using these strategies worked for them. This line of attack was designed to ensure that students understood why they must act as requested, and how critical reading works.

Seventh, direct feedback was provided both on-line during the dialogues and during the testing sessions where the students recorded their own progress. Note that the teacher provided feedback that was tailored to the students' existing levels, encouraging them to progress gradually toward full competence. An important feature of the reciprocal teaching procedure is that the students must respond when it is their turn to be the teacher, or when they answer the questions of other teachers. The students respond even if the level of which they are capable is not yet that of an expert. But because the students do respond, the teacher has an opportunity to gauge their competence, competence that is often masked by weaker students' tendencies not to respond until they are sure of themselves.

Finally, direct instruction was given in self-management, with the responsibility for the comprehension activities transferred to the students as soon as they could take charge of their own learning. Through interactions with the supportive teacher and their more knowledgeable peers, the students are led to perform at an increasingly more mature level; sometimes this progress is fast, sometimes slow, but, irrespective of the rate, the teacher provides an opportunity for students to respond at a slightly challenging level. As they master one level of involvement, the teacher increases her demands so that students are gradually called upon to adopt the adult role fully and independently. The teacher then fades into the background and acts as a sympathetic coach leaving the students to take charge of their own learning. This is the essence of expert scaffolding.

As a concrete example, consider a teacher working with two remedial reading seventh graders is the same reading group. The group is reading a passage about American snakes. One student, Charles (IQ = 70, reading comprehension grade equivalent = third grade), has a great deal of difficulty taking his turn leading the dialogue, primarily because he doesn't know how to formulate an appropriate question. He opens with, "What is found in the Southeastern snake, also the copperhead, rattlesnakes, vipers -- they have -- I'm not doing this right." The teacher responds to his difficulty and tells him the main idea. "Do you want to ask something about the pit vipers?" When he still fails to ask an adequate question, she prompts, "Ask a good question about the pit vipers that starts with the word why." When he still cannot manage it, she models, "Why do they call the snakes pit vipers?" After two tries, he copies the teacher's question and she provides praise and encouragement. Even imitating a fully formed question is difficult for Charles initially.

Four days later, Charles is still having difficulty asking questions. The teacher models one for him, but this time she waits for him to identify the main idea in his question: "How do spinner's mate spend most of his time sitting?" The teacher responds, "You're very close. The question would be, 'How does spinner's mate spend most of his time?' Now you ask it." And he does.

Seven days into the procedure, Charles forms a question, but unfortunately the answer is not in the text. The teacher helps him modify this, and by the eleventh day he takes his turn as teacher with two questions, "What is the most interesting of the insect eating plants, and where do the plants live at?" After fifteen days he produces acceptable single questions each time it is his turn to lead the dialogue. Charles -- "Why do scientists come to the South Pole to study?" Teacher -- "Excellent question -- that's what the paragraph is all about!"

In contrast to Charles, another student in the group, Sara (IQ = 84, reading comprehension equivalent = fourth grade), has a clear idea of what kinds of questions occur in schools -- "Fill in the blanks." The teacher, preoccupied with Charles, tolerates such questions until the second day and then attempts to take Sara beyond this level. Sara -- "Snakes' backbones can have as many as 300 vertebrates -- almost blank, blank, blank times as many as humans?" Teacher -- "Not a bad beginning, but that's a question about a detail. Try to avoid 'fill in the blanks' questions. See if next time you can find a main idea question and begin your question with a question word -- how, why, when..."

On the third day, Sara comes up with a main idea question, but this time she selects a line in the text, "Several varieties of snakes live all their lives in the sea," and turns it into a question, "Can snakes live their whole lives in seas?" The teacher again increases her demand, "Fine, but see if you can ask a question using your own words." For the remainder of the sessions, Sara composes questions in her own words becoming more and more like the model teacher in her turn.

As the students become more competent the teacher can gradually fade into the background. For example, consider the turn-taking rituals of the group. On early sessions, even when it is a student's turn to be the teacher, after the initial question, the turns can be described as T-S, T-S runs, that is, although it is officially a student's turn to be the teacher, the adult teacher is totally in control. The runs are adult teacher question -- student answer, just as in a regular classroom.

Look again after ten or so sessions. Now the majority of the "runs" are student-controlled, with the teacher interspersing praise and encourage- ment and management. The teacher only intercedes with advice and modeling when a student misses the point and the other students do not catch it. The teacher has moved from the pivotal role of responding individually to each child to a coach who sits in the background, offers encouragement, and occasionally pushes for a better interpretation of the text. The expert provides just the degree of scaffolding necessary for the dialogue to remain on track, leaving the students to take as much responsibility as they can. (For transcripts, see Palincsar & Brown, 1984).

These changes in the students' ability to lead the daily reading dialogue were reflected in a variety of objective measures. To summarize the main outcomes of the intervention: (1) there was clear evidence of improvement in the students' ability to paraphrase, question, clarify, and predict when called upon to do so; (2) the students progressed from passive observers to active teachers, able to lead the dialogues independently, and, in some cases, eventually to take on the role of peer tutors; (3) there was a large and reliable quantitative improvement on daily indepen- dent comprehension test, with students improving to the level set by good comprehenders on these tests (from 20% to 80% correct); (4) the effect was durable, with little drop in the level of performance six months after the program ceased; (5) the effect generalized to the classroom setting, with students progressing from below the 20th precentile to approximately the 70th percentile, i.e., reaching or surpassing the average level for their age mates on comprehension tests set as part of their regular science and social studies courses; (6) training resulted in reliable transfer to laboratory tasks that differed in surface features from the training and assessment tasks: writing summaries, predicting appropriate comprehension questions, and detecting text inconsistencies all improved; (7) sizable improvements, averaging two years, in standardized comprehension scores were recorded for the majority of subjects; (8) sizable numbers on the students were "released" from special reading classes and sent back to the mainstream as a result of a year in the program; (9) the full reciprocal teaching procedure always resulted in greater improvement and more durable performance than competing instructional procedures, such as direct instruction in the strategies or modeling along; (10) the intervention was instructionally feasible, that is, it was on less successful in natural group settings conducted by regular teachers than it was when conducted by an experimenter in the laboratory. In addition, regular classroom teachers were uniformly enthusiastic about the procedure once they had mastered it, and many incorporated it into their routine teaching reper- toires.

THE GENERALITY OF THE GUIDELINES

At this point, one might ask what such a program can tell us about motor skill learning. We reiterate that we believe that these are general guidelines that have applicability in a wide variety of training contexts, and we point to the similarity of the guidelines discussed by Horner for training complex motor responses to make this point. Given the similar- ity, and the success, of these endeavors, we feel confident that we are now in position to engineer significant, durable, and generalizable changes in the behavior of a wide spectrum of individuals coping with a wide array of tasks.

Errors and Diagnosis. As a final point, we would like to pick up on the theme that runs throughout the papers by Hogg and Horner, i.e., the importance of diagnosing the errors that are made rather than concentrating exclusively on correct performance. Error patterns provide a window through which to view the learner's understanding of the task, to view just what has been learned. Slips of the tongue have long been regarded as a mirror on the soul in the psychoanalytic literature. More prosaically, in spontaneous language, errors tell us a great deal about a child's (Bowerman, 1982; Clark, 1981; Karmiloff-Smith, 1979), or, for that matter, an adult's (Franklin, 1973), understanding of language rules. We have also found that children's error correction procedures reveal much about the problem solving skills of very young, preverbal children (DeLoache, Brown, & Kane, 1985; DeLoache, Sugarman, & Brown, in press). Like Hogg, we have found that expertise does not necessarily lead to errorless behavior. The more competent the child, the more he can tolerate a wide variety of errors, errors that he has the means to correct. Even in the "simple domain" of toddlers' manipulative play with stacking cups, we find two broad types of expertise: the cautious child, who makes fewer and fewer errors as she becomes more experienced, and the quick facile child, who continues to generate novel action sequences, often resulting in errors that are then corrected by means of flexible self-correction strategies (DeLoache, Brown, & Kane, 1985). In the example of the reciprocal teaching intervention, note how much information the teacher gets from considering the students' errors. By thus diagnosing their current level of competence, she can guide the students gradually through increasing grades of competence. Finally, as Horner points out, overgeneralization, or other forms of generalization errors, reveal a great deal about what was actually learned, perhaps as much as correct generalization patterns.

SUMMARY

By considering successful training techniques generated from both the cases of motor skills learning and cognition and instruction, the generality of central guidelines for training has been brought into high relief. Despite differences in theoretical orientation, subject populations to be served, and skills to be trained, there is considerable agreement concerning the appropriate methods of engineering worthwhile, durable, and generalizable change. Since such success stories, and convergence of ideas across disparate fields, are few, we should appreciate them when they occur. We are convinced that we are well on the way to building a theory of instruction that works for a wide range of learners tackling a broad spectrum of skills.

REFERENCES

Applebee, A. N., & Langer, J. A. (1984). Instructional scaffolding: Reading and writing as natural language activities. Language Arts, 60, 168-175.

Becker, W., Engelmann, S., & Thomas, D. (1975). Teaching: cognitive learning and instruction. Chicago: Science Research Associates.

Bereiter, C., & Scardamalia, M. (in press). Cognitive coping strategies and the problem of "inert knowledge." In S. S. Chipman, J. W. Segal, & R. Glaser (Eds.), Thinking and learning skills: Current research and open questions (Vol. 2). Hillsdale, NJ: Lawrence Erlbaum Associates.

Binet, A. (1909). Les idées modernes sur les infants. Paris: Ernest Flammarion.

Bloom, B., & Broder, (1950). Problem-solving processes of college students. Chicago: University of Chicago Press.

Borkowski, J. G., & Cavanaugh, J. C. (1979). Maintenance and generalization of skills and strategies by the retarded. In N. R. Ellis (Ed.), Handbook of mental deficiency: Psychological theory and research. Hillsdale, NJ: Erlbaum.

Bowerman, M. (1982). Starting to talk worse: Clues to language acquisition from children's late speech errors. In S. Strauss (Ed.), U-shaped behavioral growth. New York: Academic Press.

Brown, A. L. (1974). The role of strategic behavior in retardate memory. In N. R. Ellis (Ed.), International review of research in mental retardation (Vol. 7). New York: Academic Press.

Brown, A. L. (1975). The development of memory: Knowing, knowing about knowing, and knowing how to know. In H. W. Reese (Ed.), Advances in child development and behavior (Vol. 10). New York: Academic Press.

Brown, A. L. (in press). Mental orthopedics: A conversation with Alfred Binet. In S. S. Chipman, J. W. Segal, & R. Glaser (Eds.), Thinking and learning skills: Current research and open questions (Vol. 2). Hillsdale, NJ: Erlbaum.

Brown, A. L., Bransford, J. D., Ferrara, R. A., & Campione, J. C. (1983). Learning, remembering and understanding. In J. H. Flavell & E. M. Markman (Eds.), Carmichael's handbook of child psychology (Vol. 3). New York: Wiley.

Brown, A. L., & Campione, J. C. (1978). Permissible inferences from cognitive training studies in developmental research. In W. S. Hall & M. Cole (Eds.). Quarterly newsletter of the institute for comparative human behavior, 2, 46-53.

Brown, A. L., & Campione, J. C. (1981). Inducing flexible thinking: A problem of access. In M. Friedman, J. P. Das, & N. O'Connor (Eds.), Intelligence and learning. New York: Plenum Press.

Brown, A. L., & Campione, J. C. (1984). Three faces of transfer: Implications for early competence, individual differences, and instruction. In M. E. Lamb, A. L. Brown, & B. Rogoff (Eds.). Advances in developmental psychology (Vol. 3). Hillsdale, NJ: Erlbaum.

Brown, A. L., Campione, J. C., & Barclay, C. R. (1979). Training self-checking routines for estimating test readiness: Generalization from list learning to prose recall. Child Development, 50, 501-512.

Brown, A. L., Campione, J. C., & Day, J. D. (1981). Learning to learn: On training students to learn from texts. Educational Researcher, 10, 14-21.

Brown, A. L., & Palincsar, A. S. (in press). Reciprocal teaching of comprehension strategies: A natural history of one program for enhancing learning. In J. Borkowski & J. D. Day (Eds.), Intelligence and cognition in special children: Comparative studies of giftedness, mental retardation, and learning disabilities. New York: blex.

Brown, J. S., Burton, R. R., & deKleer, J. (1982). Pedagogical, natural language and knowledge engineering techniques in SOPHIE I, II and III. In D. Sleeman & J. S. Brown (Eds.), Intelligent tutoring systems. New York: Academic Press.

Butterfield, E. C., & Belmont, J. M. (1975). Assessing and improving the executive cognitive functions of mentally retarded people. In I. Bialer & M. Sternlicht (Eds.), Psychological issues in mentally retarded people. Chicago: Aldine.

Campione, J. C., & Brown, A. L. (1977). Memory and metamemory development in educable retarded children. In R. V. Kail, Jr., & J. W. Hagen (Eds.), Perspectives on the development of memory and cognition. Hillsdale, NJ: Erlbaum.

Campione, J. C., & Brown, A. L. (1984). Learning ability and transfer propensity as sources of individual differences in intelligence. In P. H. Brooks, C. McCauley, & R. D. Sperber (Eds.), Learning and cognition in the mentally retarded. Hillsdale, NJ: Erlbaum.

Campione, J. C., & Brown, A. L., & Ferrara, R. A. (1982). Mental retardation and intelligence. In R. Sternberg (Ed.), Handbook of human intelligence. New York: Cambridge University Press.

DeLoache, J. S. (1984). What's this? Maternal questions in joint picture book reading. The Quarterly Newsletter of the Laboratory of Comparative Human Cognition.

DeLoache, J. S., Sugarman, S., & Brown, A. L. (in press) The development of error correction strategies in very young children's manipulative play. Child Development.

DeLoache, J. S., Brown, A. L., & Kane, M. J. (1985). Error correct strategies in the Problem Solving of Very Young Children. Paper presented at the Society for Research in Child Development, Toronto.

Flavell, J. H. (1970). Developmental studies of mediated memory. In H. W. Reese & L. P. Lipsitt (Eds.), Advances in child development and behavior (Vol. 5). New York: Academic Press.

Flavell, J. H., & Wellman, H. M. (1971). Metamemory. In R. V. Kail, Jr., & J. W. Hagen (Eds.), Perspectives on the development of memory and cognition. Hillsdale, NJ: Erlbaum.

Feurzig, W., & White, B. Y. (1984). An articulate instructional system for teaching arithmetic procedures. Washington D.C.: National Science Foundation Final Report.

Frase, L. T., & Schwartz, B. J. (1975). The effect of question production and answering on prose recall. Journal of Educational Psychology, 62, 628-635.

Fromkin, V. A. (1973). Speech errors as linguistic evidence. The Hague, Mouton.

Gagné, R. (1965). The condition of learning. New York: Holt Rinehart and Winston, Inc.

Heller, J. I., & Hungate, H. N. (1984). Computer-based expert scaffolding. Unpublished manuscript. University of California, Berkeley.

Judd, C. H. (1908). The relation of special training to general intelligence. Educational Review, 36, 28-42.

Karmiloff-Smith, A. (1979). Micro- and macro- developmental changes in language acquisition and other representational systems. Cognitive Science, 3, 91-118.

Katona, G. (1940). Organizing and memorizing. Morningside Heights, NY: Columbia University Press.

McNamee, G. D. (1981). Social origins of narrative skills. Unpublished doctoral dissertation, Northwestern University, Evanston, IL.

McCloskey, M., Caramazza, A., & Green, B. (1980). Curvilinear motion in the absence of external forces: Naive beliefs about the motion of objects. Science, 210, 1139-1141.

Morrisett, L., & Hovland, C. I. (1959). A comparison of three varieties of training in human problem solving. Journal of Experimental Psychology, 58, 52-55.

Ninio, A., & Bruner, J. S. (1978). The achievement and antecedents of labelling. Journal of Child Language, 5, 1-15.

Orata, P. T. (1928). The theory of identical elements, Columbus, OH: Ohio State University Press.

Osgood, C. E. (1949). The similarity paradox in human learning: A resolution. Psychological Review, 56, 132-143.

Palincsar, A. S., & Brown, A. L. (1984). Reciprocal teaching of comprehension-fostering and monitoring activities. Cognition and Instruction, 1, 117-175.

Paris, S. G., Newman, R. S., & McVey, K. A. (1982). Learning the functional significance of mnemonic actions: A microgenetic study of strategy acquisition. Journal of Experimental Child Psychology, 55, 490-509.

Pylyshyn, Z. W. (1978). Computational models and empirical constraints. The Behavioral and Brain Sciences, 1, 93-99.

Ruger, H. A. (1910). The psychology of efficiency. Archives of Psychology, 2(15).

Saxe, G. B., Gearhart, M., & Guberman, S. R. (1984). The social organization of early number development. In J. Wertsch & B. Rogoff (Eds.), Children's learning in the "zone of proximal development". San Francisco: Jossey-Bass.

Scardamalia, M. (1984). Knowledge telling and knowledge transforming in written composition. Paper presented at the meetings of the American Educational Research Association, New Orleans.

Schoenfeld, A. H. (1983). Beyond the purely cognitive: Belief systems, social cognitions, and metacognitions as driving forces in intellectual performance. Cognitive Science, 7, 329-363.

Schultz, R. W. (1960). Problem solving behavior and transfer. Harvard Educational Review, 30, 61-77.

Sleeman, D., & Brown, J. S. (1982). Intelligent tutoring systems. New York: Academic Press.

Stokes, T. F., & Baer, D. M. (1977). An implicit technology of generalization. Journal of Applied Behavior Analysis, 10, 349-367.

Thorndike, E. L., & Woodworth, R. S. (1981). The influence of improvement in one mental function upon the efficiency of other functions. Psychological Review, 8, 247-261, 384-395, 553-564.

Wertsch, J. V. (1979). From social interaction to higher psychological processes: A clarification and application of Vygotsky's theory. Human Development, 22, 1-22.

Whitehead, A. N. (1915). The aims of education. Address before the Manchester meeting of the British Association for the Advancement of Science.

Woodrow, H. (1919). Brightness and dullness in children. Philadelphia: J. B. Lippincott Co.

SUBJECT INDEX

AUTHOR INDEX